THE POSITIVE
TRAIT THESAURUS:

A Writer's Guide to Character Attributes

ANGELA ACKERMAN
BECCA PUGLISI

Copyright 2013 © by Angela Ackerman & Becca Puglisi
Published by: JADD Publishing

First print edition, October 2013
ISBN-13: 978-0-9897725-1-8

Edited in part by: C. S. Lakin
http://www.livewritethrive.com

Book Cover Design: Scarlett Ruger Design 2013
http://www.thebookdesignhouse.com

Book formatting by: Mark Janssen
http://www.Janssen-Designs.com

DEDICATIONS

To my parents, who taught me who I am, who I should be, and—most importantly— who I belong to.

—Becca Puglisi

To Darian and Jarod, my greatest achievements. (Cheesy, but true!)

—Angela Ackerman

A multitude of thanks to everyone who visits our Writers Helping Writers® site. We appreciate your endless support

—A & B

MORE WRITERS HELPING WRITERS® BOOKS

The Emotion Thesaurus: A Writer's Guide to Character Expression (Second Edition)

Emotion Amplifiers: A Companion to The Emotion Thesaurus

The Negative Trait Thesaurus: A Writer's Guide to Character Flaws

The Urban Setting Thesaurus: A Writer's Guide to City Spaces

The Rural Setting Thesaurus: A Writer's Guide to Personal and Natural Places

The Emotional Wound Thesaurus: A Writer's Guide to Psychological Trauma

The Occupation Thesaurus: A Writer's Guide to Jobs, Vocations, and Careers

TABLE OF CONTENTS

FOREWORD

by Jeannie Campbell, LMFT

The Character Therapist®

I've read a lot of books about characterization, but none are so concise or all encompassing as Angela and Becca's Positive Trait Thesaurus. The introductory chapters are a veritable goldmine for authors. I'd liken them to a Cliff's Notes version of psychology textbooks and many writing craft books, condensed and super reader-friendly.

Personalities are so complex, and figuring out what makes a real person—much less a fictional person—tick is what keeps therapists like me secure in our jobs. Understanding motivations, needs, and how both positive and negative traits and behaviors develop is an integral part to understanding a person. And the first step to writing—make that writing well—has to be this deep understanding.

As a therapist, the section on how positive traits develop (which, in turn, applies to negative traits as well) was the most interesting and thought-provoking. Clearly the authors have done their research, for I might have picked up my Personality Psych book from college and read something similar. So authors, take note! It's more than just nature v. nurture. The information presented should be absorbed in such a way that it'll aid you in brainstorming.

It's highly unlikely that this will be a book you read front-to-back. I'd also recommend that you come to this book with a character in mind—you know, the one that interrupts your sleep and begs to be written. This thesaurus will help you the most when you're in the fleshing-out stages.

Each entry includes the definition, similar attributes, possible causes, associated behaviors/thoughts, and positive aspects of the trait to help you solidify your character's uniqueness. But the entries also include the negative aspects of the trait, scenarios that would challenge a person with that attribute, and other characteristics that could be in conflict with that particular trait. These sections are equally as important in helping solidify conflict and introduce external plot points to showcase your character's internal arc.

Plot-driven authors will really gain a lot from this book, but so will character-driven writers. Heck, I run a business where I profit from analyzing fictional characters, and this book was a great reinforcement to help me do what I do. From understanding the roadblocks that prevent readers from connecting with characters to developing the right character arc for your protagonist, you'll come away feeling like you took a crash course in characterization.

THE ULTIMATE HOOK: CHARACTERS WORTH ROOTING FOR

With millions of books being published worldwide every year, readers have a landslide of stories to choose from. This puts incredible pressure on writers to produce unique plot lines with dynamic, fascinating characters.

Within this flood of fiction, some books rise while others sink. Although eye-catching covers, professional editing, and a well-directed marketing campaign contribute to how well a title will do, without a great story to fill its sails, a book is doomed to drift. And what sturdy mast supports any meaningful work of fiction? Multifaceted characters who make each moment so personal and compelling that readers can't help but care about them.

Creating realistic, never-before-seen characters who take readers on an emotional journey should be the goal of every writer, yet this is no easy feat. Writers must delve into a character's personality to understand his desires, motives, needs, and fears. Both flaws and positive attributes help forge a well-constructed character. Flaws not only humanize the story's cast, they also give them something to overcome so they can achieve self-growth. Positive attributes are equally as important, because while human nature causes us to hone in on people's flaws, it is a person's strengths we admire most. Readers must feel this same admiration for characters in order to root for them.

As a result, authors must learn how to hook readers quickly, and hook them hard. Engaging the reader starts with a clever or intriguing first line and never lets up. During opening paragraphs, there are many ways to draw the audience in—eliciting sympathy by showing a protagonist's current hardship, beginning the scene at a pivotal moment that contains high stakes, or introducing a mysterious story element that makes the reader immediately wonder what is going to happen next.

These simple hooks may create interest, but eventually they play themselves out because while a character's hardship or pain may generate some sympathetic feelings from the audience, only genuine empathy can spark a reader-character bond. It's important to forge this connection as soon as possible so the reader will recognize the protagonist as honorable or deserving in some way, making him worth caring about.

So if empathy is the towrope tying readers to characters, how do writers secure this line early on and keep their audience engaged? Simple. Add punch to a hook by showing the hero's personality in a positive light.

For example, a hardened criminal digging through a trash bin for scraps might make for an unusual opening scene. But since readers know that he's a criminal, they may wonder if he's

1. http://www.bowkerinfo.com

brought his misfortune upon himself. Because they can't empathize with him, they don't care too much about his situation.

But what if he's trying to provide for a trio of orphans rescued from a child-smuggling ring? By hinting at a positive aspect of his personality right away—be it his kindness, a sense of responsibility, or the desire to protect someone vulnerable—he becomes infinitely more interesting and readers catch a glimpse of a hero who is worth believing in. The character also becomes intriguing because of the questions this new information raises: if he's a criminal, why did he save the children? Why does he care? What made him look beyond himself to help someone else?

Suggesting the *why* behind character behavior is the second half of any great hook. "Show, don't tell" still applies—meaning behavior and actions are the best vehicles for revealing a character's personality. The *why* tells us a bit about who the character is, shedding light on what morals and values he holds dear. Revealing a protagonist's positive attributes can also elicit admiration, even for an unlikable hero, and tells the audience that this is someone worth getting to know. Seeing hints of greatness through a character's actions and personality is what helps readers to become emotionally invested.

Personal growth
+ goals
+ relationships/benefit others

WHAT IS A POSITIVE ATTRIBUTE?

Many theories on the nature of personality exist, and while there are differences of opinion, people generally agree that each individual is a unique blend of traits that serve to satisfy basic wants and needs according to one's moral code. A person's upbringing, genetics, and past experiences will determine which positive, neutral, and negative traits emerge, and to what degree. Character strengths aid us in fulfilling our needs and desires and encouraging self-growth, while weaknesses often hold us back. In some situations, it can be difficult to tell a weakness from a strength, especially since flaws may form out of an understandable desire to keep us from being hurt. Within the scope of a story, the protagonist's strengths and weaknesses play important roles in his character arc, so it is critical for authors to know which traits are flaws and which are not.

Flaws are traits that damage or minimize relationships and do not take into account the well-being of others. They tend to be self-focused rather than other-focused. By this definition, *jealous* clearly belongs with the flaws. Jealous characters are focused on their own wants and insecurities; their resentment and bitterness make others uncomfortable and damage relationships.

Positive attributes are traits that produce personal growth or help a character achieve goals through healthy means. They also enhance relationships and typically benefit others in some way. *Honorable*, for instance, is easy to place on the positive side of the personality wheel. An honorable character is going to use healthy measures to achieve success, and because of his nature, he can't help but reach out to others and improve his relationships along the way.

Neutral traits are harder to categorize. Characteristics such as introverted, extroverted, and flirtatious may not necessarily aid a protagonist in achieving her goals in an obvious way, but they do encourage greater exploration of her world and allow for self-discovery. While flaws are debilitating, neutral traits don't have a highly negative impact, so we have chosen to include them in this volume with their positive counterparts.

NEEDS AND MORALS:
INFLUENCERS ON CHARACTER STRENGTHS

Personality is vastly complex, made up of actions and attitudes that show a character's likes and dislikes, ideas, thoughts, and beliefs. But what drives these individual preferences and behaviors? What causes one character to develop traits like curiosity, decisiveness, and adaptability, while another becomes thoughtful, observant, and empathetic?

The first component is **morality**, the controlling belief that certain behaviors are either right or wrong. Morals come from the deepest part of a character and cause her to place values on what she sees, experiences, and thinks. These deeply ingrained attitudes direct a character's choices so they align with her moral code, sometimes even when doing so requires self-sacrifice. Morality affects how she treats other people, what goals and desires she pursues, and how she lives her life day-to-day. As such, the most influential attributes that emerge in her personality will often be tied to a specific moral belief.

The outer world (the people and environment that influence a character) can also impact morality. Social norms, cultural values, and role models all contribute to the development of a character's belief system in regard to right or wrong. Knowing a character's morality can help an author come up with plausible temptations to incorporate into the story and challenge these deeply imbedded beliefs, generating inner turmoil and conflict.

The second factor in trait development lies in the Hierarchy of Needs. According to psychologist Abraham Maslow, individuals are driven by needs that fall into five categories:

Physiological: the need to secure one's biological and physiological needs
Safety and Security: the need to keep oneself and one's loved ones safe
Love and Belonging: the need to form meaningful connections with others
Esteem and Recognition: the need to increase one's sense of esteem
Self-Actualization: the need to realize one's full potential and achieve personal fulfillment

A character's attributes will emerge in the pursuit of satisfying her most important needs. If she is safe, secure, and loved, yet craves the recognition and esteem of others, traits such as determination, perseverance, and efficiency may develop. Thinking about what a character wants can help the writer decide which traits will best assist her in obtaining her goals.

When needs are not met, anxiety and dissatisfaction arise and behavior patterns may change. For example, take a character who has not eaten for days: her physiological needs are going unmet. A normally kind and law-abiding woman may resort to stealing so she can feed herself. Or, although she may be confident with a strong sense of pride, difficult circumstances may push her into begging for food. Driven by desperation, behaviors that are not normally part of her personality take over.

Likewise, a frugal, careful character who is overworked and held back in a dead-end job may find that her need for self-actualization is not being met. Although she is highly responsible, dependable, and consistent, she one day gets up from her desk and walks out. Later, she enrolls in business courses and goes into debt to do so, all in pursuit of satisfying her need to grow.

Core needs are potent, so writers should think carefully about how to use them to motivate their characters. In the right situation, they are even powerful enough to influence or alter one's moral compass. When needs go unmet for too long, anxiety may cause the character's morality to sway. What a person will or won't do in any given situation depends on the *depth of the need* and the character's *ability to satisfy that need.* Take a spiritual, moral character who is safe, loved, and whose physiological needs are being met. He may feel happy and complete, but what if a dangerous element like war is introduced, making his world unsafe? How far would he go to keep himself and his loved ones from harm? Would he be willing to do things that go against his moral beliefs to satisfy his need for safety?

Another benefit of using needs to determine what is most important to a character is that *the quest to meet one's needs is universal.* People generally acknowledge that satisfying one's primary needs is a worthy and understandable aspiration. This affinity with a character's inner motivation (the "why" behind the choice to pursue a goal) will foster empathy and make readers want to see the hero succeed.

THE DIFFERENT CATEGORIES OF POSITIVE ATTRIBUTES

Not all attributes are rooted in morality or needs; some stem from personal preferences resulting from experience. Every character should have a good mix of positive traits that range in intensity. When fashioning a protagonist's personality, writers should include some attributes from each of the following categories to ensure that a variety of strengths emerge.

Moral attributes are traits that are directly related to one's beliefs about right and wrong. Examples might be kindness, generosity, honor, wholesomeness, and justice. Attributes that are tied to one's beliefs will often influence the formation of other traits that align with one's moral code. For example, if a character's moral trait is wholesomeness, it is unlikely that an attribute such as flirtatious would emerge, since being a flirt would undermine her desire to be chaste and virtuous. However, it makes sense that compatible traits such as propriety, discipline, and caution could develop.

Achievement attributes align with morality but their main function is to bolster achievement. If a character has a moral sense of responsibility that determines her life goals, achievement traits such as meticulousness, dependability, resourcefulness, and organization may support her in her pursuits.

Interactive attributes emerge through experiences with one's surroundings and interactions with other people. Traits like patience, courtesy, flirtatiousness, and social awareness dictate how we relate to others and to our world. These attributes are often influenced by personal likes and dislikes. If a character wants to avoid clashes and conflict, she may adopt a friendly nature to ward them off. If she enjoys humor, she may joke when things get serious or reveal a flamboyant side to distract others from their woes. Because characters are largely social beings, this category contains the largest number of traits.

Identity attributes promote a greater sense of individual identity and often result in personal expression of some kind. Creativity and quirkiness are good examples of traits that allow a character to express themselves individually. Identity attributes can also be such a foundational part of a character's personality that they define him and end up influencing many areas of his life. For this reason, spirituality, patriotism, and introversion belong in the identity category.

Positive attributes show the reader who the character really is and that she is worth caring about. But with hundreds of traits to choose from, how do writers find the right strengths to make their characters likable and unique? The answer lies in understanding the influencers that shape an individual's personality.

HOW POSITIVE ATTRIBUTES DEVELOP

So many factors influence who a person is—from current circumstances all the way back to childhood and the formative years. To build a well-rounded, believable character, it's important to recognize all the possible contributors and see how they come together to form attributes. Only then will writers be able to create an authentic cast that will ring true with readers.

GENETICS

As important as it is for characters to take charge and make their own choices, some things are out of their control. Like it or not, they're born with certain inherent attributes. For instance, a character will likely have a natural tendency toward introversion or extroversion. He may either be enthusiastic or calm-natured without ever making the conscious decision for one over the other. Other strengths, like high intelligence or a talent for a musical instrument or a sport, are genetically imparted. While it's possible to adopt different attributes over time, there are some that a character is simply born with.

ETHICS AND VALUES

Ethics are beliefs that revolve around good and bad, moral duty, and obligation. Because of the desire to uphold what's right, a character will embrace attributes that reflect his ethics. A protagonist who would say, "If I agree to finish a project, I must see it through to the end," is someone with a strong sense of duty who places a high value on keeping his word. Resulting attributes may include responsibility, honesty, and discipline.

Values are ideals regarding the worth of people, ideas, and objects. Tied closely to morals, a character's values also determine which attributes become part of his personality. Take this value judgment, for example: "I would rather err on the side of love than on the side of justice." A character who believes this statement appreciates mercy and second chances and will likely be compassionate rather than judgmental. He places a high value on people and sees issues in varying shades of gray rather than in black and white. As a result, some of his strongest attributes may be kindness, empathy, supportiveness, and other traits that align with this belief.

UPBRINGING AND CAREGIVERS

A character's caregivers are his first role models. As a child, he will notice the values and qualities that they espouse. For example, if they held structure and order in high regard, he may come to embrace those traits. This can happen organically, simply from seeing these characteristics exhibited. Or, if his relationship with his caregivers is marked by love and respect, he may consciously choose to adopt their attributes as his own.

Even when the relationship is dysfunctional, a caregiver's traits will inevitably influence an impressionable child. In the above example, if the structured parent was also highly critical and rigid, the character may rebel by rejecting the positive attribute of structured orderliness and embrace an opposing one, such as free-spiritedness.

NEGATIVE EXPERIENCES

While negative experiences often result in the emergence of flaws, they can also cause positive traits to develop. For instance, a child who was abused by her mother may become an incredibly nurturing adult in an attempt to keep from inflicting the same pain on her children. A character may also embrace certain attributes as a way of preventing a flaw from forming, as in the case of a child—once harshly judged and criticized—who adopts tolerance so he can avoid becoming like his accusers. Negative experiences are incredibly formative; authors must have intimate knowledge of their characters' pasts if they're to understand their personalities in the present.

PHYSICAL ENVIRONMENT

Characters are influenced by their environments, both past and present. A child who grew up in a tough neighborhood is going to have different attributes from one who was raised on a farm. Traits formed in childhood usually follow a character into adulthood, but a change in environment may cause a shift in attributes, particularly when the change is drastic. Consider the case of a well-to-do girl who marries the love of her life: a construction worker whose income is a fraction of the girl's former monthly allowance. To survive in her new environment and make her marriage work, she must adopt and develop new attributes—namely, efficiency, thriftiness, and self-control.

PEERS

At certain points in life, peers become one's biggest influencers. Some characters may adopt the attributes shared by their peers as a way of fitting in and gaining acceptance. Others might truly admire their friends' attributes and choose to embrace them in an effort to improve themselves. It's important, though, to keep in mind that not every character is easily swayed by those around him.

PUTTING IT ALL TOGETHER

A character's positive attributes arise from different sources, so when building a profile, the author needs to know his protagonist inside and out—his needs, fears, desires, likes, and dislikes. Developing a backstory allows a writer to see how the character's past experiences have molded him into who he is now. Writers can get into their protagonist's mind-set by understanding his moral beliefs and seeing what needs, goals, and desires he believes to be important. Probing the past will also reveal **emotional wounds**, which will be discussed further in the *Character Arc* section.

Some writers find tools like a character questionnaire useful, so we've created one in Appendix A. Creating well-rounded characters also means pulling from moral, achievement, interactive, and identity-based attributes, so the category list in Appendix C is a good place to start when thinking about the types of attributes to incorporate. The Character Attribute Target Tool in Appendix B is a useful way to then organize each character's positive qualities, helping to ensure all four categories are represented.

POSITIVE ATTRIBUTES AND CHARACTER ARC: OVERCOMING THE FATAL FLAW

Character arc, put simply, is the evolution of a character. The most important arc is that of the protagonist, who at the start of his journey is somehow incomplete, damaged or lost. Even if he seems content, something is missing within, and only through change can he fill this lack and evolve.

Most characters, like real people, are striving for growth, to become the best version of themselves. However, working against them are their flaws—the negative attributes that hold them back in some way from reaching this perfect ideal. Flaws are a character's weaknesses, his dark side. Some are small, seemingly insignificant, while others create giant blind spots that hamper his progress time and again. Either way, these traits play a part in robbing the character of self-growth and true happiness.

Most characters have at least one fatal flaw, a negative trait that causes him to be somehow "stuck" at the start of his story. To complicate matters, he will often misinterpret this flaw as a strength, and can't see how it is keeping him from achieving what he desires most. While there should be an external force of some kind working against him, it is this internal fatal flaw that he must conquer to feel both fulfilled and complete. The only exception is in the case of a tragedy, where the character is unable to move past his greatest fear and so remains unchanged and unfulfilled. In this case, the fatal flaw becomes a tragic flaw.

So where do flaws come from? Why do they have such profound control over behavior? The answer lies in the protagonist's past and his **emotional wounds**.

A wound is an emotional hurt that has caused so much damage the character will do anything to prevent himself from experiencing the same pain again. Examples might be a woman jilted at the altar, or a man who trusted his brother with his investments, only to go broke. Because of this wounding moment, the woman refuses to give her heart away again, and the man becomes miserly and resentful. Wounds often occur in a character's formative years, and the resulting attitudes and behaviors carry forward into adulthood. A teenager abandoned by his parents may view all adults as untrustworthy and find himself unable to trust others as an adult himself. Whatever the circumstance, the wound dampens happiness and fulfillment in some way, tainting the character's view of the world and the people in it.[2]

At the core of the wound is something else: **the lie** the character believes about himself as a result of suffering the emotional wound. For example, the woman may think she was dumped at the altar because she is unworthy of love. The man who lost his savings might believe that his poor judgment is to blame. The abandoned teen may worry that his parents left because he is defective in some way. This lie is what the character fears most, and what he cannot face. Yet, this is the very thing he must confront if he is to become whole.

2. Michael Hauge, author of *Writing Screenplays that Sell*

OUTER MOTIVATION AND OUTER CONFLICT

At its most basic, the character arc consists of four pieces. The **outer motivation** is what the hero wants to achieve, and the outer conflict is the element that's blocking him from reaching that goal. In the film *The Bourne Identity*, Jason Bourne is trying to discover who he is (outer motivation) before black-ops agents catch and kill him (outer conflict).

While strengths are important in helping a character achieve his goal, due to the lie, the character often believes these qualities to be weaknesses. He sees them as negatives—a perception that is frequently reinforced by the supporting cast.

In Jason Bourne's example, everyone tied to Operation Treadstone views him as a killer, a threat who must be extinguished. And with each crime Jason commits, with each life he's forced to take to protect himself, this label is reinforced, along with his fear that he may be exactly what they say he is. Suffering from amnesia, Jason doesn't want to believe he's a killer, but the evidence piles up in the form of his inherent knowledge of combat, survival skills, and weaponry. He wants to run from what he is, but to survive, he must embrace the skills that make him so dangerous (alertness, resourcefulness, persistence, and adaptability) and use them to outwit and defeat those determined to silence him.

INNER MOTIVATION AND INNER CONFLICT

Dynamic, complex story lines also contain an inner journey that mirrors the external one. For every outer motivation, there should be an **inner motivation** (why the character wants to achieve his goal). The inner motivation is often tied to a desire for greater self-worth.

Inner motivation should be accompanied by **inner conflict**: the flaws and/or lies that stand in the way of personal growth and true happiness. As the hero wrestles with the lie, he experiences doubt and failures. Setbacks are debilitating, but they are necessary if the character's resolve is to shine through. Before he can be free of his fatal flaw, he must be burned by it, and before he can dismiss the lie, he must believe it wholeheartedly. The bigger the struggle and the deeper the pain, the more meaningful the protagonist's journey is to readers.

In Jason Bourne's case, his goal (to find out who he is) is driven by his inner motivation (to prove he is not a remorseless killer). His inner conflict (the lie) is the belief that regardless of who he is, he has done terrible things and does not deserve redemption. His fatal flaw is close-mindedness—a refusal to admit that there could be some truth to what others say about him, and more importantly, that he chose this life voluntarily.

The strongest arcs are full of ups and downs that parallel the plot's rough road. The hero should have plenty of outer conflict working against him, along with blows to his ego and self-esteem (inner conflict) that erode his personal development. Even though it might seem as if he cannot face his emotional wounds or be free of his flaws, he must. At some point, the hero should face a similar situation to the one that caused the original wound—only this time the outcome is different. His newfound strength and belief in himself keeps fear from taking hold, and he triumphs. This core of strength is where the character's positive attributes come in.

POSITIVE ATTRIBUTES HELP CHARACTERS WIN THE DAY

Resolve alone is not enough for the protagonist to achieve his goal. Jason Bourne would not have been able to succeed without his bravery, determination, and moral sense of justice. So while the hero needs flaws that make change and growth seem impossible, he must also embody attributes that will enable him to find his way out of the darkness.

A character does not have to overcome all his flaws during the journey, but if the story is to end with him becoming a stronger, more balanced version of himself, then the fatal flaw must be vanquished, or at least diminished to the point that it no longer controls his life. A complete, successful arc should show the character in opposites at the story start and finish: a protagonist jaded by the corruption around him learns to see the good in humanity; a controlling hero who viewed the world with mistrust now allows others to make decisions and help him in his efforts.

For further insight on character arc and how it fits into story structure, we highly recommend Michael Hauge's *Writing Screenplays That Sell* and *The Hero's 2 Journeys* (CD/DVD) by Michael Hauge and Christopher Vogler.

BUILDING CHARACTERS FROM THE GROUND UP: CHOOSING THE RIGHT ATTRIBUTES

While flaws create challenges and friction, attributes forge likability and allow the character to prosper. But including the right balance of positives and negatives requires skill. Too many flaws and she becomes unlikable. Too many attributes and not only will the character succeed too easily, she will be unrealistic, threatening the reader's ability to connect with the hero and the story. Here are a few ways to choose strong attribute combinations for your character:

BRAINSTORM OPPOSITES WITHIN THE BIG PICTURE

Even if you aren't an outliner, all writers should do some planning before starting a first draft. Taking the time to understand your protagonist's goals and fears will simplify the character creation process. Whether you prefer to start with a plot or a character, a few key questions will help you get started.

If you are a plot-focused writer, ask yourself: What do I want to happen in this story? Write a blurb or a few scenes that you envision, and decide what the outcome of the story is (what the protagonist wins or achieves). Once you're happy with this foundation, ask yourself: Who is the worst possible type of person to put into this situation? Knowing what terrible things you have planned will help you build a character who is unsuited for the task ahead. Think of personality flaws that will hurt, hamper, and hold him back, making success seem out of reach. Then, by using the entries in this volume, you can choose positive attributes that will eventually counteract or overpower his weaknesses. The resulting character will be perfect for your story—someone whose flaws make winning difficult, but whose positive attributes will eventually help him fulfill his goals.

If you consider yourself a character-focused writer, ask this question: Who is this character and what makes me care about him enough to write his story? Jot down notes about his quirks, attitudes, morals, and beliefs to get a sense of who he is, using this thesaurus for inspiration. Delve into his backstory. Who hurt him and why? Who showed him love or made him feel like he belonged? What challenges did he face that hardened him or weakened him? Once you have a good idea of who he is, then ask yourself: Based on what I know about this person, what is the worst thing that could happen to him?

That "worst thing" should tie into your plot. Develop it. Work against the hero and throw hardship his way. Once you know what he must do to win, give him flaws that block his path to success. These flaws should weaken him in some way, hurt his relationships with other characters, and blind him to his own deepest fears about himself.

To identify his emotional wounds, pull from his past and zero in on the hurts he's suffered. Once you have chosen flaws that set him back, double-check that the strengths you originally envisioned will help him overcome adversity. These attributes should also help him gain a better perspective and create deeper insight into himself, helping him face his internal demons and emerge whole.

The movie *Titanic* contains a strong example of how opposing flaws and attributes can be combined with great effect. Rose DeWitt Bukater is sophisticated and responsible, as befits a girl of her station in 1912. But she's also rebellious, a trait that conflicts with her attributes. This rebellious streak is what drives her choices, complicating the story and creating tension in her relationships.

USE THE FOUR CATEGORIES

Create a rounded character by choosing positive attributes that stem from his **moral beliefs**, help him **achieve** his goals, allow for healthy **interaction** with others, and clarify his **identity**. His qualities should complement one another, satisfying needs or matching his core beliefs. This will reinforce his personality type and more clearly define who he is. A handy reference that breaks down the traits by category can be found in Appendix C.

MASK STRENGTH IN THE CHARACTER'S EYES

Stories are satisfying, in part, because we get to watch the protagonist evolve and beat the odds. One way to show his growth is to give him an attribute that seems useless or makes him feel weak in some way. Seeing him recognize the trait for what it is and convert it into his greatest strength is incredibly fulfilling for readers. Get creative when picking attributes. Sometimes, the less obvious choice offers the best opportunities for him to overcome adversity.

In Stephen King's *The Stand*, Tom Cullen is frustrated by his low intelligence, wishing he could be smarter and remember things better in order to help his friends in the Free Zone as they prepare for war. However, when he is sent to Las Vegas to spy on the enemy, it is his simple nature and lack of guile that allow him to succeed when those more cunning fail.

PICK SOMETHING UNEXPECTED

Readers can usually connect to a hero's goal, the pain surrounding his past wound, or his desire to become something better. But interest can also be peaked by a character who embodies qualities that are unexpected. Maybe he has a personal quirk or preference or an unusual combination of traits. Choose an attribute (which can also manifest as a skill or talent) that is delightfully unexpected. This is a good technique for protagonists, secondary characters, and even the villain.

In the film *Willy Wonka and the Chocolate Factory*, Willy Wonka is quirky and flamboyant—traits which marry well. However, he is also an idealist; his whole point of inviting children to his factory is to find one who is responsible and good-hearted enough to carry on his legacy. The idealism is unexpected, and adds a unique twist to the story's end.

HOW MUCH IS TOO MUCH?

While it would be easier to choose just one defining attribute for your character, doing so can lead to a flat hero with little dimension. This is why you don't find many existing literary characters who only exhibit one trait. The protagonist requires the most development, and while there are no hard-and-fast rules, we recommend he have at least one main attribute from each of the four categories to round out his personality. Use your writer's intuition to find balance, and if needed, ask critique partners for second opinions.

Too many attributes can result in a messy character whose motivations and emotions are hard to define, while too few attributes puts him in danger of being forgettable. Develop all your characters thoroughly, and each will be memorable in some way. For example, Samwise Gamgee from *The Lord of the Rings* is loyal, down-to-earth, and attentive. John McClane from *Die Hard* is witty, brave, just, and persistent. Both characters are fleshed out and complete, holding their own on the screen.

A useful technique in choosing multiple attributes is to identify one as the primary and make the others secondary. This prioritization will keep clear in the author's mind which traits to emphasize most and which to use as support, adding dimension to the character's personality. For example, Hermione Granger in the *Harry Potter* series is meticulous, driven, and responsible, but readers associate her primarily with intelligence because it directly influences all of her behaviors, attitudes, and decisions.

POSITIVE ATTRIBUTES AND VILLAINS

I t might not be natural to think of villains and positive attributes in the same sentence, but it's incredibly important that our antagonists have legitimate strengths. Why? Because the stronger the villain, the more seemingly impossible it will be for the hero to best him. Seeing the main character in a high stakes situation against an indomitable foe evokes empathy in readers as they wonder how the protagonist can possibly succeed. Building this reader empathy is one of the core purposes of character creation; if you want to do it well, develop an antagonist's positive attributes to make him as strong as possible using the following techniques.

RUN A BACKGROUND CHECK

As writers, we tend to be so focused on the hero that the villain drops off the radar. To make him intimidating, develop him as thoroughly as any of your other main characters. The same influencers that form a hero's positive attributes will also impact the villain. Do your research. Create a profile using a Character Profile Questionnaire like the one in Appendix A. Flesh him out, and he'll emerge as a realistic threat to both the hero and your readers.

KNOW HIS CHARACTER ARC

A villain's character arc should contain the same elements as the hero's. Along with having a goal that is frustrated by an external source (the protagonist), his goal should be driven by an inner need for greater self-esteem resulting from a lie that he believes about himself. And, if the antagonist has been properly developed, his motivations should be traced back to an emotionally devastating wound in his past.

Take the villain Keyser Söze, from the movie *The Usual Suspects*. A petty criminal, Söze's wound is inflicted with the death of his wife and family. After killing each member of the Hungarian Mafia that he blames for their deaths, he goes underground and builds a criminal empire based on secrecy, fear, and myth. His goal is to keep his identity concealed, even from those closest to him (outer motivation), which is sometimes difficult due to the police force and the occasional eyewitness (outer conflict). Although his inner motivation isn't revealed, one could argue that he wants to hide his identity so no one will ever be able to hurt him or those closest to him again. His inner conflict remains unspoken also, but it would make sense that he accepts the blame for the deaths of his wife and children and believes himself to be beyond redemption for bringing such a bitter end upon them (the lie).

A character like this—with wounds, motivations, flaws, and ambitions—is realistic. He makes sense to readers, who see that the hero is up against someone with real issues. By exploring your villain's character arc, not only does he become more interesting and frightening to readers, the hero's situation is worsened in the form of a truly formidable and screwed-up opponent.

MAKE HIM STRONG

An author's knowledge of the villain is often limited to his major flaws and how they drive him. But just as a hero requires strengths to get what he wants, so does the antagonist. Whether the goal is monetary gain (Hans Gruber, *Die Hard*), control (Nurse Ratched, *One Flew over the Cuckoo's Nest*), or self-actualization (Buffalo Bill, *Silence of the Lambs*), a specific set of strengths is required for the villain to have a realistic shot at achieving success. It is these positive attributes that convince readers that he may indeed get what he wants, which increases their fear for the hero. It's also important to remember that the magnitude of the hero's evolution is directly related to the greatness of his opponent. If the protagonist overcomes a wimpy villain, he hasn't really accomplished much, and readers aren't impressed. But pit the hero against an intelligent, patient, vindictive antagonist who is just as driven to achieve his goals? Beating that bad guy elevates the main character to true hero status.

To create strong, realistic, intimidating villains, make sure they embody strengths that enable them to get what they want. In the case of Keyser Söze, patience, intelligence, organization, discretion, and determination are the strengths necessary to becoming a ruthless and evasive criminal mastermind. These strengths transform Keyser Söze from a theoretical bad guy to one of the most intriguing and memorable villains ever written. You can do the same for your antagonist by picking the right mix of attributes.

MAKE HIM MULTIDIMENSIONAL

Although a villain may not embody attributes from all four categories (moral, achievement, interactive, and identity), the possibility should be considered. It's as important for the antagonist to have different kinds of strengths as it is for the hero—with a few key differences.

Some may argue that villains lack morals, but most of the time this isn't true. Many fictional and historical antagonists are ruled by a moral code; it's just different from what is accepted as right and wrong by the general public. Gordon Gekko (*Wall Street*) lives by the mantra that greed is good, and therefore views it as a worthwhile pursuit. Amon Goeth, the real-life horror depicted in the movie *Schindler's List*, believed that an entire race of people held no value at all; in his mind, his actions were right and acceptable, contributing to the greater good. When choosing a moral attribute for your villain, consider how his moral code has been warped by past wounds and negative experiences. A principled villain is a truly frightening one, particularly when his moral choices are atrocious to the hero and reader.

This being said, while a moral attribute is usually the predictor of the rest of a hero's positive traits, this isn't always the case for the antagonist. Because the villain's wound is so profound, it produces a great need, increasing the likelihood that his defining attribute will come from one of the other three categories. Buffalo Bill, one of the villains from *Silence of the Lambs*, is so desperate to escape his physical body that he sets out to create a new one from the skin of his victims. It could be argued that his defining strength, although used in a twisted manner (as is true of most villains), is an identity attribute: inventiveness, out of which his other strengths form. It's also common for villains to embrace achievement attributes, since these characters are so goal oriented.

PUTTING IT ALL TOGETHER

The important thing to remember about most villains is that they're people just like anyone else. They're a mix of good and bad, with strengths and weaknesses. And while a villain may be generally offensive to you, he has wounds and needs as desperate—often more so—than the ordinary person. Figure out what makes your antagonist tick. Make him strong enough to pose a serious threat to your hero, and you'll have a worthy adversary that will have readers firmly on the side of your main character.

THINGS TO KNOW ABOUT YOUR CHARACTER'S POSITIVE ATTRIBUTES

I f you as the author are going to realistically write your character's personality, it's important to know not only what caused their attributes, but also how these traits manifest in the present. Here are a few areas you should be familiar with if you hope to clearly convey your character's personality to readers.

BEHAVIORS AND ATTITUDES

Once you've identified your protagonist's positive qualities, it becomes easier to guess how he will react in varying situations—particularly in unexpected circumstances, since these are the moments when responses are immediate. For instance, three characters who've just learned that they've won the lottery will react according to the traits they possess. An enthusiastic hero may scream, jump up and down, and pull others into the celebration. Someone with a cautious nature might express disbelief and stop to gather facts before tentatively becoming excited. An appreciative character might cry and verbally thank those who are bestowing the gift.

The interesting thing about characters is that, like real people, if you put them all in the same situation, they will react differently. Even those who share the same attribute will respond in distinctive ways due to the combination of traits they possess. Let's assume that our three lottery winners all share excitability as an attribute. The first character, who is also very generous, may promise to give his money away before he's even collected it. The excitable but boorish winner might shout gleeful obscenities and spray beer on everyone. Our third lucky hero, an excitable hypocrite, may announce his plan to pay off all his debts when he has no intention of doing so.

The options for how any individual will respond in a given situation are endless. That's why we've provided so many possible behaviors and attitudes for each attribute, to get you thinking about how your character may react.

THOUGHTS

It's important to remember that characters aren't always honest—with themselves or with others. For instance, your hero may act obedient because he believes it's the right way to be, or because he's surrounded by people who value that trait. But he might really be hiding a rebellious nature; he is compliant on the outside, but on the inside he resents anyone telling him what to do. Thoughts aren't as flashy as actions, but they're sensational in that they tend to reveal one's true nature. If you want to show your character's authentic personality to the reader, you must know what he's thinking and how his thoughts contrast with his behaviors and actions.

EMOTIONAL RANGE

When showing your character's attributes, his emotional range will factor into how he reacts. Is he demonstrative or reserved? Does he change the way he acts around different groups of people? Are there emotions that he hides? Most people aren't comfortable showing all of their feelings. A passionate character who is desperate for acceptance may downplay his emotions in an effort to be more like his peers. A happy character may be uncomfortable expressing any negativity because of his determination to live up to his cheerful reputation. Knowing your character's emotional range will allow you to convey his feelings in an authentic way.

NEGATIVES

While attributes are overwhelmingly positive, it's important to remember that they have their negative sides too. A loyal character is highly devoted to his friends, but his devotion may lead him to support someone whose motivations or actions are questionable. Loyalty can be taken too far, leading the character to lie for others or claim to agree with things he doesn't. Most attributes aren't purely positive; many times they also contain a negative component. Utilize both, and you'll deepen your character's personality in a way that will ring true with readers.

HOW TO SHOW YOUR CHARACTER'S ATTRIBUTES

Once you've identified your character's defining attributes and are familiar with all the aspects involved, you need to be able to effectively convey those traits to the reader. As with so many areas of writing, it's important to *show* these attributes rather than simply telling the reader about them. Showing takes more effort than telling, but it will pay off through the strengthening of the reader-character bond.

Telling creates distance because the reader is sitting back and being told about the character. It's the difference between someone telling you about the hot new guy in the office and you seeing him for yourself. Hearing about him may encourage interest, but you're not emotionally involved until you see him with your own eyes. This is why it's important to show who your characters are. How is this achieved?

THROUGH ACTIONS AND QUIRKS

Attributes dictate actions, so if a character is being honest with himself and with others, his behavior will reflect his positive traits. In *Anne of Green Gables*, Anne Shirley's natural inclination to look on the bright side shows the reader that she is an optimist. When Forrest Gump remains true to Jenny despite her flakiness and many disappearances, the audience infers that he is loyal, and they like him because of it. If a character behaves consistently, readers will be able to figure out what his attributes are, and what kind of person he is.

Quirks—small, original mannerisms or habits—also show personality. Captain Jack Sparrow from the *Pirates of the Caribbean* movies is memorable partly because of his individuality. Through his black eyeliner, the weird rise and fall of his voice, his drunken walk, and the flapping of his hands, it's clear that we're dealing with a flamboyant character. It's equally easy to tell that Buddy, from the movie *Elf*, is uninhibited due to his many quirky habits—from using maple syrup as a condiment to singing in public. Quirks are an effective way to reveal a character's positive side because each one is individual. When used wisely, these peccadilloes can tell the reader a great deal about the character.

THROUGH RELATIONSHIPS

A character's personality can come alive through his interactions with others. Everyone has their own biases, likes, and dislikes, which they subconsciously apply to their relationships. These differences between people can cause conflict, creating tension and stirring up trouble. Pair your hero with others who have opposing attributes or flaws, and your character's traits will come across loud and clear.

Another technique is to let the secondary characters show the reader what kind of person your hero truly is. It's been said that if you want to really know someone, don't ask him what he's like; ask the people closest to him. The hero is most comfortable with his friends, so when they're together, his guard is down and he acts more naturally. Show your character's true personality by what others have to say, through their perceptions of him. This is a good way to get past a hero's bluster and learn what he's really like.

THROUGH THOUGHTS

As was mentioned above, your character isn't always honest about his personality. In an effort to mask flaws, he may act like he has certain strengths when he doesn't. He also may try to emulate the people he admires when he's really very different. But the giveaway is the character's thoughts, because in his own mind he doesn't have to hide or pretend. If he's the point-of-view character, give readers a glimpse into his head. Show them the dissonance between his thoughts and his actions to reveal what he really thinks.

THROUGH CRISES AND CHOICES

In a crisis, stakes are raised and emotions run high, making coherent thought difficult. With no time to dissemble, a hero acts instinctively, letting his true nature show. In the zombie-apocalypse movie *World War Z*, when Gerry Lane's cohort is bitten on the hand, Gerry doesn't hesitate in chopping it off. His quick response shows that he is decisive, willing to take risks, and able to control his fear.

Choices, on the other hand, add an element of time. The character is able to think things through, weigh options, and carefully decide what he should or shouldn't do. In the original *Alien* film, Ellen Ripley is given the choice of allowing her alien-infested mate aboard the ship and possibly saving his life or leaving him outside to die to keep the aircraft free from contagion. Through the calm way she comes to her decision, we can see that she's cautious, sensible, and not easily swayed by others. Readers can learn a lot about the character not only by the choices she makes but also through the process she uses to reach her decisions.

THROUGH THE CHARACTER'S EVOLUTION

Over the course of a story, the protagonist should learn to move past or subdue his fatal flaw. But while his biggest weaknesses will change, his main attributes should be steadfast. By ensuring that strengths stay consistent, the author will reinforce these positive traits by giving readers many opportunities to see the hero exhibiting them.

WHEN READERS AREN'T INTERESTED: COMMON PITFALLS IN CHARACTER CREATION

I t's been determined that readers bond with characters who are human and evoke admiration, respect, or curiosity. The key to creating these characters is to give them positive attributes that will generate intrigue. But what if, despite our best efforts at creating interesting and realistic characters, readers aren't into them? Here are a few reasons the audience may fail to bond with your hero.

UNREALISTIC CHARACTERS

If a character comes across as unrealistic, then the problem could be that the author doesn't know him well enough. You might have the answers to numerous questions about your character, but this doesn't lead to intimacy. It's the same in real life. If you're a Brad Pitt fan, you could find tons of data about him online, but that doesn't mean you know him. You couldn't predict his actions when things get crazy, or identify the triggers from his past that will cause changes in his current behavior, or even understand what he values in his heart of hearts. With your limited knowledge, you could try to write about him, but he would come off as unrealistic and. . . very un-Brad-Pitt-like. For characters to ring true, the author needs to know them deeply so they will act consistently and make sense to the reader.

Another reason a character may seem false is if his voice isn't quite right. Speech should be as unique as the character. Due to differences in tone, quality, pitch, volume, speed, word choice, and many other factors, voices are easily identifiable from one another. Defining personality traits affect speech as well; an impatient character will talk differently than an easygoing or pensive one. Keep all this in mind when thinking about how your hero might speak. Another useful technique is to listen to movie characters who display distinctive speech elements. Karl Childers (*Slingblade*), Vizzini (*The Princess Bride*), Buffalo Bill (*The Silence of the Lambs*), and Forrest Gump (*Forrest Gump*) all have highly original voices. Note what makes them singular, and see how those elements can be applied to your protagonist.

A third possible cause for an unrealistic character has to do with his emotions. When a reader connects with a character and experiences what he's feeling, a bond is created. The reader empathizes and cares what happens to him, but only when the character's emotion is being conveyed realistically. When it's not, readers don't buy in; they pull back, creating distance. Melodrama, too little feeling, emotion that isn't clearly conveyed, and inconsistent responses will result in a character that doesn't ring true. Show your character's feelings concisely, and you'll create the opposite effect, inviting readers to share the emotional experience.

INCONSISTENT CHARACTER ARC

A character's arc is important to the overall story. When there's a major problem with the arc, it will create inconsistencies or gaps that will give the reader a sense that something is off. One of the biggest problems is when a character has no flaws. Authors can become so attached to their heroes that they don't want to think of them as weak. But without a flaw, the hero has no way to improve or fail, and the reader has nothing to root for. Imagine Hamlet without his indecision or Victor Frankenstein with no morbidity. These characters would experience no inner conflict and have nothing to overcome. Who wants to read about that? Unflawed people don't exist in the real world, and they won't exist for long on paper because readers won't stand for them. To create a hero who will resonate with readers, make sure he has some weaknesses to balance out his strengths.

FLAT CHARACTERS

There are a number of reasons a character may come across as flat. One of the biggest problems is with unoriginal or stereotypical characters. It's easy to fall back on these archetypes because they're proven. The hooker with the heart of gold, the eccentric hermit, the wise but slightly crackpot mentor—all of these templates have worked in the past. But after too many reiterations, they lose their appeal. To avoid recreating what's already been done, strive to make your character unique. Twist traditional clichés and create fresh personalities that capture interest.

One-dimensional characters with only a single defining attribute can also disappoint readers, like the studious bookworm or the athletic jock. To avoid this pitfall, build characters that have various traits, preferably from all four categories. When you succeed in identifying and blending attributes that go well together, you'll add depth that will make your hero multidimensional and interesting.

Passive heroes are another no-no. These characters react to circumstances instead of creating change for themselves. They don't make their own decisions but instead respond when things start happening around them. Readers won't respect a hero who sits back and lets other people and events determine his destiny. The character should be making his own choices and moving forward in the story, even if his decisions are wrong. Readers can relate to wrong. So make sure your hero is taking charge and not just waiting for things to happen.

INSUFFICIENT STAKES

Many times, readers tune out of a story or fall out of love with a character because they don't know what's at stake. Whether it's being stuck in prison (*The Shawshank Redemption*), living a life of solitude and isolation (*An Officer and a Gentleman*), or the end of the world as we know it (*Deep Impact*), every good story should contain high stakes. To figure out the stakes in your story, ask yourself this question: What will happen if my character doesn't achieve his goal?

If you know what's at risk but readers still aren't tuning in, it's possible that your stakes aren't high enough. For readers to fully invest in a story, they have to believe that something horrible is going to happen if the protagonist fails. This is what makes them cheer for the character and keeps them turning pages. If you fear that you've set your stakes too low, there are a few ways to make them more urgent.

First, focus on stakes that are universal. Survival, love, hunger, sex, safety, protecting loved ones—these are stakes that anyone can understand because they're so basic. Blake Snyder of *Save the Cat* fame calls them **primal stakes**, because everyone gets them on a visceral level. Consider the children's classic *Charlotte's Web*. What's at stake here? Wilbur is at stake. How is that compelling? you ask. Who cares about a pig? Well, people may not care about farm animals, but pretty much everyone is worried about death. If you can make the stakes in your story primal and universal, you'll go a long way toward ensuring that any reader is going to be invested.

While it's easy to identify the stakes in popular movies and books, it's harder to do this for our own stories. To put this into practice, let's manufacture a fictional scenario and figure out how to turn up the heat. Let's say you've got a story about a woman—we'll call her Faye—who wants to save her marriage. Protecting one's marriage or family is pretty basic, so that qualifies as primal stakes. But it's not exactly riveting. How do we give it more urgency?

The next step would be to make it clear that something awful is going to happen if the character doesn't get what she wants. In Faye's situation, we know that her marriage is at stake, and we know on a theoretical level that a marriage breakup is awful. But readers shouldn't be feeling theoretical worry; they should be biting their nails. We need to make the awfulness clear. Maybe if Faye's marriage ends in divorce, she will lose her husband's insurance coverage for her epileptic daughter, which she desperately needs to cover the medical bills.

Sometimes, even when the stakes are high, readers still don't feel a sense of urgency. They need to believe that danger is looming. To accomplish this, add a deadline or countdown so the reader can see that time is running out. A ticking clock increases the tension and keeps readers involved. In the case of Faye, let's say that the reason her marriage is in danger is because her husband believes she was unfaithful. He's agreed to go to counseling with her, but if they haven't resolved their problems by the end of two months, he's done. Two months to put a marriage back together? Impossible! Now we've got some tension.

Finally, keep throwing obstacles at your character. Without imminent danger, even primal stakes cease to be compelling. Numerous things could happen during those two months to make things more difficult for Faye. The therapist she chooses could be a dud. Her daughter's health may deteriorate. The man her husband believes was her lover may start pursuing Faye, giving her husband more fuel for the divorce fire. Or Faye could find out she's pregnant. Obstacles create uncertainty about your protagonist's ability to succeed. Make sure your character is facing roadblocks that increase in risk and intensity as the story progresses. This will ramp up the tension and give the reader more reason to fear for the hero.

INSIGNIFICANT VILLAINS

Many times it's the villain who makes the hero's situation unbearable. Reader concern for the hero often stems from the unconscionable nature of the bad guy. But if the character opposing the hero isn't terrifying, then the stakes don't seem quite so desperate. To make sure this doesn't happen, do your homework. Map out the villain's character arc so you're aware of what he wants and why he's so desperate to achieve it. Figure out his inner motivation so you know what vital piece of his internal makeup is missing or damaged. As driven as your hero is to achieve his goals, the villain should be just as determined to get what he wants. If the antagonist is willing to do whatever it takes to succeed, then your hero will be in big, big trouble. And that should play a large part in upping reader interest.

FINAL NOTES

While we've tried to include a broad range of attributes in this thesaurus, there are simply too many for the list to be complete. We recommend using the index to find the trait you're looking for since many attributes can be grouped together. For example, *cheerful, jolly, upbeat,* and *merry* are practically interchangeable, and so are all listed under the parent entry, *happy*. In other cases, the trait is so similar to an existing entry that we placed them together to avoid repetition. If you still can't find the trait that you want, consider consulting an entry that's similar, since you may find that information useful. Also, since strengths that are embedded in the psyche are the most complex and difficult to write, we chose to focus on these rather than attributes that are physical in nature (graceful, attractive, etc.).

It's important to remember that this book is meant to be used as a **brainstorming guide**. While the entries contain specific information regarding behaviors, emotions, and possible causes for attributes, characters are unique. They will react according to the combination of traits they possess, the intensity of the situation, their emotions at the time, who they're with, and any number of other factors. As such, the entries in this volume should act as a starting point rather than an exhaustive list for choosing your character's response to any given situation.

It should also be noted that while this thesaurus can be used as a stand-alone reference, we recommend using it with *The Negative Trait Thesaurus: A Writer's Guide to Character Flaws* to aid in the creation of balanced, complex characters.

Theories and opinions abound regarding the study of character and personality. For the purposes of character creation involving positive attributes, we've gone with one school of thought among many. The core causes of behavior are especially wide-ranging and often are directly tied to the individual's past experiences. The causes we've listed in these entries are simply possibilities—ideas to encourage writers to think more about how the past should affect their character's present behavior.

If there's one thing we've learned from the writing of this resource, it's that there is no limit to the number of original characters that can be created. By uncovering your character's past, factoring in their genetic makeup, and plugging in other components, you should be able to build many never-before-seen characters that are both realistic and intriguing. It is our hope and sincere belief that this resource will help you build a cast of characters so well drawn that your readers will feel compelled to share in their journey from the first page to the last. Best of luck!

THE POSITIVE TRAIT THESAURUS

ADAPTABLE

DEFINITION: showing flexibility and versatility regardless of the situation

CATEGORIES: achievement, interactive

SIMILAR ATTRIBUTES: flexible, resilient, versatile

POSSIBLE CAUSES:
Having a strong inner drive
Growing up in a dangerous or unpredictable environment
Being a caregiver to someone who has a chronic illness
Thriving on challenges
Moving from place to place frequently in childhood
Having a calm, unflappable nature
Carrying little or no emotional baggage
Having a positive attitude
Having strong self-esteem

ASSOCIATED BEHAVIORS:
Thinking quickly
Holding down more than one job
Being comfortable with responsibility
Enjoying travel and exposure to new cultures
Being highly organized
Being a team player
Sociability with others
Confidence
Being competitive with oneself
Open-mindedness
Exhibiting strong decision-making skills
Persuasiveness, either through good people skills or manipulation
Planning ahead; keeping alternatives in mind
Being prepared for anything
Not shying away from challenges
Being knowledgeable in many areas
Pursuing education or training to make oneself more prepared
Following orders efficiently
Preferring a variety of experiences over routine
Spontaneity and agreeability
Being willing to improvise
Recovering from disappointments or setbacks quickly
Having strong multitasking skills
Vocally expressing one's ideas
Being a good listener

Having a strong sense of empathy
Being thoughtful and considerate
Having broad interests and hobbies
Maintaining firm control of one's emotions
Taking advantage of opportunities
Learning from one's past mistakes

ASSOCIATED THOUGHTS:
I'd like to go out but if Margaret wants to eat in, we can do that, too.
I'll take over Rick's report. The team is waiting on it and he could be out sick for days. Since no one else is stepping up, I will.
I'm glad Marcy's planning our vacation. Wherever we end up going will be great.

ASSOCIATED EMOTIONS: confidence, curiosity, eagerness, happiness, peacefulness, pride

POSITIVE ASPECTS: Adaptable characters are reliable and responsible and can thrive in almost any situation. They enjoy challenges and new experiences and are at ease with change. Even during stressful situations, they can keep volatile emotions at bay. Adaptable characters are able to work with others or lead, whichever is needed to achieve the goal. They are quick thinkers who are able to keep their heads when others lose theirs.

NEGATIVE ASPECTS: Characters with this attribute can grow restless if they feel they are not stimulated enough. They don't always place as much importance on family and friendships as other people do; relationships may suffer if these characters are paired with people who require stability and routine.

EXAMPLE FROM LITERATURE: Jason Bourne from *The Bourne Identity* is a trained operative who has lost his memory. Seen as a threat by his government, he is hunted by other assassins and must remain versatile in order to survive. Resourceful and persistent, he fights when necessary, obtains money and documentation, and adapts to each new environment so he can react as needed and remain safe. **Other Examples from Film:** Simon Templar (*The Saint*), Hawkeye (*The Last of the Mohicans*)

TRAITS IN SUPPORTING CHARACTERS THAT MAY CAUSE CONFLICT:
compulsive, decisive, impatient, introverted, judgmental, meticulous, pensive

CHALLENGING SCENARIOS FOR THE ADAPTABLE CHARACTER:
Ambiguity (a situation, set of instructions, etc.) that one cannot prepare for
Being asked to do something that will likely result in injury, suffering, or worse
Experiencing conflicts between one's moral beliefs and the need to carry out an order
Being required to always respond to situations the same way, with no variation

ADVENTUROUS

DEFINITION: willing to try new experiences and take risks

CATEGORIES: achievement, identity, interactive

SIMILAR ATTRIBUTES: daring, risk-taking, venturous

POSSIBLE CAUSES:
Growing up with parents who had a strong sense of adventure
Being encouraged as a child to try new things and experiences
Having adrenaline-junkie tendencies
Requiring constant stimulation; being easily bored
Being an extrovert

ASSOCIATED BEHAVIORS:
Participating in extreme sports (rock climbing, sky diving, bungee jumping, etc.)
Obtaining injuries as a result of activities (broken bones, etc.)
Taking risks for fun
Initiating conversation in social situations
Researching new thrills, adventures, and experiences to attempt
Trying new foods
Having a positive attitude
Having a large social circle
Being gear-savvy; using proper equipment for an activity
Reading up on other countries and activities to experience there
Joining adventure-centric clubs or groups
Working to live, not living to work
Enjoying meeting new people
Not being tied to a single place
Asking people where they've travelled and what they've done
Preferring to spend money on experiences rather than material things
Consistently filling one's free time
Being interested in other cultures and alternative lifestyles
Having a strong sense of self-esteem
Confidence
Open-mindedness
Friendliness
Enjoying the rush of adrenaline
Being "high energy"
Exuberance
Being healthy and fit
Having more than the usual knowledge of nutritional needs and how the body works
Being multilingual

Desiring to share one's experiences with others; introducing them to new things
Training to become proficient in activities (scuba lessons, cliff diving, etc.)
Difficulty saving money due to the high costs of gear, travel, and activities

ASSOCIATED THOUGHTS:
A few more weekend climbs like this and I can take on Devil's Peak!
Renee said the diving in Australia can't be beat; that's where I'm going next.
Donnie is worrying too much. This skydiving company has an excellent reputation.
A polar bear swim! That's what I need to do.

ASSOCIATED EMOTIONS: confidence, determination, excitement, happiness, satisfaction

POSITIVE ASPECTS: Adventurous characters attract other people who share their energy and sense of fun. Willing to experiment and try new things, these characters want to experience all that life has to offer. While others might settle for what makes them content, those with an adventurous spirit will strive for complete happiness and satisfaction regardless of the risk or cost.

NEGATIVE ASPECTS: These characters commonly indulge in activities that create an emotional high. They don't often consider the consequences, which can put them in danger and bring about physical harm. Their need for adventure may cloud their judgment, encouraging them to push boundaries. When in a group of other adventurous types, peer pressure to do more and go farther can lead to poor choices.

EXAMPLE FROM FILM: Indiana Jones, the daring archaeologist from the movie franchise, is a die-hard adventurer who will go to any lengths to solve the mysteries of the ancient world. Indy easily adapts to different—often dangerous—cultures and environments and thrives on the pursuit of knowledge, risking much to obtain relics that will provide new information about the past. **Other Examples from Literature and Film:** Peter Pan (*Peter Pan*), Lara Croft (*Tomb Raider*), the Dauntless faction (*Divergent series*)

TRAITS IN SUPPORTING CHARACTERS THAT MAY CAUSE CONFLICT: calm, cynical, insecure, meticulous, needy, nervous, paranoid

CHALLENGING SCENARIOS FOR THE ADVENTUROUS CHARACTER:
Suffering an injury or illness that prevents one from getting out and doing things
Losing one's job; not having the financial means to pursue adventure opportunities
Being with a group whose risk-taking level is significantly higher or lower than one's own
Having an accident that causes a phobia that prevents the enjoyment of a favorite activity

AFFECTIONATE

DEFINITION: showing open fondness for others

CATEGORIES: identity, interactive

SIMILAR ATTRIBUTES: doting, loving, tender

POSSIBLE CAUSES:
Growing up in a loving home
Overcompensating for a lack of love in the past
Having affectionate role models
Neediness
A fear of being alone or abandoned
Having a romantic nature
Being highly empathetic
Having a desire to nurture

ASSOCIATED BEHAVIORS:
Hugging, kissing
Holding hands
Wanting to hold and be held
Holding onto another's arm to keep them close
Stroking an arm or shoulder for physical reassurance
Giving compliments and praising others
Doing favors for others (small acts of kindness, etc.)
Writing poetry for a loved one
Offering small gifts or tokens
Strong body language reading skills
A willingness to express one's feelings
Giving massages and foot rubs
Telling a loved one how special they are
Being supportive of loved ones in all their endeavors
Sitting and touching (legs touching, a hand on the other's leg, etc.)
Putting an arm around someone's shoulders
Saying words of encouragement
Sensory sensitivity, especially touch
Agreeing to do things that will please one's significant other
Adopting another's hobbies or interests as a way of increasing intimacy
Calling a loved one frequently during the day
Pursuing sexual intimacy
Saying *I love you*
Building strong relationships
Compassion
Empathy
Nuzzling

Using pet names; talking in a playful voice
Trustworthiness
Being emotionally vulnerable and open
Kindness and friendliness
Being motivated by goodwill and love
Intuitively assessing the needs and moods of others
Being open about one's emotions
Being observant; paying attention to what loved ones need
Speaking affectionately of loved ones in conversations to others

ASSOCIATED THOUGHTS:
Dave seems tense. A back rub will help him relax.
I don't care what my mother thinks. I love Amy, and I'm going to show it.
Allen is so good to me. I think I'll surprise him with a romantic dinner.
It's so sweet when my kids hold hands!

ASSOCIATED EMOTIONS: adoration, desire, elation, gratitude, love, peacefulness, satisfaction

POSITIVE ASPECTS: Affectionate characters show their emotions in very obvious ways. They're attuned to their feelings and aren't ashamed to tell others how they feel. Through their lack of inhibition, these characters build healthy and nurturing relationships that make others feel safe and loved.

NEGATIVE ASPECTS: Affectionate characters may not always properly judge when and where to indulge in public displays of affection. From a mom hugging her teenage son in front of his peers to a make-out session between co-workers at the office Christmas party, affectionate displays are not always appropriate and can cause embarrassment for others.

EXAMPLE FROM LITERATURE: In *Anne of Green Gables*, Diana Barry is the girl next door who is full of romantic ideas of friendship and love. Devoted to Anne, Diana sees her as an adventurous sister and the two become inseparable. Always hugging or holding hands to show their closeness, they stage a ceremony to declare their future as "bosom" friends. Diana becomes an important person in Anne's life by showing her the warmth and love that Anne had always longed for. **Other Examples from Film, TV and Literature:** Evelyn and Rick O'Connell (*The Mummy Returns*), Abby Sciuto (*NCIS*), Novice Aes Sedai (*The Wheel of Time*)

TRAITS IN SUPPORTING CHARACTERS THAT MAY CAUSE CONFLICT: cruel, dishonest, gullible, hostile, inhibited, proper, timid, withdrawn

CHALLENGING SCENARIOS FOR THE AFFECTIONATE CHARACTER:
Being absent from loved ones for long periods (being a soldier or having to travel for work, etc.)
Being in a relationship that is forbidden or taboo by societal or religious standards
Experiencing upsets in a marriage or committed relationship
Hiding a relationship from others
Being forced into a marriage where one doesn't feel affection for one's partner
Being drawn to someone who is uncomfortable with physical touch

ALERT

DEFINITION: being aware of and watchful for possible change or danger

CATEGORIES: achievement, interactive

SIMILAR ATTRIBUTES: aware, vigilant, watchful

POSSIBLE CAUSES:
Growing up during a period of war or turmoil
Being exposed to danger or prejudice
Having parents who taught one to be wary of danger
Being hurt or abused in the past
Living in a society categorized by uncertainty, corruption, or mistrust

ASSOCIATED BEHAVIORS:
Anticipating possible dangers before they occur
Planning ahead
Evaluating one's options
Always having an exit strategy
Asking questions
Paying close attention to what is said
Being highly observant
Having heightened senses; noticing things that others miss
Thinking about the *What if?* scenario
Avoiding risk and situations where one might be in danger
Being prepared for alternatives
Valuing one's privacy
Heeding the rules and warnings; reading the fine print
Being cautious when it comes to online safety
Locking doors
Adhering to proven, stable routines and choices
Paying attention to one's intuition
Prioritizing one's health; getting enough sleep
Controlling one's emotions
Avoiding volatile situations or people
Preferring to know what's coming rather than being surprised
Keeping an eye on one's wallet, purse, or other items of importance
Trying things out before purchasing (test-driving a car, etc.)
Being hard on oneself when mistakes are made
Noticing small changes
Exhibiting strong listening skills
Researching a vacation spot carefully before committing to visit
Having emergency kits in one's home and car
Taking extra safety measures (installing a security system, turning on lights, etc.)

Making eye contact with others
Having a difficult time opening up or showing one's vulnerability
Neighborhood attentiveness (recognizing the cars parked on one's street, etc.)
Reading the newspaper or watching the news to stay up to date
Giving full attention to one's surroundings (not texting while driving, etc.)
Being aggressive when a threat is perceived
Taking responsibility for others (watching a neighbor's child to be sure she gets on the bus safely)

ASSOCIATED THOUGHTS:
The kids left their toys out again. I'll pick them up before someone trips in the dark.
I don't remember leaving the front door unlocked.
This is a good parking spot—right under the flood light.
Everyone else might like Carrie, but there's something not quite right about her.

ASSOCIATED EMOTIONS: anticipation, determination, fear, suspicion, worry

POSITIVE ASPECTS: Alert characters are always aware of their surroundings and anticipate danger before it happens. They can be valuable in keeping others safe due to their vigilance. These characters are highly observant, noticing little things that others miss. They trust their instincts and are more concerned with safety and avoiding danger than with what others may think of their hyper awareness.

NEGATIVE ASPECTS: While alert characters are great at sniffing out trouble, they can go overboard and anticipate danger where there is none. Their worries about possible problems can limit their ability to have fun and relax; these tendencies can also feel suffocating to others. An alert character who has experienced much danger can drift into paranoia, viewing all people and uncertain situations as dangerous.

EXAMPLE FROM FILM: Dr. Richard Kimble (*The Fugitive*) is on the run both from the Chicago P.D. and the Treasury Department, determined to prove his innocence in the murder of his wife. While searching for the clues that will reveal who killed her and why, Kimble must constantly be on the alert for signs that the authorities are closing in. **Other Examples from Film and Literature:** John Rambo (*First Blood*), Frank Horrigan (*In the Line of Fire*), Jason Bourne (the *Bourne* series)

TRAITS IN SUPPORTING CHARACTERS THAT MAY CAUSE CONFLICT:
adventurous, impulsive, playful, spunky, uninhibited

CHALLENGING SCENARIOS FOR THE ALERT CHARACTER:
Feeling intense emotions that encourage rashness (rage, love, desire, etc.)
Being paired with an impulsive character who is always leaping without looking
Living in a constantly changing environment
A situation where one or more of the senses are diminished or no longer reliable
A tragedy where one misses the danger signs and blames oneself for the fallout

AMBITIOUS

DEFINITION: driven by the desire to achieve a particular goal

CATEGORIES: achievement, identity

SIMILAR ATTRIBUTES: driven

POSSIBLE CAUSES:
Confidence and pride
Being a passionate person; having big dreams
The desire to achieve something one lacked as a child
A fear of failure
Needing to prove oneself to others or desiring to leave behind a legacy
Having ambitious parents
Sibling or peer rivalry
Insecurity; worrying about not meeting expectations or not being good enough
Wanting to please others
Craving prestige or wealth that only success can bring
Having a noble purpose (to stop poverty, to oust a neighborhood's gangs, etc.)

ASSOCIATED BEHAVIORS:
Rising early
Being energetic
Determination
Efficiency
Seeking out education or training; honing the skills needed for achievement
Choosing to spend time with people who can help one become successful
Working overtime or during holidays to get ahead
Using flattery or being overly polite when dealing with those in power
Asking for help from people in a position to do so
Calling in favors
Embracing hard work
Planning for the future
Taking on greater responsibilities
Ignoring friendships in favor of working toward a goal
Being highly organized
Prioritizing one's needs
Having strong willpower
Keeping a token for inspiration (a toy Ferrari to symbolize the real thing, etc.)
Tackling tasks that others avoid or feel are beyond them
Learning quickly from one's mistakes instead of dwelling on them
Breaking down big goals into smaller milestones to mark one's progress
Researching what one will need; making a plan for success
Using others who achieved ambitious goals as role models

Making choices that lead to fulfilling one's goals
Not being satisfied with the status quo
Believing that things can always be better
Wanting to do better or become the best at something
Taking risks
Being competitive with others
Not allowing fears or worries to limit oneself
Thinking "big"
Not being overly fazed by setbacks; refocusing and moving past them

ASSOCIATED THOUGHTS:
If I go to work early, my boss will see how dedicated I am to the company.
This year, I'm going to cross "run a marathon" off my bucket list.
So I don't go out as much as Lee. That's why I'm a director and he's still a manager.
Amy's the one for me; now I just have to get her to see it, too.

ASSOCIATED EMOTIONS: anticipation, confidence, determination, hopefulness

POSITIVE ASPECTS: Ambitious characters are hardworking visionaries who don't give up easily. When others see only roadblocks, these characters see amazing futures. Ambition requires great focus and single-mindedness that enables most people with this trait to succeed at their goals.

NEGATIVE ASPECTS: Characters with ambition run the risk of putting their goals above everything else, including the people or priorities in life that should come first. When ethics and success become incompatible, achieving the goal often wins out. Many are perfectionists with unrealistic expectations who view anything short of success as failure. These characters also may set goals so high that they become unreachable, which leads to unhappiness and a lack of fulfillment.

EXAMPLE FROM FILM: Former salesman Chris Gardner (*The Pursuit of Happyness*) is unemployed and homeless with his young son when he's offered the chance to pursue a career as a stockbroker. The sole intern position is highly sought after, and Chris must fight for it despite having little money, no home, and no experience. Despite these seemingly insurmountable obstacles, Chris does everything within his power to make a better life for him and his son.
Other Examples from Film: Melanie Carmichael (*Sweet Home Alabama*), Bud Fox (*Wall Street*)

TRAITS IN SUPPORTING CHARACTERS THAT MAY CAUSE CONFLICT: obedient, lazy, pensive, pushy, scatterbrained

CHALLENGING SCENARIOS FOR THE AMBITIOUS CHARACTER:
Pursuing a goal that breaks tradition or law (a female determined to be a Catholic priest, etc.)
Being required to go against one's ethics (being part of a cover-up, etc.) to succeed
Having a competitor who is both talented and worthy
Having a physical or mental handicap
Having rivals without scruples who are willing to do whatever it takes to win
Having a responsibility that takes up a lot of one's time (caring for a sick uncle, etc.)

ANALYTICAL

DEFINITION: skilled in thinking and reasoning; having a natural instinct to study and analyze

CATEGORIES: achievement, interactive

SIMILAR ATTRIBUTES: logical, rational

POSSIBLE CAUSES:
Intelligence
Being highly curious
Being driven by the desire for order
A fear of making mistakes
Having an interest in why things work
Having parents who encouraged one to understand cause and effect
Being emotionally disconnected
Perfectionism

ASSOCIATED BEHAVIORS:
Asking questions
Reading up on a topic to attain better understanding
Studying things that evoke curiosity
Running experiments
Being well-read
Posing theories and attempting to prove them
Getting hung up on the little things
Having an interest in human behavior and psychology
Being unable to let go unless every possibility has been explored
Reading into what people say and do
Looking for patterns and cause-effect relationships
Needing to categorize and find order in one's life
Exploring how one decision creates a chain reaction
Being uncomfortable with sarcasm and jokes
Obsessing over minute details
Not being able to let something go
Needing to understand the "why" behind a process, action, or behavior
Showing less emotion than most people
Placing value on facts instead of feelings
Being organized and logical
Adhering to routines and schedules
Posing *What if?* questions
Enjoying the chance to explain how something works
Being honest even when it hurts: *Yes, you do look overweight in that dress.*
Being skeptical when presented with new ideas, beliefs, or "truths" without proof
Struggling in social situations (making small talk, etc.)

Being highly observant
Correcting misinformation or misconceptions
Sucking the enjoyment out of something by rationalizing it to others
Being good with numbers
Keeping a journal of one's thoughts and observations
Being able to quickly and accurately assess a situation

ASSOCIATED THOUGHTS:
Why ask me how she looked if she didn't want the truth?
Liam is so afraid of the dark. Something probably happened to him as a child.
I don't understand love rituals. Why not just say what you feel?
Everyone has an opinion, but no one bothers to find out the facts.

ASSOCIATED EMOTIONS: conflicted, determination, skepticism

POSITIVE ASPECTS: Analytical characters are thinkers, and can often see much deeper into a problem or situation than others. They enjoy the process of metaphorically reducing an object or issue to its base components in order to see what's working and what needs improvement. These characters work well alone, are dedicated and intelligent, and are strong problem solvers.

NEGATIVE ASPECTS: Characters with this attribute tend to get caught up in the details and miss the big picture. Their minds are always working, which can make it difficult for them to relax and enjoy social situations. Their constant desire to analyze everyone and everything can make people uncomfortable. For these reasons, analytical characters may have a hard time connecting with others on a meaningful level.

EXAMPLE FROM TV: Sheldon Cooper from TV's *Big Bang Theory* looks at everything in an analytical manner, basing almost every decision on a mathematical probability. Superiorly intelligent yet socially challenged, he lives his life according to a strict routine and has difficulty with the emotional component of friendship. A theoretical physicist, Sheldon will not support theories without in-depth empirical evidence. His actions are based on logic and fact rather than feeling. **Other Examples from Literature and Film:** Sherlock Holmes, Mike McDermott (*Rounders*), Lincoln Rhyme (*Lincoln Rhyme* series)

TRAITS IN SUPPORTING CHARACTERS THAT MAY CAUSE CONFLICT:
adaptable, adventurous, impulsive, irrational, melodramatic, paranoid, sentimental

CHALLENGING SCENARIOS FOR THE ANALYTICAL CHARACTER:
Being drawn to a hobby or activity that is illogical but brings enjoyment
Drinking alcohol
Attending frivolous events (cocktail parties with small talk, etc.)
Spending extensive amounts of time with small children
Having a fear or phobia that can't be analyzed or explained

APPRECIATIVE

DEFINITION: showing thankful recognition for what life brings

CATEGORIES: interactive, moral

SIMILAR ATTRIBUTES: grateful, thankful

POSSIBLE CAUSES:
Experiencing a life-shaping event that puts things into perspective
Being taught as a child to be grateful for what one has
Having a strong faith in God or another deity
Surviving death
Having escaped a dangerous environment or situation
Being strongly aware of one's freedom
Happiness and satisfaction
Possessing a strong spirit; feeling whole and content

ASSOCIATED BEHAVIORS:
Adaptability
Loyalty
Seeking out the world's beauty (traveling, experiencing natural wonders, etc.)
Encouraging others to let go of worries and negative emotions
Smiling
Being thankful for what one has
Not being materialistic in nature
Having a strong work ethic
Caring for others
Seeking ways to "pay it forward"
Positivity
Friendliness
Treating others with care and thoughtfulness
Finding happiness in simplicity
Being willing to help others however one can
Believing that everything will work out for the best
Not sweating the small stuff
Being non-judgmental
Having a strong connection to nature
Frequent humming or singing
Believing that every living thing has a purpose
Inquisitiveness (asking questions, showing interest in others and the world, etc.)
Praying
Having a strong sense of community
Being committed to others
Speaking with sincerity

Proactively helping or caring for others without needing to be asked
Valuing every moment and experience
Not shying away from emotional expression
Being at peace with one's circumstances
Excelling in teamwork situations
Being willing to share what one has; generosity
Seeing mistakes as opportunities to learn and grow
Sharing one's life lessons with others
Praising others for their kindness or thoughtfulness; saying *Thank you*

ASSOCIATED THOUGHTS:
I have the best family in the world. I can't imagine raising my kids without them.
Nothing is more soothing than the sound of the surf. I love living by the ocean.
Dara is a kind neighbor, bringing us cookies whenever she goes on a baking spree.
I love my critique group! What a blessing to learn from such talented writers.

ASSOCIATED EMOTIONS: eagerness, elation, gratitude, happiness, hopefulness

POSITIVE ASPECTS: Appreciative characters show gratitude for whatever comes their way. Because of their positive attitudes and adaptability, they find silver linings in hard times, see lessons in the midst of mistakes, and focus on small pleasures to remove the sting from difficult moments. These characters are centered and at ease with themselves. They make loyal friends and are good influencers, encouraging their companions to search out and find the peace that accompanies gratitude and contentment.

NEGATIVE ASPECTS: Characters who are highly appreciative can sometimes become passive, just accepting what comes their way without setting their own goals or challenging the status quo. Loved ones and co-workers can become frustrated with their complacency or label them as naïve for being so accepting. The loyalty of appreciative characters can render them vulnerable when they trust "friends" to have their best interests at heart when they do not.

EXAMPLE FROM LITERATURE: When he is saved from being eaten by his fellow cannibals, the native Friday (*Robinson Crusoe*), expresses his undying thanks by pledging himself eternally to his savior. Throughout his life, Friday remains true to Crusoe, never wavering from the promise that he made out of gratitude. **Other Examples from Film and TV:** the Vang Lor family (*Gran Torino*), Leonard Hofstadter (*The Big Bang Theory*)

TRAITS IN SUPPORTING CHARACTERS THAT MAY CAUSE CONFLICT: cocky, controlling, disrespectful, jaded, manipulative, superficial, ungrateful

CHALLENGING SCENARIOS FOR THE APPRECIATIVE CHARACTER:
Being in the debt of someone one doesn't like
Living in volatile times, such as a war, revolution, or an uprising
Feeling loyalties to opposing causes or people
Seeing others suffer and being unable to alleviate that suffering
Having a crisis of faith in God or country

BOLD

DEFINITION: having an intrepid spirit

CATEGORIES: achievement, identity, interactive

SIMILAR ATTRIBUTES: assertive, audacious, gutsy, nervy

POSSIBLE CAUSES:
The desire to prove oneself
High self-confidence
The tendency to be consumed by one's goals
Fearlessness
Being driven by a strong sense of righteousness
The belief in a higher power or purpose
Desiring to know the truth at all costs

ASSOCIATED BEHAVIORS:
Assertiveness
Coming up with unconventional solutions
Speaking one's mind even when one's opinion isn't popular
Enthusiasm; being energetic
Positivity
Taking risks
Being highly extroverted
Acting in a way that inspires others; leading by example
Making decisions without hesitation
Being the first to speak with or greet others
Having open body posture
Trying new things; seeking out new experiences
Taking the initiative (planning events, making suggestions, flirting, etc.)
Dressing and behaving confidently
Entertaining ideas that most others would dismiss (a radical career change or move, etc.)
Asking for what one wants or needs
Openness and transparency
Not beating around the bush
Pushing limits and boundaries
Having a strong gut instinct
Being one's own advocate
Taking responsibility without hesitation
Challenging rules or conditions that don't make sense
Not being held back by fear
Having strong convictions
Not caring what others think
Embracing innovation

Being goal oriented
Looking within to determine what one really wants, then pursuing it
Not being fazed by rejection or failure; bouncing back quickly
Friendliness
Encouraging others to go after their dreams
Handling stress and adversity head-on
Decisiveness
Refusing to be a people-pleaser

ASSOCIATED THOUGHTS:
I've been with this bank so long; I bet they'll waive this fee if I ask.
I don't understand Cara. If she thinks she deserves a raise, why not ask for it?
This cross-country bike tour is a once-in-a-lifetime opportunity. I can't wait!
I am so sick of these snotty boating club events. Dad will be pissed, but I'm done with them.

ASSOCIATED EMOTIONS: confidence, desire, determination, eagerness, hopefulness, pride

POSITIVE ASPECTS: Bold characters are go-getters; they know what they want and aren't afraid to go after it. When it comes to pursuing their goals, they are able to take the ups with the downs and maintain forward momentum. People are often drawn to their confidence and willingness to stand up for what they believe in. The fearlessness of these characters makes them good leaders and strong protagonists.

NEGATIVE ASPECTS: Boldness can seem overwhelming to certain kinds of people. Shy or insecure characters may find such fearless determination intimidating and even be turned off by it. Bold characters commit quickly, making things difficult for partners, co-workers, or potential love interests who want to take things slowly. Because of their convictions, these characters have a hard time backing away from what they believe to be the most direct course, and can come across as being uncooperative, self-serving, or pushy to others.

EXAMPLE FROM FILM: Despite his unconventional history as a white man brought up by Native Americans, Hawkeye (*The Last of the Mohicans*) exhibits a boldness that often results in achieving his desired results. In the face of open hostility, he remains loyal to his Mohican family. When he sets his sights on Cora, he pursues her regardless of the many obstacles in his way. In every situation, he speaks his mind with confidence, regardless of the opposition. **Other Examples from Film:** Maximus Decimus Meridius (*Gladiator*), Frank Slade (*Scent of a Woman*)

TRAITS IN SUPPORTING CHARACTERS THAT MAY CAUSE CONFLICT: calm, cautious, cowardly, irresponsible, patient, timid, whimsical, worrywart

CHALLENGING SCENARIOS FOR THE BOLD CHARACTER:
Having a rival with the same desire or goal who is equally bold and determined to achieve it
Wanting something that one cannot have (a relationship with a happily married woman, etc.)
Finding oneself in a situation where boldness is the wrong tactic (dealing with an abuse victim, etc.)
Wanting something that will do one harm (revenge, etc.)

CALM

DEFINITION: inclined toward tranquility and serenity

CATEGORIES: interactive

SIMILAR ATTRIBUTES: composed, peaceful, placid, sedate, serene, tranquil, unruffled

POSSIBLE CAUSES:
Feeling at peace with oneself and the world
Having a strong feeling of belonging
Believing in a higher power or purpose
Intuitiveness
Being naturally easygoing in nature
Having a boring personality
Having little or no imagination
Practicality
Growing up in an environment or culture where emotional temperance was valued
Having a desire for peace

ASSOCIATED BEHAVIORS:
Thinking before reacting
Speaking in a soft voice and tone
Using soothing touches and gestures that comfort others
Having excellent reasoning skills
Enjoying simple pleasures
Accurately reading people and their emotions
Not allowing circumstances to stress one out
Having strong control over one's emotions
Positivity
Resiliency
Being a good mediator or peacemaker
Making choices that are safe and predictable
Being a good judge at what people need
Being empathetic; putting oneself in other people's shoes
Comforting others through sympathy and understanding
Openness
Being risk-averse
Coping easily with stress or change
Having a relaxed manner
Not being brought down by the negativity of others
Patience and tolerance
Taking the high road: *Oh, don't worry, I wasn't offended.*
Enjoying solitary activities
Quickly letting go of the negatives

Defusing a situation by apologizing, whether one is to blame or not
Taking one's time
Dealing with a volatile situation by not tackling it head-on
Smiling; seeing the bright side
Predictability
Making time for activities that reinforce calm (reading, reflecting, meditating, etc.)
Not being afraid to say *No*
Not overcommitting oneself
Prioritizing well
Sleeping well

ASSOCIATED THOUGHTS:
Looks like rain. I'll cancel our hike and have the girls over for tea instead.
I love this song. It always makes me smile.
Jim's had such a hard time since Sue's death. I'll try not to take what he said personally.
It's too bad I didn't win. But the after party will still be fun.

ASSOCIATED EMOTIONS: confidence, gratitude, peacefulness

POSITIVE ASPECTS: Calm characters don't rock the boat. They're dependable, do what they say they'll do, and can be relied on to respond predictably in any situation. As such, they act as stabilizers for others who might have a tendency for high drama or reactiveness. Because they don't allow emotion to sway them, calm characters can be depended on to make solid decisions. Their composed, peaceful nature can be the glue that keeps a group from falling apart.

NEGATIVE ASPECTS: Because of their consistency and reliability, calm characters may also be boring. If they are too complacent and risk-averse they may miss opportunities to excel and achieve a greater level of self-growth. Their tendency to always do the right thing can render them unrealistic and forgettable.

EXAMPLE FROM TV: Spock (*Star Trek*) is an officer aboard the starship Enterprise and is known for his even demeanor and sense of calm. His Vulcan heritage enables him to put aside the emotional component of difficult situations and think logically. Regardless of danger or strife, Spock is the rock of the leadership team, anchoring others during stressful times and encouraging rationale over sentiment. **Other Examples From Film:** Mr. Miyagi (*Karate Kid*), Tony Mendez (*Argo*), Anton Chiguhr (*No Country for Old Men*)

TRAITS IN SUPPORTING CHARACTERS THAT MAY CAUSE CONFLICT:
adventurous, catty, impulsive, nagging, reckless, rowdy, spunky, temperamental

CHALLENGING SCENARIOS FOR THE CALM CHARACTER:
Falling in love with an adventurous person
Being paired with characters who are melodramatic or confrontational
Facing a life or death situation
Dealing with phobias or fears
Living in a high-stress environment where being calm or complacent could get one killed

CAUTIOUS

DEFINITION: given to prudent forethought before acting

CATEGORIES: achievement, interactive

SIMILAR ATTRIBUTES: careful, heedful

POSSIBLE CAUSES:
Living in a dangerous environment
Witnessing loved ones who suffered calamities as a result of risky behavior
Being hurt in the past
Being the victim of abuse or crime
Living with fears, phobias, or social anxiety
Fragile health
Having overly protective parents
Believing in superstition and bad luck

ASSOCIATED BEHAVIORS:
Asking questions
Investigating and researching before making decisions
Avoiding risky situations or places
Entering relationships slowly
Going over the details
Having a closed body posture
Sharing one's thoughts and opinions in a round-about way, rather than directly
Having a backup plan
Pickiness
Repeating instructions several times to ensure they will be followed
Taking the time to study new places
Doing one's research beforehand
Valuing privacy
Being confident in one's decisions, knowing that ample thought was put into them
Being pessimistic or, at best, cautiously optimistic
Showing respect for boundaries and rules
Wariness; being watchful for danger
Locking doors; not sleeping with windows open
Learning from the past and applying those lessons
Frequently changing passwords to protect oneself online
Placing cherished objects in a safe place
Hiding things from view to remove temptation (not leaving a tablet on the car seat, etc.)
Comparing different choices and scenarios
Giving trust to those who earn it
Speaking slowly; choosing one's words with purpose
Offering to clarify something one has said to ensure understanding

Needing time to reflect on one's options

Requesting a delay if one needs time to think things through

Being active and involved in one's finances and investments

Double-checking everything

Not liking surprises

Evaluating a past experience to determine if one would do the same thing again

Difficulty letting others make the decisions

ASSOCIATED THOUGHTS:

She didn't sound confident with those directions. I'll check my GPS, to make sure.

Oops. Sarah left her purse sitting in plain view. I'll hold onto it until she gets back.

I can't believe they asked for my credit card number over the phone. Do they think I'm stupid?

I'll go out with him if he agrees to meet at the restaurant instead of picking me up at home.

ASSOCIATED EMOTIONS: anxiety, confidence, suspicion, wariness, worry

POSITIVE ASPECTS: Cautious people are observant, connected to their environment, and aware of shifting dynamics. When emotions run high, these characters can restore balance and apply reasoning techniques that enable others to make decisions with a clear head. They look before they leap, think before they act, and generally are the ones still alive at the end of a horror movie.

NEGATIVE ASPECTS: Cautious characters can sometimes be seen as mood-killers when others want to be spontaneous. Worried about possible risks, these characters rely on data and fact; they need to know the variables and potential outcomes before acting. They also see it as their duty to point out risks to teammates, which isn't always taken well by others. Cautious characters may have a hard time relaxing in an environment outside their comfort zone and may be averse to trying new things. If too many factors are unknown, they are often unable to commit.

EXAMPLE FROM FILM: Ellen Ripley (*Alien*) embodies caution. When her shipmates try to bring aboard an alien life form, she takes her time, gathering information before eventually deciding to deny them access. Her decision is overridden and she finds herself trapped aboard the ship with an acid-bleeding alien. In the aftermath, it's her cautious nature that allows her to survive while her crewmates perish. Brave, intelligent, and intuitive, Ripley is able to control her fear and take care each step of the way, considering the dangers and risks before taking action. **Other Examples From Film and Literature:** Columbus (*Zombieland*), Jean Valjean (*Les Misérables*), Aragorn (*The Lord of the Rings*)

TRAITS IN SUPPORTING CHARACTERS THAT MAY CAUSE CONFLICT: compulsive, decisive, efficient, flaky, irresponsible, pushy, reckless, violent

CHALLENGING SCENARIOS FOR THE CAUTIOUS CHARACTER:

Inebriation

Being in a situation with a high-stake "ticking clock" element

Having a goal that forces one to be reckless to succeed or win

Being in a situation where a risk needs to be taken

Facing a dangerous scenario where there isn't time to plan

CENTERED

DEFINITION: maintaining a healthy life view that promotes equilibrium; emotionally stable and focused

CATEGORIES: achievement, identity, moral

SIMILAR ATTRIBUTES: balanced, temperate

POSSIBLE CAUSES:
Having strong self-esteem
Being wise
Experiencing a past imbalance that led to unhappiness and a lack of fulfillment
Having parents who encouraged one to seek out happiness and peace

ASSOCIATED BEHAVIORS:
Knowing one's priorities
Having good sense and knowing one's limitations
Satisfaction and contentment
Having a strong work-life balance
Appreciating what one has
Not being materialistic in nature
Having a good work ethic
Optimism
Respecting other people and their viewpoints
Desiring to learn and nourish the mind
Being well-read
Feeling pride in one's accomplishments, large or small
Being able to ask for help when one needs it
Getting enough exercise and interacting with nature
Making time for reflection
Having a few hobbies or special interests
Setting aside schedules and routines to focus on what's important
Striving for reasonable and attainable goals
Exploring one's feelings honestly, either internally or with others
Viewing failure as a stepping stone and learning from it
Bouncing back from disappointment
Exhibiting good judgment
Thinking before acting
Being non-competitive
Not needing to prove oneself to others
Enjoying spontaneous activities that don't include an element of risk
Practicing moderation (not eating or drinking too much, etc.)
Weighing one's options and not rushing into decisions
Knowing the value of giving back

Living without regrets
Equally enjoying time with others and being alone
Making time for vacations and getaways
Doing what feels right instead of what others think one should do
Thinking deeply on certain topics that pertain to life in general
Feeling peace with one's place in this world
Taking disappointment in stride
Giving back to others in a way that feels comfortable
Not working weekends
Being able to say *No* when one is overcommitted or overwhelmed

ASSOCIATED THOUGHTS:
The orchard will make a great day trip so the kids can see where apples come from.
I'll get my errands done today and then make tomorrow a beach day.
Lorna is always working. Sure, she's climbing the corporate ladder, but at what cost?
I guess a round of golf is out, but rainy days are always great for baking.

ASSOCIATED EMOTIONS: curiosity, eagerness, gratitude, happiness, peacefulness, satisfaction

POSITIVE ASPECTS: Centered characters exude confidence because they know themselves intimately and make decisions that lead to happiness. They do not get pulled into unhealthy activities like office politics, drama, or toxic relationships because these things threaten their centered state. Characters who are internally balanced have good priorities and steady emotions. The happiness of a centered character often prompts others to take control of their lives and find a better balance themselves.

NEGATIVE ASPECTS: Characters who derive satisfaction from their current lives are not as driven as those who are willing to make sacrifices to get what they want. In a job where hard work, dedication, and ambition are critical success factors, centered characters may find themselves passed over for promotions in favor of someone more driven.

EXAMPLE FROM FILM: In the movie *Chocolat*, Roux is a gypsy who floats along the river, stopping at towns along the way to work odd jobs and buy supplies. Though his people are feared and persecuted by many, Roux is comfortable with his beliefs and way of life. He works when he needs to, nurtures the healthy relationships that develop, and recognizes the value of kicking back and relaxing. **Other Examples from Literature and Film:** Nurse Thelma (*The Bone Collector*); Mr. Miyagi (*The Karate Kid*)

TRAITS IN SUPPORTING CHARACTERS THAT MAY CAUSE CONFLICT:
controlling, disciplined, jealous, judgmental, perfectionistic, pushy, reckless, workaholic

CHALLENGING SCENARIOS FOR CENTERED CHARACTERS:
Facing a financial crisis that requires one to work long hours
Being pressured by others to put more time and energy into one area of life
Experiencing a crisis of faith that causes one to doubt oneself and question priorities
Being asked to commit to many projects at once and feeling obligated to comply

CHARMING

DEFINITION: having a pleasing personality; being appealing to others

CATEGORIES: achievement, identity, interactive

SIMILAR ATTRIBUTES: alluring, appealing, captivating, charismatic, magnetic

POSSIBLE CAUSES:
Possessing confidence and a strong sense of self
Having a positive outlook on life
Being highly intuitive and empathetic
Having a kind nature
Being highly social; getting energy from being with other people

ASSOCIATED BEHAVIORS:
Having a good sense of humor
Being attentive to others; having good listening skills
Playfulness
Greeting others with enthusiasm
Being polite (holding the door, letting others enter first, etc.)
Having good recall of faces, names, and past interactions
Curiosity
Using a person's name during conversation
Friendliness
Being respectful of others
Patience
Being a hospitable and caring host
Smiling and nodding in encouragement as someone speaks
Speaking in a voice that has warmth and energy
Noticing personal details and offering compliments
Building people up when talking about them
Offering honesty and behaving in a trustworthy fashion
Accepting compliments with grace and modesty
Including others; never excluding them
Attentiveness; making sure the needs of others are being met
Offering light touches while socializing
Inviting people into one's personal space
Deftly handling negative people by refocusing on positive avenues
Generosity
Being aware of one's image
Being well-dressed and well-groomed
Appearing relaxed and at ease
Having good posture
Maintaining strong eye contact

Asking questions to show that one is paying attention and interested

Having worldly knowledge that allows one to offer opinions and add to conversations

ASSOCIATED THOUGHTS:

I bet she'll thaw a bit if I ask about her family. Everyone likes to talk about their kids.

Dad looks totally uncomfortable. Maybe a joke will make him feel better.

That poor woman, herding six kids through the bus station. I'll see if I can carry her bags.

Claire always wears that brooch. I'll have to ask why it's so important to her.

ASSOCIATED EMOTIONS: amusement, confidence, eagerness, happiness, pride, satisfaction

POSITIVE ASPECTS: Charming characters always seem to know what to do or say to put people at ease and win trust. They can be caring and considerate and make the people around them feel special and unique. These characters are the center of attention not because of how they look or the power they wield, but because people are attracted to their energy and appealing manner.

NEGATIVE ASPECTS: Charming characters can use their intuitive senses for good or for ill. Even if they resist the temptation to use manipulation to get what they want, they can unknowingly intimidate others. Those who are less charismatic may feel that they will never measure up or be loved and respected as much as the charming character. Taken a step further, these resentful feelings could easily turn to envy and jealousy, making these characters vulnerable to attack.

EXAMPLE FROM FILM: Ferris Bueller (*Ferris Bueller's Day Off*) has a knack for winning people over. When he feigns illness and skips school, his classmates are so overcome with concern that they organize a fundraiser in support of his recovery. His parents are just as smitten with Ferris, seeing him as the ideal child and never noticing his constant deceptions and insistence on breaking the rules. Ferris is even able to convince his best friend into borrowing his dad's Ferrari for the day. With the exception of his sister and the dean of students, there doesn't seem to be anyone that Ferris can't charm. **Other Examples from Film:** James Bond, Alex "Hitch" Hitchens (*Hitch*)

TRAITS IN SUPPORTING CHARACTERS THAT MAY CAUSE CONFLICT: abrasive, catty, cynical, gullible, hostile, insecure, introverted, jealous, loutish, melodramatic, rowdy, spoiled, vindictive, whiny

CHALLENGING SCENARIOS FOR THE CHARMING CHARACTER:

Engaging with a discerning person who sees through the charismatic character's charm

Dealing with jaded or bitter people

Recognizing that one is being manipulated by someone else

Having one's charming behavior be misinterpreted as romantic interest

Trying to be a good host while hiding one's personal dislike of someone

CONFIDENT

DEFINITION: being fully assured of oneself

CATEGORIES: achievement, identity, interactive

SIMILAR ATTRIBUTES: secure, self-assured, proud

POSSIBLE CAUSES:
Being talented or gifted in some way
Growing up in a loving, affirming environment
Not being overly concerned with what others think; being happy with oneself
Having faith in one's abilities to achieve one's goals
Having experienced many successes in the past

ASSOCIATED BEHAVIORS:
Standing tall with the shoulders back
Looking people in the eye
Walking with purpose
Meeting challenges head-on
Not compromising when challenged or opposed
Trying new things
Good-natured flirting; friendliness
Facing change without fear or doubt
Being able to laugh at oneself: *Wow, I did a great job spilling the wine, didn't I?*
Learning from failure
Being assertive
Having a strong work ethic
Congratulating others on their success
Initiating conversation with ease
Not being intimidated by someone's power, stature, or wealth
Striking out on one's own, if necessary
Knowing what one believes and standing firm on those values
Not being swayed by others
Not taking oneself too seriously
Curiosity
Asking for help when one needs it
Complimenting others; lifting them up instead of tearing them down
Seeing others as partners and mentors instead of competitors
Being socially adept
Accepting criticism with dignity
Focusing on the positive rather than the negative
Being open-minded
Finding solutions to problems instead of being stymied by them
Educating oneself so as to become more competent in a given area

Admitting when one has made a mistake
Acknowledging weaknesses while playing to one's strengths
Focusing on what is within one's control to change
Smiling
Taking compliments well
Not always knowing one's limitations

ASSOCIATED THOUGHTS:
I studied like crazy. Time to ace this test.
This is what I was born to do.
Someone's got to manage this office. Why not me?
Even Bill Gates started at the bottom. I'm not afraid of hard work.
Wow, she's beautiful. I'm going over and saying hello.

ASSOCIATED EMOTIONS: amusement, curiosity, eagerness, happiness, satisfaction

POSITIVE ASPECTS: Confident characters know who they are and what they're capable of. Because of their self-assurance, they don't fall into the trap of worrying about what others think. They aren't often threatened by people or difficult situations, instead seeing them as opportunities to grow and improve. Because confidence is such an enviable quality, others will naturally be drawn to the these characters.

NEGATIVE ASPECTS: Confident characters can be threatening to those suffering from insecurity, who may see them as cocky or conceited. Their confidence can indeed lead these characters to think too highly of themselves, causing them to look down on others and have difficulty connecting with them. Their self-assuredness can also compel them to overestimate their abilities, setting them up for failures that wash their confidence in self-doubt.

EXAMPLE FROM FILM: In *The Hunt for Red October*, Jack Ryan knows his stuff. He's an expert on naval intelligence and, specifically, Soviet Captain Marko Ramius. In his quest to prove Ramius' good intentions, he takes on the president's National Security Advisor, twice defies his fear of flying, and confronts Ramius himself, never doubting what he knows despite opposition by people in power. **Other Examples from Film:** John McClane (*Die Hard*), Jimmy Markum (*Mystic River*), Deloris Wilson (*Sister Act*)

TRAITS IN SUPPORTING CHARACTERS THAT MAY CAUSE CONFLICT: catty, frivolous, humble, jealous, needy, oversensitive, suspicious, timid

CHALLENGING SCENARIOS FOR THE CONFIDENT CHARACTER:
Being in a scenario that reveals and magnifies one's Achilles' heel
Experiencing a failure or tragedy that shakes one's confidence
Encountering a problem that one is incapable of mastering
Discovering that a personal achievement is a false victory due to another's meddling
Encountering repeated failures that erode one's confidence

COOPERATIVE

DEFINITION: willing to work or collaborate with others

CATEGORIES: achievement, interactive, moral

SIMILAR ATTRIBUTES: agreeable, helpful, obliging

POSSIBLE CAUSES:
Growing up with several siblings and sharing household chores
Living in a military family (or having a military background)
Being people-friendly
Being naturally community-minded
Having strong leadership abilities
Growing up in a family that ran a business

ASSOCIATED BEHAVIORS:
Having an open mind
Asking questions to start the collaborative process
Knowing people by name
Having strong social skills
Being helpful and forthright
Having a strong sense of responsibility
Taking pride in one's work
Honesty
Being polite
Choosing a career that relies on group efforts (being a chef in a restaurant, etc.)
Accountability
Encouraging others along the way: *Great job with the flyer. It's just what we need.*
Being invested in the goal
Having an upbeat mood and positive outlook regarding the work needing to be done
Giving others a chance to speak or weigh in
Saying *Yes*; generally being agreeable
Being willing to work hard
Being community-minded
Working with others with enthusiasm and energy
Carrying out tasks without argument
Being a peacemaker
Appreciating other people and their skills and saying *Thank you*
Being willing to try new things or new ideas
Being able to compromise
Showing up on time
Being prepared
Listening to what others have to say
Being able to follow another's direction if needed

Putting the good of the team first
Dedication and loyalty
Noticing what needs to be done and stepping up to do it
Enjoying the feeling of camaraderie
Being respectful of the time and effort other members are putting forth
Dividing tasks based on the strengths and weaknesses of others
Taking pride in building, creating, or completing something
Paying attention to when people are struggling and finding a way to help

ASSOCIATED THOUGHTS:
Shredding all these files is going to take forever, but it has to be done.
Mark's a fast worker. Between the two of us, we'll have this place clean in no time.
I'm so glad Brenda is on my team. I've wanted to work with her since forever.
Lisanne likes to start early, so I'll change my schedule.

ASSOCIATED EMOTIONS: determination, eagerness, gratitude, hopefulness, satisfaction

POSITIVE ASPECTS: Cooperative characters are easy to get along with, dedicated to the task, and invaluable team members. They understand that they can accomplish more by pooling the talents and resources of others than working alone. They are good listeners, respect their teammates, and take pride in group accomplishments.

NEGATIVE ASPECTS: Cooperative characters can sometimes assume that others are just as committed and willing to work as they themselves are, which can lead to trouble. Blindly depending on others to provide information and leadership can result in a less-than-satisfactory result. If others in the group lack dedication or passion, cooperative characters may find themselves taking on more than their share of responsibility in order to finish the job.

EXAMPLE FROM FILM: Dan Burns (*Dan in Real Life*) isn't one to rock the boat. Although recently widowed, he agrees to go on a blind date when his family sets one up. When he does meet someone interesting and discovers that she's dating his brother, he tries to bow out. His inclination is to go with the flow and keep peace, making him a cooperative, though passive, hero. **Other Examples from Film and TV:** Sam Weinberg (*A Few Good Men*), Stu Redman (*The Stand*), Mike Weston (*The Following*)

TRAITS IN SUPPORTING CHARACTERS THAT MAY CAUSE CONFLICT:
ambitious, apathetic, controlling, free-spirited, hostile, independent, spoiled, suspicious, whiny

CHALLENGING SCENARIOS FOR THE COOPERATIVE CHARACTER:
Working with someone who is used to getting his or her way
Being in a group or organization that lacks leadership and vision
Working with people who don't seem to care about the goal
Working with a partner who creates drama for everyone involved
Dealing with personality clashes within a team or group

COURAGEOUS

DEFINITION: possessing the mental or moral resilience to face opposition, danger, or difficulties despite one's fear

CATEGORIES: achievement, interactive, moral

SIMILAR ATTRIBUTES: brave, dauntless, heroic, valiant

POSSIBLE CAUSES:
The desire to honor role models by living up to their moral standard and/or sacrifice
The belief that one must not let fear stand in the way of what is right
Wanting to protect others from harm or suffering
Having a strong moral code
Believing one person can make a difference and the future is determined by one's actions

ASSOCIATED BEHAVIORS:
Doing what is right instead of what is easy
Facing danger, uncertainty, or hardship with strength
Being strong for others
Being confident
Standing up for those who are not equipped to stand up for themselves
Stepping up when leadership is needed
Facing fear to achieve a goal
Understanding one's shortcomings
Enduring pain or suffering with a show of strength
Telling the truth when it's important
Speaking up when others stay silent
Facing the unknown
Showing compassion and empathy for others
Putting oneself in danger so others will be safe
Following one's beliefs even when it's dangerous to do so
Living one's life according to one's beliefs
Having a strong sense of one's purpose
Believing in justice and equality
Determination
Having a strong mental focus when it's needed
Having high stamina and perseverance
Accepting responsibility for one's actions
Being willing to step outside of one's comfort zone
Giving someone a second chance, or asking for a second chance
Not being defeated by rejection or failure
Having strong convictions
Knowing when to speak and when to stay silent
Being in control of one's emotions

Putting others before oneself

Focusing on the end goal; not allowing oneself to be sidetracked

Knowing what one believes and not allowing others to sway those beliefs

Resiliency; the ability to keep trying even after multiple failures

ASSOCIATED THOUGHTS:

Jon's going to be devastated. But the news should come from me, not a stranger.

Mom and Dad might be disappointed, but this is something I need to do.

Mrs. Bloom shouldn't treat Marc differently than me. I'm going to talk to her.

This isn't exactly safe, but Rick's sister is in there and someone's got to get her out.

That kid is struggling in the current. I need to get out there now!

ASSOCIATED EMOTIONS: determination, guilt, resignation, somberness, wariness, worry

POSITIVE ASPECTS: Courageous characters will make up for what is lacking in any circumstance. After reflection or a moral assessment, they will step up, no matter the odds, because they know that it's the right thing to do. People who show courage have a core of inner strength and a strong moral compass. They're willing to put the welfare of others first when it counts most. They feel fear, but can master it, and do not allow it to alter their decisions. Characters who are courageous lead by example, even if they are unsuited to a task. Others are inspired by their courage and often strive to honor it by showing courage themselves.

NEGATIVE ASPECTS: Courage, while commendable, is not always smart. Characters with this trait sometimes don't see beyond the immediate situation to the long-term impacts of a choice or action. When pausing to think might be the best course of action, courageous characters can be impulsive and respond emotionally, letting their desire to act override wisdom.

EXAMPLE FROM LITERATURE: Frodo, the simple hobbit from *The Lord of the Rings* trilogy, is the least suited for a dangerous mission against a deadly, powerful foe. Yet his willingness to set forth provides an incredible lesson in courage. Lacking the strength of humans, the battle training of dwarves, and the magic of wizards, Frodo makes his way to Mount Doom to destroy the one ring before it can send Middle Earth into darkness. His fortitude and strength comes from within, and despite his fear, he ultimately saves the world. **Other Examples from Literature and Film:** Harry Potter (*Harry Potter* franchise), Herman Boone (*Remember the Titans*)

TRAITS IN SUPPORTING CHARACTERS THAT MAY CAUSE CONFLICT: gullible, manipulative, reckless, self-destructive, selfish, timid, violent, weak-willed

CHALLENGING SCENARIOS FOR THE COURAGEOUS CHARACTER:

Facing a situation where one has failed in the past

Dealing with a phobia

Having to choose between doing what's right and doing what's popular

Facing a decision that will mean life or death for someone else

Showing courage despite a hardship, disability, or great personal cost

COURTEOUS

DEFINITION: mannerly; considerate of others

CATEGORIES: interactive, moral

SIMILAR ATTRIBUTES: chivalrous, conscientious, considerate, gallant, genteel, polite, respectful, well-mannered

POSSIBLE CAUSES:
Being brought up in an environment where politeness was seen as a virtue
Being inherently thoughtful and kind
Being taught to place others before oneself
Having empathy for others
The desire to be respected in turn; adhering to "The Golden Rule"
Fear (of disapproval, broken relationships, conflict, violence, etc.)

ASSOCIATED BEHAVIORS:
Being neat and orderly
Having a strong work ethic
Being thoughtful and kind
Exhibiting good manners
Respecting the personal space of others
Being intuitive of the needs of others
Showing interest in others to make them feel important
Congratulating others for their accomplishments
Treating people fairly
Giving compliments: *That color really suits you.*
Factoring in the moods of others before bringing something up
Having a gentle manner
Offering to pitch in and help
Using a considerate tone
Giving people credit for their work and their ideas
Giving people one's undivided attention (not taking phone calls or texting, etc.)
Showing appreciation for another's time or effort
Having good table manners
Letting others go first (at the check-out counter, in traffic, when entering a room, etc.)
Serving others
Friendliness
Using a warm, inviting voice
Not abusing the power one may have over others
Deferring to others
Trying to foresee what others may need and providing it
Avoiding topics that make others uncomfortable
Not interrupting or laughing too loudly

Smiling and nodding encouragement as others are speaking
Respecting the privacy of others
Making introductions when someone new enters the conversation
Socializing with more than just one person at an event
Making others feel included and valued
Joking and lightly teasing only if it will put someone at ease or is appropriate
Apologizing if one has hurt someone's feelings
Making suggestions without being pushy
Treating everyone with respect
Holding one's tongue instead of lashing out

ASSOCIATED THOUGHTS:
Nicole looks flushed. Maybe I should offer to take her coat.
I see a few empty glasses. I better grab another bottle of wine.
I'll run over and say hi to Emma so she's not standing there all alone.
Mark's divorce is still fresh; I'll hang out with him and make sure he has fun tonight.

ASSOCIATED EMOTIONS: gratitude, happiness, hopefulness

POSITIVE ASPECTS: Courteous characters put the people around them at ease through their polite attentiveness. They can be relied on to behave appropriately in social situations and are often respected by others. In fictional scenarios when tensions run high, someone who is attentive and caring can defuse the situation and encourage others to open up about their fears and worries. When other characters show themselves to be self-absorbed, power hungry, or goal-driven, this trait can be a refreshing counterweight and supply contrast.

NEGATIVE ASPECTS: Because courteous characters often think of others first, sometimes their own needs are not met. This can lead to a lack of fulfillment and personal happiness. These characters can also be targeted by others who view them as weak and decide to take advantage of them.

EXAMPLE FROM LITERATURE: Atticus Finch (*To Kill a Mockingbird*) is a true southern gentleman. Although his principles set him at odds with many of his oldest friends and family, he remains courteous. He has more right than most to be angry and reactive, but whether he's speaking to Mrs. Dubose, who has heinously insulted him, or standing between a lynch mob and an innocent man, Atticus maintains his composure and treats others with respect. **Other Examples from Film:** Hoke Colburn (*Driving Miss Daisy*), Chon Wang (*Shanghai Noon*)

TRAITS IN SUPPORTING CHARACTERS THAT MAY CAUSE CONFLICT:
inflexible, know-it-all, proper, pushy, selfish

CHALLENGING SCENARIOS FOR THE COURTEOUS CHARACTER:
Dealing with disrespectful, dishonest, or drunk people
Being paired with a mistrustful person who was taken advantage of in the past
Being thrust into a survivalist situation where every person must fend for himself
Suffering a humiliation that gravely wounds one's dignity

CREATIVE

DEFINITION: having the power or inclination to bring new things into existence

CATEGORIES: achievement, identity

SIMILAR ATTRIBUTES: artistic

POSSIBLE CAUSES:
Having nurturing, creative parents
The desire to make an imprint or leave something behind
Intense curiosity
Needing to connect with others in an emotional way
Being emotionally sensitive
Innate giftedness
Living in a creative community
Finding a void and wanting to fill it
Seeing and appreciating beauty in untraditional forms
The desire to be unique and wholly individual

ASSOCIATED BEHAVIORS:
Eccentricity
Finding beauty in things that people take for granted
Being highly imaginative
Putting a unique spin on everything that one does
Having a strong social conscience
Expressiveness
Creative problem solving
A desire to know people's stories and what makes them who they are
Being self-disciplined when it comes to one's art
Persistence; sticking with a project until one's goal has been achieved
Having an ear for pleasing sounds, such as music
Experiencing strong (sometimes manic) emotions
Adaptability
Being adventurous; wanting to experience different things
Spontaneity
Suffering self-doubt if others do not connect deeply with one's creative works
Being intuitive and empathetic
Having an interest in mysteries and the unknown
Becoming excited when a new idea hits
Growing quiet or seeming lost in thought
Intense concentration
Feeling hurt if others don't take an interest in one's work when it's shared
Forgetting to attend to other details (skipping appointments, not eating properly, etc.)
Experimentation
Getting lost in daydreams

Thinking in metaphors

Wanting to evoke an emotional response in others

Having difficulty expressing oneself without an art medium (drawing, writing, etc.)

Seeing things the way they could be rather than how they currently are

Having a healthy attitude toward failure

Being creative in one's appearance (through clothing choices, hairstyles, etc.)

ASSOCIATED THOUGHTS:

Look at that old panhandler—there's so much strength and beauty in his lined face.

Her red hair is so bright with the sun shining through it, like a phoenix rising from the ashes.

The sound of the wind scattering the dead leaves is so musical.

They named their dog "Blackie?" Couldn't they come up with something more original?

ASSOCIATED EMOTIONS: curiosity, desire, determination, eagerness, excitement, peacefulness

POSITIVE ASPECTS: Creative characters usually see the world a little differently than most and almost always have a fresh perspective to offer. The power of creation doesn't come easily, so those who seek to create are usually determined, hardworking, and driven. These characters have a long-distance perspective that enables them to work through criticism, discouragement, and rejection.

NEGATIVE ASPECTS: Because creative types tend to focus on their gifts, they may be somewhat out of touch with reality. This can lead to awkwardness or insecurity in social situations. Their focus on the muse can distract them from day-to-day practicalities, like housecleaning, paying the bills, and grocery shopping. The need to create can become so all-consuming that it leads to the neglect of important relationships, bringing about isolation. The path to creation is also rife with naysayers, turning some creative characters negative and jaded or instigating thoughts of self-doubt that lead to depression.

EXAMPLE FROM HISTORY: Michelangelo, one of the most famous artists in history, was an accomplished Italian sculptor, painter, and architect during the Renaissance. Despite being highly intelligent, he set aside a future as a scholar and dedicated himself to studying the arts. Following his passion for creating, he went on to sculpt "David" for the Florence Cathedral and painted the ceiling of the Sistine Chapel. **Other Examples from History:** Pablo Picasso, Wolfgang Amadeus Mozart, William Shakespeare

TRAITS IN SUPPORTING CHARACTERS THAT MAY CAUSE CONFLICT:
analytical, callous, efficient, haughty, hypocritical, lazy, perfectionist, proper

CHALLENGING SCENARIOS FOR THE CREATIVE CHARACTER:

Experiencing a handicap that affects one's skill (losing one's eyesight, etc.)

Finding beauty in something that goes against cultural norms and wanting to share it

Living in a culture where art is viewed as frivolous or a waste of time

Being so weighed down by responsibility that one has little time or energy to create

Living in the shadow of someone whose talents far surpass one's own

Knowing someone who takes his talent for granted

CURIOUS

DEFINITION: marked by the desire to investigate and learn

CATEGORIES: achievement, identity, interactive

SIMILAR ATTRIBUTES: inquisitive

POSSIBLE CAUSES:
Having a naturally inquisitive outlook
Growing up in an environment where exploration and asking questions was encouraged
The belief that there is always something more to be learned
Having a thirst for knowledge
The desire to right wrongs or make things better
Possessing an adventurous spirit

ASSOCIATED BEHAVIORS:
Asking questions
Having strong observation skills
Pursuing knowledge (reading, researching, going to school, etc.)
Showing interest and enthusiasm when insight is shared
Seeking out people with similar interests
Taking things apart to see how they work
Going off on tangents rather than following a set plan
Listening in on the conversations of others
Difficulty paying attention on a task if something more interesting is present
Applying trial and error; learning by doing
Experimenting with new ideas or techniques; ingenuity
Collecting things
Showing disdain for rules, boundaries, and limits
Not becoming bored easily
Solving problems in innovative ways
Being intense when pursuing an interest
Mimicking or modeling similar discoveries in order to learn
Occasionally overstepping (asking questions that are inappropriate or too pointed, etc.)
Being willing to try new things
Impulsiveness
Wanting to improve and strengthen, or to create better processes
Losing track of time
Using errors, weaknesses, and flaws as a way to improve or innovate
Verbally working through one's theories or questions
Joining groups or clubs
Taking risks to satisfy one's curiosity
Making sacrifices in order to learn (interning or researching for no pay, etc.)
Deriving pleasure and satisfaction from new discoveries and experiences

Enjoying riddles, puzzles, and the unknown
Thinking about the *What if?*
Breaking rules in order to follow an idea or interest
Open honesty with others about one's interests and aims
Obsessive tendencies
Trying something to see what it feels like or doing something to see what happens

ASSOCIATED THOUGHTS:
Look at the two of them whispering. I'll corner Ella later and find out what's going on.
Every day that woman comes alone to the playground. I wonder what her story is?
Interesting, how different animal species huddle together in specific environments.
The vacuum is still making that sound. Let's take it apart and see what's going on in there.
Before Harold casts his fishing line, he rolls his wrist. I need to ask him why he does that.

ASSOCIATED EMOTIONS: confidence, curiosity, eagerness

POSITIVE ASPECTS: Curious characters are drawn to problems or inconveniences that other people would choose to avoid. Their curiosity can make them adventurous, spurring them on to do things others wouldn't do. They are often knowledgeable, either in a general way or about something specific. Characters who are curious easily stumble upon mysteries or involve themselves in dangerous matters; as such, they can conveniently introduce conflict into a story line.

NEGATIVE ASPECTS: Curious characters are often impulsive, acting without thinking. They can be single-minded to a fault—focusing on their pursuit (or being hopelessly distracted) and following whatever rabbit trail appears before them. Those who are curious are frequently more interested in their current topic of exploration than their relationships and may not understand or appreciate those without a similar level of curiosity.

EXAMPLE FROM LITERATURE: Pippin Took, one of Frodo's hobbit companions, is notoriously curious, which often leads to trouble. *In The Fellowship of The Ring*, the companions are inside the dwarven city of Moria when Pippin touches an ancient sword, sending the fragile bones of a nearby skeleton clattering down an empty well. The noise that ensues summons a horde of orcs, and the fellowship is forced to fight to secure their freedom. Later, in *The Two Towers*, Pippin's insatiable desire to look inside the magical palantír leads him to steal the seeing stone from a sleeping Gandalf. By touching it, the hobbit accidentally forges a connection with Sauron himself, putting everyone in peril once more. **Other Examples from Literature and Film:** Alice in Wonderland, Fievel Mouskewitz (*An American Tail*), Curious George

TRAITS IN SUPPORTING CHARACTERS THAT MAY CAUSE CONFLICT: cautious, ignorant, impatient, irrational, know-it-all, pessimistic, stubborn, unhelpful

CHALLENGING SCENARIOS FOR THE CURIOUS CHARACTER:
Dealing with people who are protective of their knowledge
Living in a society where free thinking is discouraged
Being given tasks that require strict attention and focus
Working with people who lack drive or the desire to explore

DECISIVE

DEFINITION: having the ability to make quick, efficient decisions; lacking hesitation

CATEGORIES: achievement

SIMILAR ATTRIBUTES: resolute

POSSIBLE CAUSES:
Bearing responsibility from a young age
Having absent or reluctant parents
Having control issues
Being driven by the need to succeed
Having a strong sense of responsibility
The desire to lead

ASSOCIATED BEHAVIORS:
Acquiring knowledge or skills to make informed decisions
Seeing things as black or white
Surrounding oneself with people who are skilled
Asking pointed questions: *Can you guarantee that timeline?*
Confidence
Needing a plan of action at all times
Appearing certain even when one is not
Demanding honesty and compliance
Placing one's trust in only those who have earned it
Choosing to lead rather than follow
Becoming frustrated with people who can't commit or make decisions
Disliking ambiguity
Fully committing to every decision; not second-guessing oneself
Being strong-willed
Knowing what one wants and needs in a given situation
Being highly logical and rational
Being goal oriented
Placing the mission before other people's emotions
Tackling problems and situations directly
Being in tune with one's emotions
Being able to motivate others
Having a strong work ethic
Independence
Being organized
Having confidence and self-esteem
Not being ruled by fear or regret (but sometimes being in denial)
Taking risks
Assertiveness

Being a strong problem solver
Taking advantage of opportunities
Feeling anger or frustration if one makes a mistake
Accepting responsibility and learning from one's missteps
Having a positive attitude
Determination
Making day-to-day decisions quickly (what to wear, what to order off the menu, etc.)
Trusting one's gut instinct

ASSOCIATED THOUGHTS:
Why does she make this so difficult? Just pick a restaurant and be done with it.
Becky knows she has homework. Why doesn't she just sit down and do it?
I like what the candidate had to say. He's the logical choice to vote for.
If we elope, we can avoid the million details and family drama and get on with our lives.

ASSOCIATED EMOTIONS: confidence, determination, impatience, irritation, scorn

POSITIVE ASPECTS: Decisive characters inspire confidence because of their faith in their decisions. Once they commit to a course of action, they look firmly ahead, never doubting their choices. These characters are responsible and make good leaders. They are often a driving force for change in the world.

NEGATIVE ASPECTS: Unfortunately, these characters can be so invested in their decisions that they're reluctant to change direction, even when events take a turn for the worse. Since they usually do make good decisions, it can be difficult for them to admit it when they've made a mistake. Because these characters draw their conclusions based on logic, they can grow impatient with others who place a more emotional value on their choices. This can lead to friction and frustration on all sides.

EXAMPLE FROM FILM: James T. Kirk of the *Star Trek* franchise thinks on his feet and makes decisions quickly. He doesn't prevaricate or second-guess himself. When trouble arises, he assesses the situation, seeks counsel from trusted colleagues when necessary, weighs his options, and takes action. Sometimes his decisiveness makes him rash and reckless, but in his high-risk position as a commander of a Starfleet ship and crew, his ability to make quick decisions serves him well.
Other Examples from History and Film: George S. Patton, Gordon Gekko (*Wall Street*), Captain Miller (*Saving Private Ryan*)

TRAITS IN SUPPORTING CHARACTERS THAT MAY CAUSE CONFLICT: defensive, easygoing, flaky, foolish, forgetful, gullible, indecisive, irresponsible, lazy, worrywart

CHALLENGING SCENARIOS FOR THE DECISIVE CHARACTER:
Having to make choices with a partner who is wishy-washy
Working in a field where one is restrained by rules, safety committees, and regulations
Having to make a decision in an area where one lacks knowledge
Knowing the right thing to do but being held back by a partner who refuses to listen to reason
Making decisions only to have them overridden by one's employer

DIPLOMATIC

DEFINITION: skilled at handling people while respecting their needs

CATEGORIES: interactive, moral

SIMILAR ATTRIBUTES: tactful

POSSIBLE CAUSES:
Growing up with two or more siblings
Being responsible for people whose views, attitudes, and needs differ
Working in management or politics
Obtaining a position of power and wanting to keep it
Having a strong sense of teamwork and community
Valuing fairness and respect
Being strongly empathetic
Having an intuitive nature
Being the peacemaker in a family that often clashes
Acting as a caregiver or support worker for those with chronic illnesses or mental instabilities

ASSOCIATED BEHAVIORS:
Acknowledging others and their needs as valid and important
Showing respect
Being a strong listener
Thinking before acting
Being able to put oneself into someone else's shoes
Being trustworthy
Treating everyone fairly and without bias
Speaking in a neutral tone
Having an aptitude for reasoning and logic
Repeating the facts so there are no misunderstandings for anyone
Defusing high emotions by remaining calm and reasonable
Building people up in a genuine manner
Offering opinions that show respect for everyone involved
Speaking tactfully about past mistakes
Not assigning blame unless it can be done in an instructive way
Offering opinions on how to work together for the best outcome
Holding to one's beliefs and ideals
Avoiding negative language such as *I don't like that*, or *That won't work*, etc.
Offering ideas and solutions for change
Positivity
Hesitating in order to choose one's words carefully
Not being aggressive
Respecting other people's boundaries and personal distance
Maintaining strong eye contact

Offering a joke or comment to defuse tension
Showing kindness when correcting someone's misconception or mistake
Offering honesty—but carefully, in a way that won't cause offense
Avoiding arguments; having strong negotiating skills
Leading by example
Being willing to compromise
Being highly aware of people's emotions and working to avoid hurt feelings
Sharing a personal struggle in an effort to put people at ease
Paying close attention to and accurately interpreting the body language of others

ASSOCIATED THOUGHTS:

Brenda's mad about not being invited to Erica's party. I'll step in if this gets ugly.
I need to show them they can help one another since they're both after the same thing.
If the kids swap chores every few weeks, then no one can complain about it being unfair.
When Dad visits, I'll show him how safe the city is. He'll feel better about my move here.

ASSOCIATED EMOTIONS: confidence, determination, hopefulness, resignation, satisfaction

POSITIVE ASPECTS: Diplomatic characters are often wise, far-seeing, and intelligent. They can remove themselves emotionally from a situation and are skilled at providing insight that helps others make good decisions. Natural peacemakers, these characters don't let passion rule them. They are careful with their words, seeking out information, investigating, and obtaining feedback before weighing in or offering potential solutions. A diplomatic character is able to be supportive, loyal, and trustworthy without judging, and so make good confidantes.

NEGATIVE ASPECTS: Diplomacy can be draining; when a diplomatic character has strong feelings and needs to vent, he may be reluctant to do so out of fear of damaging his reputation. Friends may frequently bring their disputes, beefs, and arguments to him, expecting to be heard and counseled. This can lead to high stress and unhappiness, as well as a sense of frustration born from knowing that whatever is decided, someone will always be dissatisfied with the outcome. A diplomatic character can also be viewed by others as manipulative, since his ability to read and persuade others can be used to his personal advantage.

EXAMPLE FROM FILM: Alfred Pennyworth, Bruce Wayne's serving man in the *Batman* franchise, tactfully handles all manner of affairs for his employer whilst maintaining the secrecy of Bruce's identity. As a confidante, he fulfills his role while being both a mentor and moral compass for Bruce, whose judgment is sometimes clouded by the negativity of Gotham City's criminal underworld. **Other Examples from Literature and Film:** Gray Grantham (*The Pelican Brief*), Sean Maguire (*Good Will Hunting*)

TRAITS IN SUPPORTING CHARACTERS THAT MAY CAUSE CONFLICT:

defensive, dishonest, impulsive, jaded, suspicious, sweet, unhelpful, whimsical

CHALLENGING SCENARIOS FOR THE DIPLOMATIC CHARACTER:

Remaining diplomatic when one has personal stakes in the outcome
Trying to help others find middle ground when one is morally opposed to their goal
Being diplomatic in the face of disrespect, confrontation, threats, and manipulation

DISCIPLINED

DEFINITION: exhibiting willpower and self-control

CATEGORIES: achievement, identity

SIMILAR ATTRIBUTES: self-controlled

POSSIBLE CAUSES:
Being strongly dedicated to a goal or belief
Being raised in a devout household
Participating in competitive sports
Having role models who were disciplined and dedicated

ASSOCIATED BEHAVIORS:
Adhering to long-term routines or patterns
Making sacrifices to achieve one's goals
Honing one's skills in an effort to improve
Being strong-willed
Having a strong moral barometer
Resisting temptation in all forms
Being a hard worker
Integrity and focus
Making sacrifices for what is important
Self-respect
Difficulty compromising
Being able to filter out distractions
Cutting out relationships and influencers that go against one's goals
Having a serious demeanor when it comes to seeking achievement
Seeking out mentors who can help one improve
Willingness to train or hone one's talents or traits
Challenging one's limits; pushing oneself to strive harder
Taking pride in one's accomplishments and hard work
Avoiding situations where one might be tempted to break one's resolve
Carefully controlling one's emotions
Having a sense of duty (to oneself or others)
Being encouraged by small improvements
Putting business before pleasure
Working out or adhering to a diet to meet one's goal
Making concessions in other areas to stay on track
Using one's time productively
Feeling accomplished when one defeats temptations
Optimism and determination
Refusing to give up or give in
Having a plan to reach one's goal

Having well-defined priorities
Being a good manager of one's time
Being attentive to details

ASSOCIATED THOUGHTS:
I'd like to go out, but I need to get to bed early so I'm ready for tomorrow.
If I save up my tips for the next three months, I can take that trip to Mexico.
Working through the weekend will help me get this project back on schedule.
It would be easy to give up, but I'd always regret it.
I'd love some dessert, but my diet's going so well. I don't want to sabotage it.

ASSOCIATED EMOTIONS: confidence, desire, determination, hopefulness, satisfaction

POSITIVE ASPECTS: Disciplined characters are focused and determined with concrete goals. They're strong planners, choosing the best and most direct course of action in order to achieve a desired result. Because discipline is a trait that many people desire but few can honestly claim, characters exemplifying this attribute are often admired and respected by their peers.

NEGATIVE ASPECTS: Disciplined characters are sometimes so focused on what they want that they marginalize friends and loved ones; this can be especially hurtful when these supporting characters have sacrificed in order to further the character's desires. In addition, disciplined characters don't always set reasonable boundaries when it comes to their passions; when this happens, their dedication can put them in danger or bring about physical harm. Discipline can escalate into an unhealthy obsession, and if one gives in to temptation as a reward, feelings of failure and self-loathing may follow.

EXAMPLE FROM FILM: He may not be the smartest guy on the block, but Rocky Balboa (*Rocky*) has strength of will when it comes to training. He gets up early every morning to run, eats an unappetizing but protein-packed breakfast of raw eggs, and puts his body through the ringer to get into peak physical shape. He even attempts to remain celibate during training, but... well, he's a boxer, not a saint. **Other Examples from Film:** Captain Von Trapp (*The Sound of Music*), Kate Moseley (*The Cutting Edge*)

TRAITS IN SUPPORTING CHARACTERS THAT MAY CAUSE CONFLICT: dependent, gentle, influential, innocent, manipulative, needy, proper, sentimental, whiny

CHALLENGING SCENARIOS FOR THE DISCIPLINED CHARACTER:
Remaining disciplined during times of doubt and insecurity
Facing a temptation that is as tantalizing as one's original goal
Having an identity crisis that forces one to reevaluate the current path
Suffering an emotional hurt or physical setback
Having one's discipline take an unhealthy turn (weight obsessions, perfectionism, etc.)

DISCREET

DEFINITION: intentionally unobtrusive; conducting oneself with care, sound judgment, and a respect for privacy

CATEGORIES: interactive

SIMILAR ATTRIBUTES: circumspect, prudent

POSSIBLE CAUSES:
Loyalty
Growing up during a time when secrets were important (the Cold War, WWII, etc.)
Working within an industry where sensitive information must be protected
Being exposed to danger (civil unrest, political takeovers, high crime, etc.) in the past
Being raised in the public eye (growing up in a political, famous, or wealthy family, etc.)

ASSOCIATED BEHAVIORS:
Keeping secrets
Controlling the flow of information for the greater good
Being careful with one's words; being tactful
Protecting others by omitting the truth
Wearing clothing that is nondescript or unremarkable
Moderating one's movements to avoid being the focus of attention
Thinking logically and planning ahead
Being careful with one's personal information
Maintaining control of one's emotions
Avoiding situations where it's easy to lose control (drinking too much, etc.)
Being observant and watchful
Asking careful questions while keeping one's motivation to oneself
Being trustworthy and reliable
Respecting privacy
Thinking before acting; being risk-averse
Being protective
Taking on sensitive duties to ensure they're done correctly
Being slow to trust others
Self-restraint
Modesty and humility
Advising when necessary; keeping the confidences of others
Answering questions in a generic way
Trivializing to avoid revealing anything: *I won't bore you with the details.*
Being gifted at diplomacy
Having a quiet demeanor or air of mystery
Using flattery to put people at ease
Dealing sensitively with people
Ignoring or deftly handling pointed inquiries or information demands

Avoiding disruptions through careful planning
Gathering information without being obvious
Having a good sense of timing

ASSOCIATED THOUGHTS:
I wish she wouldn't ask such personal questions. Those secrets aren't mine to tell.
I'll keep Lorna away from Dan so he doesn't accidentally blab about her surprise party.
If I take the late train, I shouldn't run into anyone who knows me.
All he needs to know is to be outside the restaurant at eight. I'll handle the rest.
Listen to Mike brag about how much money he makes. He's going to alienate his friends.

ASSOCIATED EMOTIONS: determination, reluctance, resentment, skepticism, sympathy, worry

POSITIVE ASPECTS: Discreet characters are aware of the social climate and the possible dangers to their well-being and the well-being of others. They are protective of privacy, be it their own or a loved one's, and have sound judgment in knowing what to say and do to properly handle the flow of information. These characters make decisions based on strong observation skills, they know what to say and to whom, and they're careful not to ruffle feathers as they work to maintain a low profile.

NEGATIVE ASPECTS: Because discreet characters have an objective of keeping certain information away from others, they may appear to be closed-off or secretive, which isn't a strong foundation for friendship. Out of necessity, discreet characters may manipulate others, which can hurt their integrity or the integrity of those they are protecting. These characters tend to be very private; when they accomplish something special, others may never know of their role in the event, which can lessen the satisfaction for a character longing for appreciation and recognition.

EXAMPLE FROM FILM: In *Argo* (a film loosely based on real events), Tony Mendez is a CIA operative who goes undercover to rescue six trapped American diplomats from Iran. Acting as a movie producer scouting locations for a fictitious film, he handles Iranian officials by saying and doing exactly what is needed to maintain his cover. Keeping a low profile, he carefully educates the diplomats so they can pull off their fake film crew roles and escape. Once on American soil, Tony remains secretive about his involvement in the rescue for the greater good of protecting American prisoners of war still in Iran. **Other Examples from Film:** Father Bobby Carillo (*Sleepers*), Aaron/Roy Stampler (*Primal Fear*)

TRAITS IN SUPPORTING CHARACTERS THAT MAY CAUSE CONFLICT: alert, impulsive, intelligent, nosy, reckless, suspicious, tactless, uncooperative, uninhibited

CHALLENGING SCENARIO FOR THE DISCREET CHARACTER:
Catching a trusted friend in a lie
Making a mistake that causes conflict for the person one is trying to protect
Being asked to breech another's privacy for the greater good
Finding oneself caught between opposing people or goals
Having one's privacy invaded and one's secrets revealed as a result

EASYGOING

DEFINITION: casual in manner and mindset

CATEGORIES: identity, interactive

SIMILAR ATTRIBUTES: carefree, happy-go-lucky, lackadaisical, laid-back, mellow, relaxed

POSSIBLE CAUSES:
Having fun-loving parents who went with the flow
Being confident in oneself
Being naturally contented and satisfied
Believing that things happen for a reason and one must let go of things beyond one's control
Growing up in an overly strict or highly stressful environment and choosing to live differently

ASSOCIATED BEHAVIORS:
Happiness
Having a non-competitive nature
Acting as a peacemaker when there are conflicts
Having a calm and agreeable demeanor
Having fun without worrying about the judgment of others
Avoiding stress
Being willing to show one's emotions
Honesty
Being low maintenance
Not taking pains with one's appearance
Working to live, not living to work
Enjoying holidays and weekends
Making time for one's interests
Encouraging others to not worry and enjoy life
Enjoying achievements when they happen
Thoughtfulness
Spontaneity
A sense of fairness; being uncompetitive
Doing things last minute as opposed to planning ahead
Working well in a group setting
Not feeling compelled to lead; being content to follow
Preferring loose timelines rather than set deadlines
Tardiness
Easily overlooking offenses; forgiving and forgetting
Sleeping in
Being free of most worry
Thinking positively
Patience
Having a good sense of humor

Being even-keeled; not being easily upset
Not worrying about success; just enjoying the experience
Being friendly and accepting of others
Having a go-with-the-flow attitude that allows one to fit in with many different groups
Being slow to anger
Deriving energy from the happiness of others
Having an open mind
Being at peace with oneself
Preferring to let others make decisions

ASSOCIATED THOUGHTS:
Whatever movie Debbie picks, I know I'll enjoy it.
The other team deserves to win. They definitely outplayed us today.
I don't think I could do Rick's job, with all those deadlines and long hours.
This camping trip will be so much fun. Even if it rains, we'll play cards and catch up.

ASSOCIATED EMOTIONS: amusement, confidence, happiness, indifference, satisfaction

POSITIVE ASPECTS: Easygoing characters are comfortable to be around. They're laid-back and take life as it comes. Rather than stress over things that are out of their control, they go with the flow and enjoy the positives. Characters with this trait don't worry about winning or losing or chasing success; they simply enjoy the experience.

NEGATIVE ASPECTS: Easygoing characters don't always have the same priorities as other people. Their mellow approach to life may lead others to believe that they're apathetic or lack passion. Being easygoing means not being concerned with things that may be important to others, like punctuality, orderliness, or ambition. This difference in priorities can cause conflict with characters who value such things.

EXAMPLE FROM FILM: In the course of his life, Forrest Gump encounters more than his share of danger and stress. But he takes everything in stride. Whether he's being forced to wear "magic shoes," saying goodbye to his best friend in the middle of a firefight, caring for a bitter paraplegic, or raising his young son on his own, Forrest doesn't get rattled. He faces each challenge with a positive attitude and an open mind, ready to learn from what the day has to offer. **Other Examples from Literature and Film:** Novalee Nation (*Where the Heart Is*), Will Freeman (*About a Boy*)

TRAITS IN SUPPORTING CHARACTERS THAT MAY CAUSE CONFLICT:
ambitious, introverted, judgmental, melodramatic, needy, nervous, obsessed, suspicious, workaholic

CHALLENGING SCENARIOS FOR THE EASYGOING CHARACTER:
Seeing a friend or loved one in chronic pain and being unable to help
Suffering an injustice (not being covered by insurance due to an administrative error, etc.)
Having a desire or need so important that one would do anything to obtain it
Experiencing a tragedy or disaster that pulls one out of one's temperate emotional range

EFFICIENT

DEFINITION: carrying out tasks effectively; being productive with one's time

CATEGORIES: achievement

SIMILAR ATTRIBUTES: productive

POSSIBLE CAUSES:
Having a "type A" personality
Having a strong drive to succeed
Growing up in a busy, active family
The need to be productive
Being highly active and involved; needing to manage one's time and energy wisely

ASSOCIATED BEHAVIORS:
Having a good sense of time
Making lists
Being highly productive
Prioritizing well
Making decisions quickly
Feeling a sense of accomplishment at finishing tasks
Always moving and doing
Thriving under stress
Being able to temper one's emotions as needed
Being logic-driven
Setting achievable goals
Being highly organized
Being able to multitask well
Keeping a neat home, bedroom, or office space
Setting deadlines and timeframes
Delegating tasks to others
Avoiding distractions
Being highly focused
Getting straight to the point
Planning ahead
Saving money and time whenever possible
Thinking and acting proactively
Becoming frustrated with overly chatty neighbors and small talk
Seeking out knowledge when it's needed
Being comfortable with technology
Adhering to a schedule
Rushing
Rising early; setting one's alarm
Being punctual

Having high expectations
Asking for help when needed
Creating a plan and sticking to it
Having a strong sense of responsibility
Not getting caught up in small details; staying focused on the goal
Being frustrated by wasted time, energy, or resources

ASSOCIATED THOUGHTS:
I may as well clean up my email while I watch this movie with the kids.
Since I pass the post office on the way to work, I'll drop off this package tomorrow.
While Jim's at ball practice I'll zip over to the detailing shop and have the car cleaned.
How does Lori track expenses with all these loose receipts? She should make a spreadsheet.

ASSOCIATED EMOTIONS: agitation, annoyance, confidence, determination, pride, satisfaction

POSITIVE ASPECTS: Efficient characters are task-oriented, organized, and can get a lot accomplished in a short period of time. They make decisions quickly and so don't usually get bogged down in the details. They're often good at implementing systems to streamline projects and processes, and will many times assume a leadership role just to get things moving.

NEGATIVE ASPECTS: Characters with this trait can grow frustrated with people who lack their speed and proficiency. Likewise, friends who don't work as quickly might bristle under an efficient character's impatience or annoyance. These characters can be so focused on finishing that they don't pay close attention to detail and end up sacrificing quality for time.

EXAMPLE FROM FILM: The futuristic robot from *The Terminator* is systematic and efficient in finding and hunting down Sarah Connor and her son. Emotionless and ruthless, the cybernetic organism uses all its resources to stay on task and execute its mission of terminating its targets. **Other Examples from Film and TV:** Harold Crick (*Stranger than Fiction*), Aaron Hotchner (*Criminal Minds*), Special Agent Cho (*The Mentalist*)

TRAITS IN SUPPORTING CHARACTERS THAT MAY CAUSE CONFLICT: compulsive, flaky, indecisive, insecure, scatterbrained, self-destructive, verbose, whiny

CHALLENGING SCENARIOS FOR THE EFFICIENT CHARACTER:
Being friends with someone who is lazy and unmotivated
Being surrounded by people who constantly whine and complain
Letting someone important down because one sacrificed quantity for quality
Being so overcommitted that one is forced to cut corners to complete one's assignments
Having to rely on unreliable people
Being in a relationship with someone who is emotionally needy

EMPATHETIC

DEFINITION: able to recognize and identify with the emotions of others

CATEGORIES: interactive, moral

SIMILAR ATTRIBUTES: sensitive, understanding

POSSIBLE CAUSES:
Being deeply attuned to emotion
Having heightened intuition
Being strongly self-aware
Feeling in sync with the energy of other people
Having a compassionate nature
Being taught the importance of love and compassion at a young age

ASSOCIATED BEHAVIORS:
Experiencing another's emotion as if it was one's own
Having a strong connection to other people
Trustworthiness and honesty
Having a quiet, contemplative nature
Being genuine; showing an interest in others
Influencing the attitudes of others by projecting certain feelings and moods
Being sensitive to the emotional pain of others
Offering comfort when it is needed
Listening actively
Enjoying working with animals or being around them
Being able to sense "fake" emotions
Seeing past actions and words to discern the truth
Being altruistic
Finding it difficult to put one's needs first
Reluctance to share emotions too fully for fear of being overwhelmed
Deeply respecting all living things
Pondering the meaning of life and one's role within it
Wisdom
Being able to describe what another's emotion feels like (visceral sensations, etc.)
Having strong values and ideals
Wanting to help others or fix their problems
Avoiding places where painful emotions are abundant (cancer wards, prisons, etc.)
Wanting to share happiness and positivity
Championing humane causes
Understanding the importance of giving and receiving
Sometimes feeling overwhelmed by emotion
Being an introvert
Treating others the way one wishes to be treated
Spiritualism

Volunteering; participating in projects of goodwill

Feeling overwhelmed by emotions; needing to retreat to a quiet place

Experiencing pain echoes (true empaths)

Needing time alone to recharge and clear one's head

Having a difficult time letting go of the pain of others

Forming deep, meaningful relationships

Avoiding toxic people and situations

ASSOCIATED THOUGHTS:

Devon acts strong, but I know he's just worried that people will think he's weak.

The hate pouring off that man is incredible. I can see right through his false smile.

I need to help that family who lost their home. What a horrible thing to go through.

A funny movie will get Max out of his funk.

ASSOCIATED EMOTIONS: anguish, conflicted, desire, eagerness, gratitude, love, sympathy

POSITIVE ASPECTS: Characters with a strong sense of empathy make good friends and lovers. They are good listeners, genuinely care, and want the best for other people. They try to foster positivity and enjoy the communal energy of sharing their happy emotions. Their ability to walk in other people's shoes allows them to have a deeper understanding of problematic situations and react in a way that will improve the emotional landscape for everyone involved. These characters can also convert their empathy into a passion for change, making them strong champions for causes that improve the quality of life for others.

NEGATIVE ASPECTS: While positive emotions affect empathetic characters in an uplifting way, negative emotions can be toxic, dragging them into a dark place. Unless they are able to shield themselves, some may pick up the emotions or pain of others and experience the same hurt themselves. This can make interacting with others difficult, leading them to withdraw and become reclusive. In addition, being sensitive and showing true concern can be a double-edged sword for empathetic characters when others use them as a dumping ground for their worries, fears, and frustrations. Too much of this can lead to emotional strain and depression.

EXAMPLE FROM FILM: Oskar Schindler (*Schindler's List*) begins his story as a war profiteer in Germany, but upon witnessing the Nazi liquidation of the Kraków ghetto, he finds himself compelled to help the Jews who remain. By the end of the war, although he has saved over a thousand lives, he is heartbroken at the thought of the lost ones he might have helped had he done more. **Other Examples from Film:** Dr. Malcolm Crowe (*The Sixth Sense*), John Coffey (*The Green Mile*), Deanna Troi (*Star Trek: The Next Generation*)

TRAITS IN SUPPORTING CHARACTERS THAT MAY CAUSE CONFLICT:

analytical, antisocial, cautious, confrontational, cruel, hateful, melodramatic, volatile, withdrawn

CHALLENGING SCENARIOS FOR THE EMPATHETIC CHARACTER:

Interacting with those who lack empathy, such as someone with antisocial personality disorder

Being exposed to many conflicting emotions at once

Being paired with someone who lacks morals and doesn't value life

Living with someone who is chronically ill

ENTHUSIASTIC

DEFINITION: frequently feeling or exhibiting much excitement

CATEGORIES: identity, interactive

SIMILAR ATTRIBUTES: ardent, ebullient, excitable, exuberant, hyper

POSSIBLE CAUSES:
ADHD/ADD
Being highly creative and passionate
Being free-spirited
Being excessively energetic
Curiosity
Immaturity
Having an optimistic outlook
Needing action or adventure; being an extrovert
The desire to perform or prove oneself to others
Medication or diet
Being a highly intelligent person who is consistently under-stimulated

ASSOCIATED BEHAVIORS:
Preferring to be part of a group
Infectious laughter
Speaking rapidly
Touching for effect
Impatient movements
Acting without thought
Agreeing without always thinking things through
Organizing fun events and gatherings
Being energized by music and people
Volunteering to help with whatever needs doing
Giving one's all to a project that one is excited about
Generating lots of ideas and voicing them
Showing pride in one's town, sport teams, country, etc.
Impatience if other people are slow to move or act
Talking incessantly about the object of one's enthusiasm
Bouncing back quickly from negative experiences
Getting involved with projects in one's community
Attempting to win people over and join in one's enthusiasm
Focusing on the future more than the past
Enjoying the moment
Asking questions
Smiling often
Engaging in wrestling and horseplay

Wanting to see and experience new things
Making others feel valued through enthusiastic greetings
Forming fast friendships
Using lots of hand gestures
Not always knowing where personal boundaries are
Movements that exude energy (bouncing a foot, tapping the tabletop, etc.)
Speaking in a loud, boisterous voice
Rushing through responsibilities that don't generate excitement

ASSOCIATED THOUGHTS:
Our float is going to be the best one in the parade!
The boating trip will be awesome. I wish the weekend would hurry up and get here!
What an incredible organization. I can't wait to see how I can help.
Look at that offensive line. Our team's gonna win!

ASSOCIATED EMOTIONS: confidence, desire, excitement, happiness, hopefulness

POSITIVE ASPECTS: Enthusiastic characters are passionate. Whatever idea or organization they espouse, they are loyal and dedicated to it, often taking on undesirable roles or background positions that others may reject. Their zeal is infectious and their exuberance can be the catalyst to spurring fence-sitters into action.

NEGATIVE ASPECTS: Enthusiastic characters may be passionate, but they don't always think things through. Their excitement for an organization or upcoming event may give them an unrealistically rosy view and render them blind to faults and red flags. Others might view these characters as childish and simple and may not take them seriously. Enthusiastic characters may become so excitable that they take projects over, creating friction with other team members.

EXAMPLE FROM FILM: It's Buddy the elf's (*Elf*) nature to face each day with enthusiasm. Although momentarily dismayed upon discovering that he's not an actual elf, he recovers quickly, throwing himself into the adventure of finding his real dad in the strange and wonderful world of New York City. **Other Examples from TV and Film:** Barney Fife (*The Andy Griffith Show*), Rod Tidwell (*Jerry Maguire*)

TRAITS IN SUPPORTING CHARACTERS THAT MAY CAUSE CONFLICT: abrasive, cocky, grumpy, irresponsible, patient, pessimistic, temperamental

CHALLENGING SCENARIOS FOR THE ENTHUSIASTIC CHARACTER:
Participating in activities where emotional displays are a detriment (poker, etc.)
Learning that the object of one's enthusiasm is not what it appeared to be
Being the only enthusiast in a crowd of naysayers and wet blankets
Enthusiastically supporting an organization that most people believe to be a sham

EXTROVERTED

DEFINITION: outgoing; socially adept

CATEGORIES: identity, interactive

SIMILAR ATTRIBUTES: gregarious, outgoing, sociable

POSSIBLE CAUSES:
Genetics
Being an adrenaline junkie
Getting one's energy from other people
An adventurous upbringing (being exposed to new cultures and experiences, etc.)

ASSOCIATED BEHAVIORS:
Having an outward focus (on other people, experiences, etc.) rather than an inward one
Feeling confident in social situations
Being friendly and chatty
Being motivational
Seeking new pursuits and experiences
Being adventurous
Enjoying large venues, events, and crowds
Being reward-focused
Being socially adept and gifted at small talk
Becoming easily bored
Thinking while speaking; working things out verbally
Buying tickets to concerts or entertainment events
Making the first move (approaching others, striking up a conversation, etc.)
Impulsiveness
Stepping outside of one's comfort zone
Being outgoing
Competitiveness
Being productive with one's time
Enjoying traveling and meeting new people
Going to parties and hosting events
Laughing and joking with others
Texting and calling people to stay connected
Needing constant activity and stimulation
Asking direct questions rather than beating around the bush
Being a thrill seeker
Having many friendships rather than only one or two
Cheerfulness and high-spiritedness
Spontaneity: *Let's head out to the farm and have a bonfire!*
Having difficulty expressing one's feelings
Always moving and doing

Feeling energetic and enthusiastic in social situations
Seeking and taking advantage of opportunities
Being trendy (buying the latest technology, staying current with fashions, etc.)
Enjoying team sports
Craving attention
Openly sharing ideas and opinions
Listening to loud music
Being active on social media

ASSOCIATED THOUGHTS:
Perfect temperature for a swim. I'll call around to see who's up for water polo.
I can't wait for Zack's party. It's going to be epic!
That's it—I'm ditching this conference. There must be something fun to do in this town.
I love these tights, but if I show up in them, the girls will laugh me out of the office.

ASSOCIATED EMOTIONS: confidence, eagerness, excitement, happiness, pride, satisfaction

POSITIVE ASPECTS: Extroverted characters are almost never alone; they thrive in the company of others. They enjoy getting out, trying new experiences, and meeting new people. These characters are confident in most social situations and can mingle well. They often have a large group of friends and can be very spontaneous and open-minded. Their enthusiasm will affect others and bring up the energy level of any gathering.

NEGATIVE ASPECTS: Extroverted characters are easily bored and require almost constant stimulation. This can be exhausting for friends who are not so outgoing or lean toward being introverted. Their desire for something new and exciting can lead to rashness and poor decisions. They are also reward-driven and can be very competitive, causing friction among friends and colleagues.

EXAMPLE FROM FILM: In the movie *The Talented Mr. Ripley*, wealthy Dickie Greenleaf is living in Italy to escape his stuffy and controlling parents back in the United States. In constant need of excitement and adventure, Dickie is a natural extrovert, getting his energy from being out with his many friends at jazz clubs and bars. He travels extensively, moving to new locales when his current scene gets boring. **Other Examples from Film and Literature:** Elle Woods (*Legally Blonde*), Bridget Vreeland (*The Sisterhood of the Traveling Pants*)

TRAITS IN SUPPORTING CHARACTERS THAT MAY CAUSE CONFLICT: calm, introverted, patient, perfectionist, proper, reckless, sentimental, untrusting

CHALLENGING SCENARIOS FOR THE EXTROVERTED CHARACTER:
Being forced to attend long, drawn-out ceremonies (Sunday mass, weddings, funerals, etc.)
Being stuck (in an elevator, for instance) with no stimulation until help arrives
Falling in love with an introvert
Having a job that requires one to be alone for long periods of time (a truck driver, etc.)

FLAMBOYANT

DEFINITION: striking or colorful in behavior and appearance

CATEGORIES: identity, interactive

SIMILAR ATTRIBUTES: colorful, dashing, glamorous

POSSIBLE CAUSES:
Having a strong sense of identity
Needing to express oneself as an individual
Growing up in a home that encouraged exploration
Being highly creative
The desire to create drama
Playfulness

ASSOCIATED BEHAVIORS:
Dressing distinctively in any situation
Having a totem symbol for one's individuality (a fedora, mismatched socks, etc.)
Being fashion-forward; creating trends rather than following them
Making an entrance
Using grand gestures
Being showy or flashy
Enjoying attention
Extravagance
Having a big personality
Getting energy from other people and being on display
Posing for effect
Raising one's voice to be heard over a crowd
Expressiveness
Having a strong sense of humor
Being hygienic
Keeping strong eye contact
Using the voice distinctively (using dramatic pauses, tone shifts, an accent, etc.)
Choosing a signature look (a haircut no one else is brave enough to try, etc.)
Optimism and a positive outlook
Taking criticism well
Being attentive to detail
Having a passion for life and an adventurous spirit
Accessorizing with jewelry or adornments to make oneself stand out
Testing boundaries and traditional ideas
Having strong social skills
Enthusiasm
Entertaining others
Bringing up the energy in a room

Enjoying shock value: *For Halloween I'm going to be a fishing net!*
Being highly imaginative and creative
Owning one's look; confidence
Growing bored by the same look

ASSOCIATED THOUGHTS:
My hair is so blah. I'm going to shake things up and dye it orange.
A cape is perfect for the prom. I love it!
Looks like Jay's ready to highjack the DJ's booth. Time for my grand entrance!
The only way to pull off a look like this is to own it.
After I show up in this body paint, book club will never be the same.

ASSOCIATED EMOTIONS: amusement, anticipation, confidence, eagerness

POSITIVE ASPECTS: Flamboyant characters are high-spirited and have a flair for the dramatic. They bring up the energy of the room and are skilled at drawing every eye to them. These characters are often admired for their individuality, their confidence, and their sense of fun and flash.

NEGATIVE ASPECTS: Characters with a flamboyant flair draw attention—but not always the positive kind. People who are more reserved may alienate or ridicule them. These characters may also be pressured to conform rather than be admired for their willingness to be themselves. There is also a danger for flamboyant characters to become addicted to attention and take excessive pride in their sense of style, leading to narcissism.

EXAMPLE FROM FILM: Captain Jack Sparrow from *The Pirates of the Caribbean* franchise has a flair for the dramatic, dressing much better than the average pirate and frequently adopting poses and gestures that draw an audience. He wears kohl eyeliner to make his eyes more intimidating and utilizes his voice to pull attention, deepening his tone for effect and emphasizing certain words to get emotion and meaning across. **Other Examples from Film, Literature, and Pop Culture:** Oda Mae Brown (*Ghost*), Caesar Flickerman (the *Hunger Games* trilogy), Lady Gaga

TRAITS IN SUPPORTING CHARACTERS THAT MAY CAUSE CONFLICT:
empathetic, haughty, introverted, judgmental, proper, sophisticated, temperamental, withdrawn

CHALLENGING SCENARIOS FOR THE FLAMBOYANT CHARACTER:
Dealing with others who make assumptions about one's sexuality (especially for males)
Interacting with people who believe that one's actions are inappropriate
Having a crisis of faith over one's identity
Living in a culture where freedom of expression is highly discouraged
Having to blend in out of necessity (serving a jail term, government scrutiny, etc.)
Facing hate, ignorance, or discrimination because of one's stylistic choices

FLIRTATIOUS

DEFINITION: inclined to provocative teasing and suggestive attention

CATEGORIES: identity, interactive

SIMILAR ATTRIBUTES: amorous, coquettish, provocative

POSSIBLE CAUSES:
Having a strong sense of playfulness
Being confident in one's sexuality
Feeling a biological need to find a mate and reproduce
Having control issues

ASSOCIATED BEHAVIORS:
Making suggestive comments that can be taken sexually
Choosing a target and conveying interest through words and actions
Lavishing praise and compliments
Leaning in toward another person
Entering someone's personal space
Drawing attention to the mouth (licking one's lips, playful biting a straw, etc.)
Offering a suggestive smile
Looking people in the eye
Laughing in a deep, sensual way
Playful joking
Being more touchy-feely than normal
Speaking in a lower-pitched voice
Dressing to attract (sexual) attention
Wearing perfume or cologne in hopes that it will be noticed and enjoyed
Suggesting a future meeting: *We should go to a movie sometime,* or *You like Italian?*
Light teasing
Blushing
Employing coquettish mannerisms (a darting glance, a shy smile, etc.)
Stroking the hair, exposing the throat, pointing one's body toward the other person
Offering lingering touches
Asking questions to judge a target's interest level
Furtively looking someone up and down
Sharing things (lunch, a locker, one's personal items, etc.)
Asking or answering questions that require honesty and vulnerability
Focusing on someone's physical attributes: *I love your dress. It looks...wow.*
Tilting the head and giving a slight smile
Borrowing an item so one will have a reason to return it and see the person again
Trading numbers, emails, or contact information
Showing confidence (open body posture, chest thrust out, asking brazen questions, etc.)
Acting silly and suggestive

Enjoying the effect one has on a target

Showing an interest in what the other person finds important

Touching the lips, neck, or face

"Accidentally" bumping into someone to manufacture an opportunity to talk

Asking for someone's help or advice as a way of starting a conversation

Acting protective in small ways (walking a date to her car, etc.)

Frequent and playful texting

ASSOCIATED THOUGHTS:
I think I'll just bump into Matt at the bus stop and see what happens.
Lori's finally alone. Now's a good time to buy her a drink.
If I act like I came here with someone, maybe she'll be jealous.
If Bill lets me borrow his jersey for the game, I can swing by his place later to return it.

ASSOCIATED EMOTIONS: amusement, confidence, desire, embarrassment, excitement, happiness

POSITIVE ASPECTS: A bit of flirting can add a sense of fun to social interactions. This level of playfulness brings people closer and encourages everyone not to take things too seriously. When done skillfully, flirting can make others feel important. It is an attractive quality to most people.

NEGATIVE ASPECTS: Characters who are flirty by nature may not know when to stop flirting, which can cause jealousy to flare. Their actions can easily be misconstrued, making an interested party believe that the flirtatious character's feelings run deeper than they actually do. Flirts can also take their behavior too far and run the risk of ruining their reputations.

EXAMPLE FROM FILM: Jessica Rabbit, the sultry singer from *Who Framed Roger Rabbit,* is an iconic bombshell flirt. This animated character has curves and knows how to use them. Exuding confidence, she moves and dresses in a way that draws all male eyes to her assets. **Other Examples from Film:** Mae Mordabito (*A League of their Own*), Joan (*Mr. Mom*)

TRAITS IN SUPPORTING CHARACTERS THAT MAY CAUSE CONFLICT: callous, catty, cautious, devout, innocent, overconfident, oversensitive, proper, sleazy, timid, vain, vindictive

CHALLENGING SCENARIOS FOR THE FLIRTY CHARACTER:
Being interested in someone who seems immune to one's flirting

Having a significant other who flirts with everyone

Being attracted to someone who is turned off by flirtation

Having to compete for someone's attention because of other interested parties

FOCUSED

DEFINITION: having fixed concentration and attention

CATEGORIES: achievement

SIMILAR ATTRIBUTES: intense

POSSIBLE CAUSES:
Intelligence
A studious nature
Having a deep interest in learning how things work
A desire to apply oneself; being goal-oriented and achievement-driven
A need for success or acclaim

ASSOCIATED BEHAVIORS:
Making time for a subject of interest
Knowing what one wants
Being able to shut out distractions (music, people talking, the internet, etc.)
Intense concentration
Paying close attention and being alert for change
Leaning in or bending close to one's subject of study
Losing track of time
Planning ahead
Having the stamina and endurance to see something through
Making a list of what needs to be done to stay on task
Having a clear head; being free of distracting emotional worries
Shutting out those who are negative or show a lack of understanding for one's goals
Following a routine or training regimen
Having a strong work ethic when it comes to the subject of one's focus
Understanding the scope of one's mission or goal
Productivity
Feeling passion for one's interest, goal, or career
Being a doer rather than a dreamer
Exhibiting strong willpower
Being able to organize one's thoughts
Getting started right away rather than procrastinating
Knowing what needs to be done
Taking the lead
Seeking answers to one's questions
Persistence and determination
Prioritizing well
Appreciating structure and planning
Believing in oneself and one's abilities
Wanting to do a good job

Getting lost in one's work; not being aware of one's surroundings

Showing devotion to a task or goal

Reading and researching to apply oneself more fully

Tackling one thing at a time rather than multi-tasking

Feeling frustration at those who are scatterbrained or chatty

Self-awareness (knowing one's strengths and weaknesses)

ASSOCIATED THOUGHTS:

Two years until the next Olympics. It won't be easy, but I can do it.

My job is to keep my eye on the ball. Nothing else.

My legs want to give out, but I can push through it.

Allie doesn't get it—I have to study. I want to go to Harvard, not some community college.

ASSOCIATED EMOTIONS: confidence, curiosity, desire, determination, pride, satisfaction

POSITIVE ASPECTS: Focused characters are able to drive out negative self-talk along with external distractions and get down to work. Their determination and persistence allow them to stretch themselves to really discover what they are made of, excelling in ways that most only hope to do. They take themselves and their goals seriously and think big in terms of what challenges they wish to take on. Their desire to do well means they may go slowly, sacrificing efficiency for thoroughness.

NEGATIVE ASPECTS: While focused individuals are able to get down to business quickly and stay on task, their ability to block out everything but the mission sometimes means shutting out people. Focused characters may become so fixated on their inner world that they ignore or neglect loved ones and friends. Obsessions can develop, leading to an unbalanced lifestyle where all of one's time goes into the goal, leaving little energy for anything else. Productive when focused, these characters may let other things slide in order to maintain a high productivity level in a specific area. They may lose track of time, miss appointments, and forget to attend family events.

EXAMPLE FROM FILM: Doc Holliday in *Tombstone* has a passion for gambling. This interest is all-consuming, sometimes causing him to stay up for days at a time in order to gamble. His extreme focus has turned him into a gifted player—one who can read opponents as well as cards—but it also puts his health at risk. Obsessed with the game and the drinking and smoking indulgences that go with it, Doc's body slowly breaks down, unable to cope with the strain. **Other Examples from Film and Literature:** Evelyn Salt (*Salt*), Darby Shaw (*The Pelican Brief*), Hermione Granger (*Harry Potter* series)

TRAITS IN SUPPORTING CHARACTERS THAT MAY CAUSE CONFLICT:

easygoing, empathetic, extroverted, inattentive, jealous, needy, socially aware, temperamental, unstable, willful

CHALLENGING SCENARIOS FOR THE FOCUSED CHARACTER:

Having dual goals or desires that split one's focus

Experiencing repeated failures which threaten to weaken one's resolve

Dealing with fallout from putting work before family

Being the target of a prankster

FRIENDLY

DEFINITION: showing friendship; acting in a way that befits a friend

CATEGORIES: interactive, moral

SIMILAR ATTRIBUTES: affable, amicable, congenial

POSSIBLE CAUSES:
Living in a loving, supportive environment
Enjoying people and interaction
Confidence
Deriving pleasure from interaction and relationships
Being raised by parents who had a strong sense of community and caring
Having strong social skills
Believing in peace and goodwill
Craving acceptance; wanting to fit in

ASSOCIATED BEHAVIORS:
Greeting people
Smiling
Being comfortable around others
Generosity
Asking questions to encourage conversation
Treating people fairly and with respect
Displaying trustworthiness and a willingness to trust others
Easily engaging in small talk, even with strangers
Displaying welcoming, open body posture
Having a positive attitude
Putting others at ease
Politeness
Talking about things in a positive light
Making time for people
Being thoughtful (bringing a gift for the hostess, etc.)
Being attentive in groups; making sure everyone is having a good time
Giving compliments
Cooperation
Showing support in good times and bad
Being open to new relationships
Using a warm tone
Speaking with energy and enthusiasm
Taking the time to find out a person's interests
Being approachable and easy to talk to or confide in
Showing hospitality
Being a good neighbor

Following through on promises and commitments
Inviting others to meet one's family or come into one's home
Giving more than one takes
Trying new things, especially to support a friend (going rock climbing, etc.)
Reaching out to others when they need help
Respecting the independence of others
Not being judgmental
Showing appreciation
Not projecting one's own baggage onto others

ASSOCIATED THOUGHTS:
Looks like a long wait. I'll just talk to the people behind me to pass the time.
That girl is all alone at her table. I'll eat lunch with her.
I can't wait to meet the girls in my dance class.
Bill knows a ton about cars. I'll ask his opinion on the best models.

ASSOCIATED EMOTIONS: curiosity, gratitude, happiness, love, peacefulness, satisfaction

POSITIVE ASPECTS: Friendly characters are kind, thoughtful, respectful, and open, naturally drawing people to them. One-on-one or in a crowd, they make those around them feel included and special. Characters who are friendly are highly sociable and genuinely care about the feelings of others, inspiring the people around them to become the very best versions of themselves.

NEGATIVE ASPECTS: Friendly characters are naturally helpful, making them a target for manipulative people, users, and predators. Some friends may also abuse these characters by counting on them too heavily, treating them as a sounding board for all of their problems. Not only can this cause moodiness and frustration, but it can result in the friendly character's needs going unmet.

EXAMPLES FROM LITERATURE: Arthur Weasley (the *Harry Potter* franchise) is very amicable and attentive. He asks questions to show his interest in others, is caring and kind, and his friendly nature puts him in good standing within most of the wizarding community. Trustworthy and helpful, Arthur reaches out to those in need and becomes something of a surrogate father for Harry. **Other Examples from Film:** Buddy (*Elf*), Giselle (*Enchanted*), Josh Baskin (*Big*)

TRAITS IN SUPPORTING CHARACTERS THAT MAY CAUSE CONFLICT: abrasive, controlling, cruel, inattentive, inflexible, manipulative, morbid, pushy

CHALLENGING SCENARIOS FOR THE FRIENDLY CHARACTER:
A moral conflict that requires a choice between a friendship and doing what's right
Being highly competitive
Having a friendship that grows toxic over time (due to inequality, jealousy, etc.)
Needing to set aside friendships in order to lead others, make decisions, or be diplomatic

FUNNY

DEFINITION: comical; causing amusement or laughter

CATEGORIES: identity, interactive

SIMILAR ATTRIBUTES: amusing, comical, entertaining, humorous, jovial

POSSIBLE CAUSES:
Growing up in a family where one was expected to entertain younger siblings
The desire to entertain, make people laugh, or be in the spotlight
Having a quirky and humorous outlook on life
Being exposed to comedians and entertainers
Growing up in an environment that was filled with laughter
Needing attention or affirmation

ASSOCIATED BEHAVIORS:
Making witty comebacks and observations
Cracking jokes and making people laugh
Observing the strangeness of life in a comical way
Speaking in funny voices or accents
Using comical facial expressions
Having an excellent sense of timing
Thinking on the fly
Reveling in the unexpected
Being a strong storyteller
Embellishing stories to make them funnier
Being able to poke fun at oneself
Purposely acting like a klutz
Making light of a serious situation to defuse tension
Awkwardness that is comical and endearing
Engaging in clever wordplay
Offering wry commentary: *Well, she'll never win a gold medal for the balance beam.*
Eccentricity
Noticing things that others miss
Using an object in a funny or inappropriate way
Drawing a crowd at social events
Using humor to bring people together and boost morale
Employing sarcasm that is funny rather than personal or hurtful
Making use of universally funny topics (potty humor, silly stereotypes, etc.)
Encouraging others to join in and add to the humor of the moment
Applying a truism in an unintended way: *Make ourselves at home? Okay...off go the pants!*
Making mistakes on purpose
Enjoying a good prank
Mischievousness
Confidence

Enjoying and pointing out irony
Pausing for effect
Spontaneity
Poking fun at personal calamities or situations
Knowing when to stop before something goes too far
Being highly social
Having good instincts about people (knowing what they might find funny or offensive, etc.)
Having one's own style of humor; not copying someone else's
Noting body language to judge the reaction to a joke

ASSOCIATED THOUGHTS:
Where'd that guy learn his table manners—from watching Survivor?
Buddy, a white suit? I'd love to see a car blast through a puddle right about now.
You know what would be funny? A clown with a phobia of clowns.
Everyone's so serious. A good fart would lighten the mood.

ASSOCIATED EMOTIONS: amusement, curiosity, happiness

POSITIVE ASPECTS: Because everyone loves a good joke, characters with a strong sense of humor usually have no shortage of friends. When life gets serious or someone wants to let off steam, it's easy to kick back and have a good time with someone funny. Humor is generally appreciated, so amusing characters can sometimes joke themselves out of a serious situation and escape unwanted consequences.

NEGATIVE ASPECTS: Some characters may not know when to stop being funny; this can create the perception that they're unable to take anything seriously. Funny characters who go too far can cause anger or embarrassment for others, creating rifts in relationships. In addition, friends and potential lovers may have trouble getting close to these characters as they wonder if the humor is simply a mask that hides the funny character's true self.

EXAMPLE FROM TV: Jerry Seinfeld began his career as a stand-up comedian, making the late night TV circuit and impressing the likes of Johnny Carson and David Letterman with his unique brand of funny. He then channeled his humor into the creation and writing of *Seinfeld*, a sitcom that went on to become a commercial success and pop culture sensation. Popular Seinfeldisms such as the master of your domain, yadda-yadda-yadda, regifting, Festivus, and spongeworthy are still quoted to this day. **Other Examples from Pop Culture:** Richard Pryor, Ellen DeGeneres, Lucille Ball, Eddie Murphy, Chris Rock

TRAITS IN SUPPORTING CHARACTERS THAT MAY CAUSE CONFLICT: defensive, focused, haughty, humorless, insecure, predictable, proper, pushy, studious

CHALLENGING SCENARIOS FOR THE FUNNY CHARACTER:
Working beneath a serious person (a boss who evaluates employees for promotion, etc.)
Facing a personal tragedy or seeing others experience one
Being paired with another funny character who gets bigger laughs
Living in a culture where one's humor is considered inappropriate, offensive, or not funny
Belonging to a family where one's actions are scrutinized (a political or royal family, etc.)

GENEROUS

DEFINITION: liberal in giving

CATEGORIES: interactive, moral

SIMILAR ATTRIBUTES: altruistic, bighearted, charitable, giving, philanthropic

POSSIBLE CAUSES:
Having a strong sense of gratitude
Desiring to share, lift up, and help others
Wanting to pay back or pay forward
Growing up in a giving family or community
Having a strong sense of morality
Experiencing the generosity of others in a way that changed one's life for the better

ASSOCIATED BEHAVIORS:
Sharing whenever doing so might help
Offering gifts with no conditions
Kindness
Thoughtfulness
Deriving pleasure at lifting someone's spirits
Donating one's time, energy, and money to charitable causes
Giving time to help organize events or socials
Being trustworthy and assuming the trustworthiness of others
Taking on extra duties or responsibilities to give someone else a break
Offering to use one's connections or influence to help someone
Giving compliments
Making time for people
Hoping others will be inspired to act generously if one does so first
Seeing the needs of others and doing something about it
Opening one's home to others
Being non-materialistic
Giving because one can
Humility; playing down one's generosity
Being actively concerned about the welfare of others
Spreading happiness and positivity
Treating others like family
Thinking about how one can better help or aid a person or cause
Being proactive
Giving back to one's community and workplace
Gaining energy from giving
Taking the lead role in a cause that is dear to one's heart
Living humbly
Inspiring others

Being dedicated to others
Being passionate about one's giving
Treating people with equality
Showing a genuine interest in others
Being a good listener
Empathy
Friendliness
Appreciating what one has
Learning more about a cause through involvement (working in a soup kitchen, etc.)

ASSOCIATED THOUGHTS:
That homeless man always wears the same threadbare coat. Maybe one of mine would fit.
Mary's had a hard pregnancy. I think I'll make up some casseroles for her freezer.
Someone has to organize the Christmas party; since I'm home this year, I can help.
I'll tuck a spare twenty in Lucas' jacket before he leaves. It will be a nice surprise.

ASSOCIATED EMOTIONS: confidence, determination, gratitude, love, satisfaction

POSITIVE ASPECTS: Generous characters are fulfilled by bringing comfort, satisfaction, and happiness to others. Content with what they have, they hold a high appreciation for their circumstances and the important people in their lives. They often make good listeners and are very observant. If they see a need, they step forward to fill it to the best of their ability, rather than wait for someone else to do so. These characters inspire kindness and philanthropy in others through their unselfish acts. They see giving as simply part of being a decent human being.

NEGATIVE ASPECTS: Generous characters view the world through a positive filter, seeing the best in people. This naïveté regarding the human condition can leave them open to being taken advantage of by those without scruples. These characters find it difficult to say no, and often overcommit rather than risk disappointing those depending on them. They can also be generous to a fault, giving so sacrificially that their own welfare suffers.

EXAMPLE FROM POP CULTURE: Santa Claus is possibly the most iconic example of generosity. According to the well-loved story, Santa and his elves work the year through to make presents for the good children of the world until Christmas Eve, when they deliver them house-to-house via magical reindeer. Cheerful, good-natured, and hardworking, Santa is always ready with a kind word of praise. **Other Examples from Film:** Oskar Schindler (*Schindler's List*), George and Mary Bailey (*It's a Wonderful Life*)

TRAITS IN SUPPORTING CHARACTERS THAT MAY CAUSE CONFLICT: grumpy, irresponsible, manipulative, stingy, stubborn, temperamental, timid

CHALLENGING SCENARIOS FOR THE GENEROUS CHARACTER:
Wanting to give something to a person with extreme pride
Being too ill or overburdened to continue with one's charity projects
Having to say no to a worthy cause
Being confronted by family members who don't feel like they're a priority

GENTLE

DEFINITION: not harsh, brusque, or violent

CATEGORIES: interactive

SIMILAR ATTRIBUTES: benign, docile, mild

POSSIBLE CAUSES:
Being raised by loving caregivers
Being naturally sensitive to the feelings of others
Being protected or shielded from the world as a child
Valuing all life

ASSOCIATED BEHAVIORS:
Graciousness
Kindness
Being soft-spoken
Patience
Exhibiting good manners
Being considerate and loving
Showing thoughtfulness for others
Comforting those in need
Modesty
Being even-keeled
Showing unconditional love
Keeping to oneself
Preferring quieter environments
Having a non-threatening demeanor
Speaking thoughtfully
Rarely raising one's voice
Being respectful of the privacy of others
Offering slow smiles
Having a positive attitude
Speaking in a calm, comforting tone
Using careful movements and easy touches (patting an arm to show closeness, etc.)
Taking moments for quiet reflection
Enjoying being alone with one's thoughts
Avoiding crowds and noise
Humming or singing softly during times of contentment
Avoiding high drama and stressful situations
Forging close friendships with a few people rather than having many friends
Trustworthiness
Being able to calm others and enable them to let down their guard
Displaying concern for people, animals, or nature

Optimism
Being intuitive and observant
Not being competitive
Indulging in daydreams
Showing an appreciation of beauty and art
Reserving one's opinion until it is requested
Being noncombative; refusing to argue

ASSOCIATED THOUGHTS:
Hank is so stressed out. Maybe a walk after dinner will help him relax.
I love it when I make Jill smile. She tries to hide it, but losing her job has taken a toll.
If I stay calm, maybe everyone will stop shouting at each other.
That poor cat's skin and bones. I'll coax her out with a can of tuna and take her home.

ASSOCIATED EMOTIONS: curiosity, desire, gratitude, happiness, hopefulness, nostalgia

POSITIVE ASPECTS: Gentle characters are soft-spoken, reflective, and observant. They are attuned to the emotions of others and can often help defuse tense situations. Thoughtful and respectful, they make great friends and can forge loving relationships. Their gentle nature often compels others to protect them and pay greater heed to their emotional needs.

NEGATIVE ASPECTS: Gentle characters can have quieter personalities, which, from a literary standpoint, can put them in danger of fading on the page. They may have difficulty voicing their own desires and needs or pursuing them to the point of feeling fulfilled. If they live in a loud, busy environment that is not suited to their personality, they may become overly dependent on others. This can make characters like these appear weak to readers.

EXAMPLE FROM FILM: When becoming stranded on a hostile planet, most aliens would go on the defensive. Instead, gentle E.T. (*E.T. the Extra-Terrestrial*) befriends a trio of siblings. He faces many indignities, such as having to live in Elliot's closet, being disguised with flowery frocks and cosmetics by Gertie, and having to flee faceless government officials. But he consistently responds with kindness and empathy, shattering countless alien stereotypes and creating a truly unforgettable character. **Other Examples from Literature:** Black Beauty (*Black Beauty*), John Coffey (*The Green Mile*)

TRAITS IN SUPPORTING CHARACTERS THAT MAY CAUSE CONFLICT: cruel, flaky, nervous, possessive, temperamental, volatile, repressed

CHALLENGING SCENARIOS FOR THE GENTLE CHARACTER:
Being faced with turmoil within the community (lawlessness, riots, impending war, etc.)
Having others in danger and being forced to fight to save them
Dealing with people who have no respect for those with quiet dispositions
Having to play peacemaker between feuding family members
Being betrayed by a loved one

HAPPY

DEFINITION: upbeat and content

CATEGORIES: identity, interactive

SIMILAR ATTRIBUTES: cheerful, content, jolly, lighthearted, merry, upbeat

POSSIBLE CAUSES:
Having a loving home environment
Being satisfied in one's job
Having balanced and fulfilling relationships
Being safe and secure
Having strong purpose
Feeling at peace with who one is

ASSOCIATED BEHAVIORS:
Staying connected with family and friends
Kindness and thoughtfulness
Showing gratitude for what one has
Being optimistic about the future; focusing on the positive
Feeling satisfied at doing good and helping others
Coping with life's ups and downs in a healthy way
Pursuing mental and physical health
Contentment
Thinking about the bigger picture and how one fits into it
Looking at the bright side when something bad happens
Minimal stressing and worrying
Putting things into perspective
Generosity and kindness
Having a good sense of humor
Enjoying other people and the unique talents and ideas that they offer
Working well with others
Humming or singing
Friendliness and politeness
Enjoying learning new things
Forgiving others for wrongs
Deriving pleasure from all that life brings
Being willing to commit to the people and causes that one cares about
Setting goals that will continue or increase one's satisfaction and happiness
Feeling at peace with one's world
Taking control of one's life
Not comparing oneself to others
Making time for hobbies and engaging in creativity
Being considerate of others
Laughing and smiling

Honesty and truthfulness
Being trustworthy
Loving others unconditionally
Being persistent; pursuing the things one loves to do
Self-confidence
Not taking life or people for granted
Challenging oneself
Being proactive
Noticing and appreciating beauty
Daydreaming about the future

ASSOCIATED THOUGHTS:
What a sunrise! After I finish my coffee I'll treat Grandma to a pancake breakfast.
If I work hard all summer, I can pay for snowboarding lessons this winter.
What a great day. I can't believe how beautiful it is outside.
I did it! I didn't drink pop for a whole month. I bet I could do it for another month.

ASSOCIATED EMOTIONS: amusement, confidence, eagerness, gratitude, happiness, satisfaction

POSITIVE ASPECTS: Happy characters are content and fulfilled. Satisfied with their life's direction, they take a straightforward approach to fixing the things that bother them so they can keep charging ahead. When wronged, happy people are able to forgive. They love unconditionally; this, paired with the contagious nature of happiness, makes them desirable as friends.

NEGATIVE ASPECTS: Happy characters will sometimes steer clear of inconveniences that would dispel their good mood. This can frustrate others, who may feel that these characters aren't taking the situation seriously or being a team player. If a friend who is down wants to be left alone, being overly cheery and determined to bring him "up" may be the last thing he wants or needs. When the happy character's attempts to improve his mood is rebuffed, it can lead to hurt feelings and a damaged friendship.

EXAMPLE FROM FILM: The popular character Mr. Bean from the *Mr. Bean* franchise is always upbeat and optimistic, no matter how simple the situation or what calamities befall him. He makes the best of any scenario, smiles often, and gains joy via problem solving and innovation as he deals with humorous mishaps. **Other Examples from TV and Pop Culture:** Andy Taylor (*The Andy Griffith Show*), Santa Claus

TRAITS IN SUPPORTING CHARACTERS THAT MAY CAUSE CONFLICT: grumpy, haughty, needy, oversensitive, resentful, superstitious, ungrateful

CHALLENGING SCENARIOS FOR THE HAPPY CHARACTER:
Dealing with grief or betrayal
Having to decide if a stagnating relationship should be salvaged or cut loose
Facing a situation that causes doubt about one's ability to succeed
Seeing others in pain or unhappy
Having one's fortune come with a price (being promoted because a co-worker was let go)

HONEST

DEFINITION: honorable in intentions; straightforward in conduct

CATEGORIES: interactive, moral

SIMILAR ATTRIBUTES: authentic, direct, frank, genuine, sincere, straightforward, truthful

POSSIBLE CAUSES:
Having a strong sense of honor
Having firm opinions about right and wrong
Having no filter; saying what comes to mind without thought
Wanting healthy, functional relationships
Not being affected by what others may think or feel
Being hurt in the past by the concealment of truth
Being responsible
Valuing trustworthiness
Being pure and innocent (e.g. children)

ASSOCIATED BEHAVIORS:
Owning up to one's mistakes
Acknowledging one's weaknesses
Striving to balance honesty and tact
Failing to find balance and exhibiting a lack of tact
Redirecting the conversation in an effort to avoid lying
Respecting the privacy of others
Being uncomfortable with keeping secrets or knowledge from others
Being authentic
Working through problems in relationships by talking things out
Keeping meticulous records so as to dispel any accusation of dishonesty
Looking others in the eye
Speaking in an even tone; using minimal hand gestures
Using facial expressions that match one's words
Not making excuses; simply relaying the facts
Returning found items
Admitting to one's feelings if asked
Showing empathy for others
Thanking others for their honesty
Viewing things in black or white
Sticking to one's commitments
Offering an honest opinion whether it's requested or not
Having a strong conscience
Whistle-blowing when one encounters dishonesty (plagiarism, cheating, etc.)
Being unbiased and lacking prejudice
Living free of most guilt or shame
Respecting others enough to be truthful

Speaking without hesitation
Being emotionally stable and non-reactive
Generally being a rule follower
Getting right to the point instead of working up to it
Repeating details the same way during multiple retellings
Feeling freed by telling the truth
Happiness and fulfillment
A strong sense of fairness and justice

ASSOCIATED THOUGHTS:
This is the second time Brian's numbers have been off. I'll let accounting know.
I know I'm supposed to play hard to get, but that's not who I am.
Tim's supposed to be on work disability, so what is he doing fixing his roof?
Oh my. I've got to catch Marta and tell her she's got a dryer sheet stuck to her dress.
I guess I should ask Rita to meet me for lunch so I can tell her how I feel.

ASSOCIATED EMOTIONS: confidence, curiosity, determination, pride, reluctance, resignation, satisfaction

POSITIVE ASPECTS: Characters who are honest are generally happy and content because they live each day staying true to who they are. This authenticity means not having to fabricate a story, line, or excuse, and not fearing being caught in one's lies. If a candid evaluation or opinion is needed, honest characters are gold beyond measure. They say what they mean and can be relied on to not put friendship before truth, making them trustworthy and reliable.

NEGATIVE ASPECTS: Honest characters don't always know when directness is unwanted or unnecessary. Sometimes they view things in such extremes of black or white that their forthrightness comes across as being overly blunt. It's easy for honest characters to give advice unsolicited; on occasions when a listening ear would be preferred, they have difficulty not evaluating the problem and offering opinions.

EXAMPLE FROM FILM: In *Kate and Leopold*, leading man Leopold is a duke, an idealist, and a highly principled character. He finds any form of dishonesty repugnant, whether it be marrying a woman he doesn't love or endorsing a product he despises. His integrity provides much conflict when it clashes with the ideals of less principled characters in the story, such as his career-driven love interest. **Other Examples from Film and TV:** Spock (*Star Trek* franchise), Sheldon Cooper (*The Big Bang Theory*)

TRAITS IN SUPPORTING CHARACTERS THAT MAY CAUSE CONFLICT: gossipy, nagging, nosy, sentimental, tactless, temperamental

CHALLENGING SCENARIOS FOR THE HONEST CHARACTER:
Being honest in the face of drastic personal consequences
Choosing honesty even if it means a guilty person or criminal walks free
Suffering a past hurt yet being honest about one's feelings and risking hurt once more
Being entrusted with a secret that impacts others
Needing to break the law because it is the right thing to do

HONORABLE

DEFINITION: characterized by noble principles; displaying integrity

CATEGORIES: identity, interactive, moral

SIMILAR ATTRIBUTES: ethical, principled, reputable, respectable, upright

POSSIBLE CAUSES:
Having a strong sense of empathy
Being raised in an environment where ethics and honor were valued
Having role models that put duty and country first

ASSOCIATED BEHAVIORS:
Loyalty
Speaking the truth when asked
Standing up for one's beliefs even when it's unpopular to do so
Giving without expecting anything in return
Treating people (even opponents) with respect and fairness
Taking the high road
Forgiving people
Giving someone the benefit of the doubt
Transparency; acting without manipulation
Honesty
Graciousness
Thanking an opponent after a game; wishing them well
Being up-front about what one wants or needs
Requesting help when it's needed
Helping others when one is able to do so
Humility
Adhering to a code of ethics
Seeking out truth and knowledge
Fact-checking
Having good manners
Keeping one's ego in check
Not taking advantage of other people or unlawful opportunities
Maintaining control of one's emotions
Accepting responsibility
Making changes to bring about positive improvement
Having a strong sense of right and wrong
Living by example
Having strong self-esteem
Treating others as equals
Protecting those who need it
Respecting and upholding the law

Keeping one's promises
Making sacrifices so others are safe
Having a strong sense of loyalty to one's community or country
Never asking others to do what one is not willing to do first

ASSOCIATED THOUGHTS:
I've been honest from the get go. He should have taken me at my word.
I'm no hero; I just did the right thing, that's all.
Amy's new, but I'll trust her on this. I would want the same if our roles were reversed.
I should take Mark home before his drinking gets out of hand.

ASSOCIATED EMOTIONS: confidence, determination, gratitude, hopefulness, pride, satisfaction

POSITIVE ASPECTS: Honorable characters have an inner strength and integrity that makes them highly trusted and respected. They do what they believe to be right, no matter what the cost to themselves. Someone who acts with honor will put personal ego aside and behave with complete transparency, showing his strength of character.

NEGATIVE ASPECTS: Because honorable characters try to see the best in people, they can be targets for those who are unprincipled. This may lead to them being duped or taken advantage of. Some honorable characters may blindly trust in organizations and people and fail to see that these individuals aren't worthy of such loyalty. If they don't continually evaluate the groups and individuals they're aligned with, their actions can actually do harm instead of good.

EXAMPLE FROM FILM: Jean Valjean, the freed slave from *Les Misérables*, tries to do the right thing and view everyone as equal. His respect extends to people from all walks of life as he empathizes with their struggles for survival and freedom. He treats people with dignity and embodies forgiveness—even for Javert, the ruthless policemen who hounds him over the decades despite the honorable life Jean has lived since his original transgression. **Other Examples from Film and Literature:** Marko Ramius (*The Hunt for Red October*), Aragorn (*The Fellowship of the Ring*), Cameron Poe (*Con Air*)

TRAITS IN SUPPORTING CHARACTERS THAT MAY CAUSE CONFLICT: ambitious, hypocritical, impatient, loyal, sleazy, unethical

CHALLENGING SCENARIOS FOR THE HONORABLE CHARACTER:
Choosing between family and the law
Having one's trust betrayed
Desiring to seek retribution after a preventable loss (the death of a child to drunk driving, etc.)
Doing the right thing when it conflicts with one's desire

HOSPITABLE

DEFINITION: welcoming to others; showing generosity to guests

CATEGORIES: interactive, moral

SIMILAR ATTRIBUTES: neighborly

POSSIBLE CAUSES:
Having a large family that gathers often to socialize
Living in a close-knit community where everyone looks out for one another
Having parents or caregivers who opened their home to whoever was in need
Being raised as a socialite where "playing the host" was a frequent role
Being a nurturer
Having a strong sense of community

ASSOCIATED BEHAVIORS:
Opening up one's home to others
Hosting events to bring people together
Greeting people with warmth and enthusiasm
Generosity
Being optimistic and open-minded
Offering comforts to guests (food, drink, a bathroom to freshen up in, etc.)
Including others
Striking up conversations to make others feel important and welcome
Being non-judgmental
Showing respect for one's guests
Being able to put oneself in someone else's place
Offering protection to others
Treating newcomers like family
Being genuine
Wanting people to feel comfortable
Willingly serving others
Reaching out to neighbors who might be in need
Seeking out ways to help others
Setting aside one's schedule to attend to others
Being a good listener
Showing an active interest in other people's lives; asking questions
Sharing silly stories about oneself to make others feel at ease
Freely offering one's trust
Making travel recommendations (the best restaurants, local sites to see, etc.)
Being thoughtful in small ways (baking muffins for someone's breakfast, etc.)
Seeing the best in other people
Having a friendly manner
Enjoying the exchange of experiences, ideas, and perspectives

Being helpful and kind
Following through on promises
Showing others that it is safe to be vulnerable
Treating others the same way one would like to be treated
Giving someone the benefit of the doubt
Acting as a tour guide for someone who is unfamiliar with the area
Making people feel secure and safe
Sharing one's possessions and resources with others
Enjoying fellowship with others
Caring more about people than one's possessions

ASSOCIATED THOUGHTS:
There's a couch in the basement. I'll ask Mark if his friend would like to stay here.
I loved hearing about Nepal last night. Jess has been to some amazing places!
Poor Sam, losing his home. We should clean up Carl's old room and offer it to him.
I'm going to invite the new neighbors over for dessert.

ASSOCIATED EMOTIONS: anticipation, curiosity, excitement, gratitude, happiness, love, pride, satisfaction, sympathy

POSITIVE ASPECTS: Hospitable characters are loving and open and have a strong sense of community. Their desire to connect with people in a meaningful way makes others feel valued, safe, and welcome. Hospitable characters promote trust and fellowship through their generosity, kindness, and self-sacrifice.

NEGATIVE ASPECTS: Hospitable characters can be so open and willing to serve others that too much of their time and energy is spent satisfying the needs of friends, acquaintances, and strangers, leaving not enough one-on-one time with family. Their generosity can also put them at the mercy of selfish or entitled guests who would take as much as they can get without giving in return. And while hospitable characters gain real satisfaction from making others feel welcome, frustration and disillusionment can occur when their kindnesses aren't reciprocated.

EXAMPLE FROM FILM: Vianne Rocher (*Chocolat*) greets with a smile all the guests who frequent her chocolate shop, offering them free samples of this or that and trying to guess what their favorite confection might be. An outcast herself, she recognizes the sting of rejection and is determined that everyone she meets will feel welcomed and accepted. **Other Examples from Literature:** Bilbo Baggins (*The Hobbit*), Mr. And Mrs. Beaver (*The Lion, the Witch, and the Wardrobe*), the Abegnation faction (*Divergent series*), Bishop Myriel of Digne (*Les Misérables*)

TRAITS IN SUPPORTING CHARACTERS THAT MAY CAUSE CONFLICT: antisocial, disrespectful, entitled, paranoid, suspicious, unfriendly, ungrateful, withdrawn

CHALLENGING SCENARIOS FOR THE HOSPITABLE CHARACTER:
Playing host to people who do not trust one another
Trying to be hospitable while grieving for the loss of a loved one
Being asked to entertain or help someone who has hurt a family member in the past
Wanting to help and care for others but being incapacitated (from an illness, etc.)

HUMBLE

DEFINITION: not haughty, arrogant, or superior

CATEGORIES: interactive, moral

SIMILAR ATTRIBUTES: demure, meek, modest, unpretentious

POSSIBLE CAUSES:
Being naturally introverted
Growing up in the shadow of talented parents or siblings
Living in an environment where one shouldn't call attention to oneself
Having an honest desire to see others receive recognition and praise
Coming from a religious background that teaches honoring others rather than oneself
Having low self-esteem or confidence
Being shy

ASSOCIATED BEHAVIORS:
Avoiding the spotlight
Taking background roles
Downplaying one's skills and abilities
Talking up the accomplishments of others
Feeling satisfaction at being part of a team
Expressing discomfort when complimented
Deferring to others when disagreements or stalemates arise
Speaking in a quiet voice
Using unassuming movements that don't draw the eye
Engaging in hobbies and activities that don't call attention to oneself
Not bragging about one's successes
Having a strong work ethic
Responding to internal rather than external motivators
Doing one's work without grumbling or complaint
Generosity
Using words that are uplifting and encouraging
Being supportive
Giving compliments
Underestimating oneself
Playing it safe; not taking risks
Doing the jobs that no one else wants to do
Not expressing one's opinions until asked to do so
Listening first, then speaking
Minimizing one's role in success to avoid attention
Keeping secrets about one's successes or achievements
Becoming embarrassed when others bring up one's talents or abilities
Turning praise around to the giver; diverting attention

ASSOCIATED THOUGHTS:

She's worked so hard on this project. I hope she gets the proper credit.
Please don't call on me... Please don't call on me...
I'm so proud to be part of this team.
I wish they wouldn't go on about my involvement; it was a group effort.

ASSOCIATED EMOTIONS: confidence, happiness, insecurity, nervousness, satisfaction

POSITIVE ASPECTS: Humble characters defer to others, allowing them to take the credit. They're happy to be involved in a process that leads to something good and are satisfied to play a part without needing to share in the acclaim. These characters often prefer supportive roles, seeing themselves as cogs in the machine, and do not seek to elevate themselves above others. Because generosity goes hand in hand with humility, these characters are usually highly thought of by their peers. Humble characters often deflect when addressed directly, singing the praises of those around them as the "real heroes." This kindness is appreciated by others and creates a strong reciprocal feeling of loyalty and friendship.

NEGATIVE ASPECTS: It can be very difficult to thank or give a boon of appreciation to those who are overly humble since they see themselves as unworthy of such attention. Similarly, their unwillingness to take more credit than is due can create unnecessary awkwardness. Trying to repay a favor or do a good turn for a character who is unable to accept such kindness can lead to frustration. It's also possible that, due to their desire to remain in a supporting role, humble characters may fail to live up to their full potential.

EXAMPLE FROM FILM: George Bailey (*It's a Wonderful Life*) spends his life serving others and supporting his successful friends and family members. Instead of recognizing the powerful role he plays in the lives of the people around him, he sees himself as a simple family man and owner of a "cheap, penny-ante building and loan." Despite having repeatedly sacrificed for the people of Bedford Falls, he is genuinely shocked at the end of the story by their tangible outpouring of gratitude for all that he has done. **Other Examples from Literature:** Melanie Wilkes (*Gone with the Wind*), Ma Ingalls (*Little House on the Prairie* series)

TRAITS IN SUPPORTING CHARACTERS THAT MAY CAUSE CONFLICT:
ambitious, charming, defensive, extravagant, flamboyant, flashy, gossipy, proud, pushy

CHALLENGING SCENARIOS FOR THE HUMBLE CHARACTER:
Being forced into a leadership position
Having to step out of the shadows in order to right a wrong
Being paired with a flamboyant or quirky character who's always drawing attention
Experiencing success in a very public fashion that makes one uncomfortable
Being part of a team whose values or work ethic conflict with one's own

IDEALISTIC

DEFINITION: seeing the world as it could be; pursuing noble goals, beliefs, or a higher purpose

CATEGORIES: achievement, identity

SIMILAR ATTRIBUTES: noble

POSSIBLE CAUSES:
Having visionary parents or mentors
The desire to change the world for the better
Wanting to leave a legacy
Having a deep love for people, the world, or a specific belief or cause
Witnessing corruption, danger, or hardship
Having passionate convictions

ASSOCIATED BEHAVIORS:
Having a strong imagination
Asking *What if?*
Being highly observant
Creative problem solving; innovation
Being highly intuitive
Understanding what needs to be improved and how it can be done
Valuing the happiness of others
Believing in the good of humanity
Having deep values and beliefs
Being honorable and principled
Dreaming big
Being curious about the world and the people in it
Tenaciously pursuing one's goals
Being a deep thinker
Seeing the potential in everything
Generosity
Encouraging and inspiring others
Having a reflective nature
Bouncing back from disappointments or setbacks
Making independent choices rather than being swayed by others
Self-confidence
Boldly holding to one's beliefs
Hopefulness; optimism
Positively reinforcing others
Being consistent in one's pursuits
Having high personal expectations and standards
Finding joy in one's life and sharing it with others
Being satisfied with one's path

Avoiding conflict whenever possible
Being a strong mediator or peacemaker
Backing up one's beliefs with action
Trying to leave things better than one found them
Professing an interest in the meaning of life
Expressing one's feelings well
Having a job that focuses on helping others (social work, fundraising, etc.)
Being a good listener
Being considerate of others
Being spiritual

ASSOCIATED THOUGHTS:
There has to be a way to help that orphanage. Kids shouldn't have to live like that.
I want to do something meaningful, not just clock in and out every day.
Something's bothering Dean. Maybe we can work through it together.
If we all pitch in, we can clean up this lake. Then other communities would follow.

ASSOCIATED EMOTIONS: anticipation, confidence, curiosity, desire, eagerness, happiness, hopefulness

POSITIVE ASPECTS: Idealistic characters are valued for their honesty, their ability to listen, and their genuine, caring natures. They make strong peacemakers and advisors by ignoring the fluff, focusing instead on the heart of a problem and what it will take to make those involved more happy and fulfilled. They are resilient and determined when it comes to their convictions and cannot easily be brought down by disappointment or failure. These characters have big dreams and the courage to chase them, which often leads to change for the better.

NEGATIVE ASPECTS: While they're able to easily visualize the big picture, idealists sometimes have a hard time ironing out the details. Their inability to see how to make the dream a reality on a practical level can frustrate both them and the people dedicated to helping them succeed.

EXAMPLE FROM FILM: Sam Childers, a former gang member in *Machine Gun Preacher*, finds God and becomes a champion of orphaned children in the south Sudan. Despite the danger of raids from the Lord's Resistance Army, Sam builds an orphanage to keep children from being forced into recruitment as child soldiers. As the struggle intensifies, Sam becomes consumed by his mission, sacrificing his business, personal finances, and family relationships to pursue what he believes to be right. **Other Examples from History and Film:** Mahatma Gandhi, Martin Luther King, Jr., Jerry Maguire (*Jerry Maguire*), Dave Kovic (*Dave*)

TRAITS IN SUPPORTING CHARACTERS THAT MAY CAUSE CONFLICT: argumentative, cynical, fanatical, impatient, pessimistic, suspicious, unhelpful

CHALLENGING SCENARIOS FOR THE IDEALISTIC CHARACTER:
Having a relative who repeatedly discourages the idealistic character "for their own good"
Experiencing setbacks that make one doubt or question one's goal
Feeling the need to pursue a goal that puts oneself or one's family at risk
Living in a society that is tightly regimented and controlled

IMAGINATIVE

DEFINITION: having an active imagination; forming clear mental images of things that have not been previously considered

CATEGORIES: achievement, identity, interactive

SIMILAR ATTRIBUTES: inspired, inventive

POSSIBLE CAUSES:
Wanting to escape one's current situation
Genetics
Having a highly active mind
Being naturally curious
Being generally dissatisfied with the status quo; knowing that things can always be better

ASSOCIATED BEHAVIORS:
Verbalizing one's ideas with enthusiasm and energy
Looking at what's common or plain and seeing something special
Solving problems creatively
Being artistic
Daydreaming
Being able to visualize something without props or plans
Sketching, journaling, or making notes about one's ideas
Having no shortage of ideas
Being creative
Being intrigued by fantasy or that which is not yet a reality (advances in science, etc.)
Enjoying mysteries and the unknown
Being fascinated by inventiveness and the innovations of others
Enjoying movies and/or reading fiction
Thinking about the *What if?*
Optimism and a positive outlook
Believing in things that aren't real
Being driven to turn an idea into a reality
Staring off at nothing while thinking
Being drawn to color and movement
Believing that anything is possible
Experiencing more epiphanies than most people
Eccentricity
Being fun-loving and playful; acting silly in order to explore ideas
Curiosity
Resourcefulness
Dreaming vividly
Having a strong awareness of the world and oneself; seeing what others miss
Being able to entertain oneself (and often others, as well)

Finding inspiration from many sources
Fearlessness
Rarely suffering from boredom
Being unworried about what others think
Indulging in role-playing games

ASSOCIATED THOUGHTS:
What if there really was something in the closet? What if it's watching me right now?
When you think about it, how could aliens not be real?
I have to get this story idea down on paper—it's brilliant!
This zoo fundraiser is dull. Why can't the monkeys break out and swarm the dining hall?

ASSOCIATED EMOTIONS: amazement, confidence, curiosity, eagerness, excitement

POSITIVE ASPECTS: Imaginative characters are always looking for a way to entertain themselves. Their thoughts are vivid, as clear to these characters as if they were watching a movie, and they often feel compelled to share their ideas with others. This can make them the life of the party and create spontaneous fun with friends. For them, there is no idea too big or too preposterous. Once inspired, they become compelled to turn their dreams into realities. This leads to incredible innovation.

NEGATIVE ASPECTS: An imaginative character who lets his imagination run amok can become his own worst enemy. Living too fully among one's ideas and not enough in the real world can lead to social anxiety disorders, compulsive behavior, and a blurred line between what's real and what's not. Those who have a strong imagination may appear eccentric to others, becoming isolated. And while they're responsible for incredible innovations, not all new ideas are positive. Weapons of mass destruction, chemical warfare, and torture techniques like water boarding are all examples of innovation that brought about dark results.

EXAMPLE FROM HISTORY: Walt Disney was a man with great vision. Never satisfied with the status quo, he was always thinking up bigger ideas. Comics, animation, cartoon shorts, full-length feature films, amusement parks—his imagination was boundless. He took many risks pursuing his endeavors, many of which ended in failure. But he always kept going, thinking outside of the existing box to come up with new ideas that, once considered impossible, have become commonplace in today's culture. **Other Examples from Film and History:** J.M. Barrie (*Finding Neverland*), Stephen Hawking, Albert Einstein, Benjamin Franklin

TRAITS IN SUPPORTING CHARACTERS THAT MAY CAUSE CONFLICT: analytical, fussy, inhibited, proper, superstitious, uncommunicative

CHALLENGING SCENARIOS FOR THE IMAGINATIVE CHARACTER:
Having one's idea stolen by someone else
Coming up with a new idea at the same time that someone else puts it forth
Living so much in one's imagination that the line between fantasy and reality blurs
Envisioning something original and amazing but not being able to make it a reality
Not being believed due to one's imaginative nature

INDEPENDENT

DEFINITION: thinking and acting for oneself; resisting influence

CATEGORIES: achievement, identity, interactive

SIMILAR ATTRIBUTES: autonomous, self-reliant, self-sufficient

POSSIBLE CAUSES:
Having trust issues
Needing to be in control
Shyness
Being introverted
Having a rebellious streak
Experiencing oppression in the past
Believing in oneself and one's abilities
A history of personal success and capability
Desiring to be beholden to no one

ASSOCIATED BEHAVIORS:
Self-reliance
Accepting others
Exhibiting inner emotional strength
Trustworthiness
Striving for what one wants; not settling
Having a strong work ethic
Being able to do things on one's own
Enjoying solitude and being alone
Seeking out information and then making up one's mind
Trusting one's intuition
Being centered; knowing who one is and what one's role is in the world
Not being affected by peer pressure
Choosing not to meddle in other people's lives
Being passionate about an activity or a cause
Not wasting time
Cutting out negative influences (toxic friends, jobs that are draining, etc.)
Not getting upset easily
Patience
Recognizing when something isn't working and making changes to correct it
Protecting one's privacy and territory
Knowing what is best for oneself
Respecting the rights of others
Moving on from one's past; letting go of emotional baggage
Being financially responsible
Finding it difficult to ask for help
Being highly disciplined

Taking pride in one's achievements
Being competitive with oneself
Having a good work-life balance; not being overcommitted or stressed out
Placing a high value on personal freedom
Having a clear vision
Taking the initiative
Striving to put doubters in their place through proving them wrong
Avoiding debt; being financially responsible

ASSOCIATED THOUGHTS:
It took ten months, but this canoe is ready. I can't wait to take it out on the lake.
I wish my parents would stop trying to rule my life. I know what's best for me.
Buying a house will strain my finances, but renting out the top floor will help pay the bills.
I know Vic's got more money than me, but I can afford to pay for my own dinner.

ASSOCIATED EMOTIONS: confidence, defensiveness, happiness, loneliness, relief, satisfaction

POSITIVE ASPECTS: Independent characters see themselves clearly. They know what they can do and are comfortable taking action when others might be cowed. Past successes prove their capability, so they're able to work alone and often prefer to do so. These characters are sure of themselves and aren't overly concerned about the perceptions of others. As a result, they're able to focus on their goals and the job at hand. Forward-thinkers, they're able to move past the status quo to embrace ideals that are ahead of their time.

NEGATIVE ASPECTS: Because they are so often alone, independent characters may have difficulty working with or relating to others. Their lack of concern with what people think may create a perception about them of aloofness, smugness, or superiority. Their self-reliance may give loved ones the idea that they aren't needed or even much wanted and may widen the gap between these characters and the people in their lives.

EXAMPLE FROM FILM: Thanks to his experiences as a Green Beret in Vietnam, John Rambo (*First Blood*) knows how to fend for himself. His skills come in handy when he returns from the war to a hostile culture where he has difficulty relating to others or getting a decent job. When things get tough, he withdraws from society, traveling from place to place and taking care of himself rather than relying on others. **Other Examples from Literature:** Laura Ingalls (the *Little House* books), Erin Brockovich (*Erin Brockovich*)

TRAITS IN SUPPORTING CHARACTERS THAT MAY CAUSE CONFLICT:
controlling, cowardly, judgmental, needy, nervous, self-destructive, spoiled, timid

CHALLENGING SCENARIOS FOR THE INDEPENDENT CHARACTER:
Having dependent family members (a sibling needing financial support, etc.)
Having a mental disorder that makes one dependent on others
Suffering a blow to one's finances (being robbed, a bad investment, etc.)
Having a friend who needs emotional support over a long period of time
Incurring a debilitating injury that requires help from others (having to learn to walk again, etc.)

INDUSTRIOUS

DEFINITION: working with devotion and determination

CATEGORIES: achievement, interactive

SIMILAR ATTRIBUTES: diligent, hardworking, tireless

POSSIBLE CAUSES:
Having a "type A" personality
The desire for fulfillment; being goal driven
Having a strong passion or sense of purpose
Having a strong motivation to succeed
Craving power, status, or influence

ASSOCIATED BEHAVIORS:
Rising early and working late
Being organized, punctual and efficient
Having high standards
Talking often about one's passions
Reaching targets ahead of schedule
Competitiveness with oneself or with others
Working well with others when required to
Pursuing ideas that will improve the end result
Practicing more if needed
Shuffling appointments to accommodate one's work
Streamlining one's processes to be more efficient
Experiencing satisfaction from even small wins
Perseverance
Directness; not beating around the bush
Socializing with people from work to discuss work
Adhering to routines
Not wasting time or procrastinating
Anticipating what's needed
Double-checking; worrying over small mistakes
Dependability and consistency
Reflecting on an event to evaluate how it went
Not complaining about the labor involved in completing a project
Skipping meals when one is busy
Needing to be constantly active and engaged in tasks
Being prepared (even over-prepared) for events or meetings
Suffering from muscle strain and sore muscles (if tasks are physical)
Feeling mentally and physically wrung out at the end of the day
Sleeping less than other people
Rewarding oneself (having a beer after work, watching the game, etc.)

Taking work calls at home after hours
Being restless between projects
Studying the techniques of others who have succeeded at the same thing
Blowing off steam to balance out tense, long hours of work
Curbing bad habits or behaviors to be better at one's job (staying out late, etc.)
Using self-talk to encourage oneself to work harder

ASSOCIATED THOUGHTS:
If I train hard all summer, I'll be ready for the dance competition this fall.
By adding five laps to every swim session, I'll drop those extra pounds in no time.
It's 8:00 am and Dawn's still sleeping? Time to wake up, Sleeping Beauty!
Rick is Bob's favorite because he's so dedicated. I need to put in more hours, too.

ASSOCIATED EMOTIONS: confidence, desire, determination, excitement, impatience, overwhelmed, satisfaction

POSITIVE ASPECTS: Industrious characters are dependable and hardworking, pouring all their energy into a task or goal. When a job needs to be done, they step up and pull their weight. They make good use of their time and are good role models. Industrious characters generally see success and feel strong satisfaction at putting their best effort into all they do. They have the drive to complete what they've started and often end up being involved in innovation and change.

NEGATIVE ASPECTS: Industrious characters may sometimes become so caught up in their work that it damages their health and relationships. Long work hours and stress will disrupt sleep patterns and weaken their immune systems. Family and friends may feel resentment when an industrious character gives all of his time and energy to a job or project, leaving nothing for them. The pursuit of success, power, or prestige can become all-consuming, leading to a very unbalanced and exhausting lifestyle.

EXAMPLE FROM FILM: Rudy Ruettiger (*Rudy*) is a young man who dreams of playing football at the University of Notre Dame. Although he lacks the grades, the finances, and the physique of a football player, he refuses to give up. He works feverishly to earn income and overcome his dyslexia while attending a neighboring college, raising his grades enough to transfer to Notre Dame. Rudy volunteers to work for free as a groundskeeper to get closer to the team he loves and finally gains a spot on the practice squad. Due to his hard work, drive, and incredible heart, he's allowed to dress as one of the team for the final home game. **Other Examples from Literature and Film:** Ruby Thewes (*Cold Mountain*), Vince Papale (*Invincible*)

TRAITS IN SUPPORTING CHARACTERS THAT MAY CAUSE CONFLICT:
easygoing, flaky, lazy, needy, playful, rebellious, rowdy

CHALLENGING SCENARIOS FOR THE INDUSTRIOUS CHARACTER:
Experiencing a family crisis that demands one's time and attention
Losing one's job, and with it, one's sense of identity
Being unable to achieve conflicting goals; having to fail at one to succeed at the other
Being given a task one cannot complete despite a strong work ethic (due to lack of skill, etc.)

INNOCENT

DEFINITION: being of pure intent and motive

CATEGORIES: identity, interactive, moral

SIMILAR ATTRIBUTES: blameless

POSSIBLE CAUSES:
A sheltered upbringing
A developmental disability (e.g. Down Syndrome)
Never having experienced evil, cruelty, or hatred
Seeing only the good in humanity
Mental deterioration and old age

ASSOCIATED BEHAVIORS:
Candidness
Honesty
Curiosity
Being exceptionally trusting of others
Not being superficial
Kindness
Seeing the positive in every situation
Vulnerability
Respecting others
Showing genuine confusion when others lie or deceive
Friendliness
Trustworthiness
Making mistakes without realizing it
Answering questions directly, without couching
Looking people directly in the eye
Being excitable or enthusiastic
Seeing things in a practical light
Wearing one's emotions on one's sleeve
Being confused by sarcasm and irony
Telling others precisely how one feels
Asking questions that unknowingly cross boundaries into another's privacy
Listening with enjoyment to people telling stories or recounting their adventures
Having difficulty with concepts beyond one's experience (hate crimes, war, famine, etc.)
Being emotional without being embarrassed
Being passionate about one's interests even if others are not
Admitting when one has made a mistake
Being willing to help others
Being a peacemaker; being uncomfortable when one is at odds with others
Optimism

Smiling and laughing easily
Taking things literally
Believing people have one's best interests at heart

ASSOCIATED THOUGHTS:
Mom and Dad will know what to do.
Why is Jim upset? Of course Elijah will pay him back as soon as he can.
It's too bad Marie broke her leg, but at least she can catch up on her reading.
Kara said she was sorry. Why won't Lewis forgive her?

ASSOCIATED EMOTIONS: adoration, curiosity, excitement, happiness, love

POSITIVE ASPECTS: Innocent characters are pure and trusting. They take what they see at face value, always finding something worthwhile where others may only see the negative. Regardless of age, they're often perceived as childlike—good, yet vulnerable, which makes them easy to like and protect.

NEGATIVE ASPECTS: In their determination to only see the good, innocent characters may not view the world and other people as they truly are, which puts them at a disadvantage. While some may admire their innocence, others will see it as a weakness to be exploited, making them an easy mark. Still others view innocence as a fault that needs to be eradicated for the innocent character's "own good," and they set out to do so by revealing harsh truths to destroy their childish delusions.

EXAMPLE FROM FILM: Edward, the emotionally fragile character in *Edward Scissorhands*, lives isolated in a gothic mansion, an artificial man with scissor blades for hands. When he is shown kindness by his neighbor, he falls in love with Kim and begins to open up and interact with the townspeople. With the good comes bad, and he is betrayed by people wishing to use him. After a final altercation that ends in the accidental death of Kim's boyfriend, Edward recognizes that he is not capable of handling the tumult of emotion that exists beyond the walls of his home and chooses isolation once more. **Other Examples from Literature and Film:** Tom Cullen (*The Stand*), John Coffey (*The Green Mile*), Fraulein Maria (*The Sound of Music*)

TRAITS IN SUPPORTING CHARACTERS THAT MAY CAUSE CONFLICT: bold, controlling, cruel, flirtatious, gullible, manipulative, mature, persuasive, selfish

CHALLENGING SCENARIOS FOR THE INNOCENT CHARACTER:
Witnessing a crime
Discovering that one has been lied to or betrayed in some way
Living in an environment where people hide who they really are (high school, etc.)
Being told to lie in order to protect a close family member or friend

INSPIRATIONAL

DEFINITION: encouraging others, through one's example, to strive for change and fulfillment

CATEGORIES: identity, interactive

SIMILAR ATTRIBUTES: motivational

POSSIBLE CAUSES:
Being successful or accomplished
Having an extremely positive outlook
Having wisdom or insight into the human condition
Having an encouraging, supportive mentality
Having big dreams and the willingness to go after them
Being passionate about a topic and wanting to raise awareness

ASSOCIATED BEHAVIORS:
Making the time to create meaningful connections with other people
Leading by example
Having a strong work ethic
Believing in oneself and others
Having high self-esteem and confidence
Being goal driven
Cheering on the big and small successes of others
Taking control of one's destiny no matter what setbacks occur
Seeing worth in other people and appreciating them for who they are
Creating challenges in order to foster growth
Honesty
Creating awareness or sharing information that one believes others should know
Encouraging others to explore their individuality and find fulfillment
Being open, even with acquaintances or strangers
Believing in the best side of people
Discussing one's vulnerability in an effort to connect with others
Being genuine
Feeling empowered by helping others make positive changes
Not being derailed by hardship or adversity
Striving for growth and a deeper understanding of oneself
Being articulate or thoughtful when speaking
Including others rather than excluding them
Being highly energetic and focused
Living one's beliefs and encouraging others to stand up for what they believe in
Being a deep thinker
Knowing what is important and prioritizing accordingly
Sharing one's story and how one's choices and determination have opened doors
Offering words of encouragement to those who need it

Giving more than one takes
Being willing to help
Having patience
Having faith in one's actions, that they will lead to reaching one's goals
Desiring to learn, gather information, and share it with others

ASSOCIATED THOUGHTS:
This won't be easy, but I can do it.
I should tell Carol my story; maybe it will encourage her to keep trying.
I don't know how I'll pay for it, but I'm going to go to college.
People need to know the truth!

ASSOCIATED EMOTIONS: confidence, desire, determination, gratitude, happiness, peacefulness, satisfaction

POSITIVE ASPECTS: Inspirational characters are doers who aren't afraid to follow their dreams and stand up for what they believe in. They are focused on goals that often lead to self-growth and willingly champion causes that bring about positive change for others. Characters like this are hard working, dedicated, and supportive in nature, cheering on others and encouraging them to be better. They unwittingly motivate people and frequently make a positive impact on others.

NEGATIVE ASPECTS: Sometimes inspirational characters can be so focused on the goal that they forget to enjoy small accomplishments and other constants in their lives. The inspiring character may become so accomplished that family and friends start to feel as though they are not striving hard enough themselves and that they should be accomplishing more. This may lead them to struggle with doubt or resentment and low self-esteem.

EXAMPLE FROM HISTORY: Born without the ability to see, hear, or verbally communicate with others, Helen Keller could easily have lived her entire life in darkness, cut off from everyone around her. But due to her stubbornness, her intelligence, and the determination of a visionary teacher, Helen was able to overcome her deficiencies and become one of the most inspiring people who ever lived. **Other Examples from History and Film:** Martin Luther King, Jr., Anne Frank, Joan of Arc, Terry Fox, Mahatma Gandhi, Atticus Finch (*To Kill a Mockingbird*), Oskar Schindler (*Schindler's List*), William Wallace (*Braveheart*)

TRAITS IN SUPPORTING CHARACTERS THAT MAY CAUSE CONFLICT:
controlling, frivolous, haughty, indecisive, introverted, jealous, laid-back, lazy, proper, unethical, unmotivated

CHALLENGING SCENARIOS FOR THE INSPIRATIONAL CHARACTER:
Wishing to persevere but not having the resources or health to do so
Experiencing repeat failures that cause a crisis of faith
Being so weighed down by responsibility for others that one's own dreams are sidelined
Experiencing an injury that causes a goal to become seemingly impossible

INTELLIGENT

DEFINITION: having a high mental capacity; cerebral

CATEGORIES: achievement, identity

SIMILAR ATTRIBUTES: brainy, bright, smart

POSSIBLE CAUSES:
Genetics
Having access to education and opportunities
Living in a nurturing environment during formative years
Being highly motivated to learn

ASSOCIATED BEHAVIORS:
Adhering to logic and reasoning
Thinking quickly
Having strong problem-solving skills
Impatience
Having good recall
Being able to focus intently
Asking pointed and thoughtful questions
Having an aptitude for languages
Curiosity
Seeking constant stimulation
Having deep knowledge of a hobby or interest
Taking pride in one's achievements
Being goal driven
Enjoying mysteries or puzzles
Being innovative
Having an aptitude for a specific subject (math, geology, programming, etc.)
Being able to absorb or process information well
Having an affinity for technology
Enjoying recreational activities that contain an educational component
Being well-spoken with a strong vocabulary
Believing in facts over faith or intuition
Drawing apt conclusions from an analysis of facts
Being respected by others
Showing respect for other intelligent people
Setting aside personal feelings so a task can be accomplished
Being objective
Avoiding slang and shortcuts
Having original ideas
Asking for precise instructions or directions
Catching onto a punch line before it's revealed (nodding beforehand, etc.)

Thinking efficiently
Having a noticeable flaw due to one's obvious intelligence in other areas
Puzzling out calculations in one's head (determining taxes, etc.)
Reflecting on ideas that are complex or unusual
Becoming lost in thought
Losing track of a conversation when one's mind is active

ASSOCIATED THOUGHTS:
By splitting the bill twelve ways, we'll each owe twenty-two dollars, including tax.
If I buy Professor Bell a coffee, I can pick his brain about quantum mechanics.
There are three grammatical errors in this bulletin. Why don't people proofread?
I can't wait to tell Jeremiah I've come up with a solution for his problem!

ASSOCIATED EMOTIONS: confidence, contempt, frustration, happiness, pride, satisfaction

POSITIVE ASPECTS: Highly intelligent characters have a lot of knowledge and can therefore offer information when it's needed. Most are also good problem solvers, which is always helpful in a pinch. Really smart characters are good at research and are able to get to the root of things. They aren't often led astray by slanted or biased viewpoints. Intelligence is a highly respected trait, so these characters will often be admired and emulated despite their negative characteristics.

NEGATIVE ASPECTS: Because intelligent characters are able to think quickly, they often become frustrated with or contemptuous of those who can't keep up. Smart characters know they're smart; for those who just want to fit in, this can lead to negative behaviors such as hiding their intelligence, underachieving, and settling for mediocrity. Intelligent characters are often exceptional in some way; this can cause underdevelopment in other areas, creating an imbalance.

EXAMPLE FROM FILM: Will Hunting (*Good Will Hunting*) lives life as a simple janitor, but in reality, he's a genius. Not only does he have a photographic memory, but his mind is also capable of solving mathematical queries that few in the world can begin to understand. With a brain like his, the sky should be the limit, but wounds formed by his abusive past keep him from realizing his potential. Will is a great example of how a deliberate combination of positive attributes and flaws can result in a truly memorable character. **Other Examples from Film and Literature:** John Nash (*A Beautiful Mind*), the rats of NIMH (*Mrs. Frisby and the Rats of NIMH*), Ender Wiggins (*Ender's Game*)

TRAITS IN SUPPORTING CHARACTERS THAT MAY CAUSE CONFLICT: childish, disorganized, foolish, idealistic, irresponsible, lazy, prejudiced

CHALLENGING SCENARIOS FOR THE INTELLIGENT CHARACTER:
Being placed in a group where one's teammates take advantage of one's intelligence
Having parents with excessively high standards and expectations
Being treated as a simpleton because of misconceptions or prejudice
Working in an environment where luck and chance are big factors
Lacking other skills (such as street smarts) that are necessary to achieving one's goal

INTROVERTED

DEFINITION: being inclined to explore one's inner mental landscape more so than the outer world

CATEGORIES: identity, interactive

SIMILAR ATTRIBUTES: introspective, reserved

POSSIBLE CAUSES:
Genetics (an oversensitivity to dopamine)
Having a strong sense of self

ASSOCIATED BEHAVIORS:
Only speaking when one has something important to say; avoiding small talk
Needing time alone to recharge after being around others
Preferring to socialize one-on-one rather than in groups
Being highly self-sufficient
Avoiding loud, noisy, or chaotic events (rock concerts, big parties, etc.)
Respecting people's boundaries and privacy
Forgetting to check a phone or email for messages
Looking forward to being alone and having time to do nothing
Being a deep thinker
Speaking slowly and thoughtfully
Becoming more uncomfortable than is normal when one's personal space is invaded
Hiding from people (not answering the phone or door, etc.)
Clock-watching to know when it's finally okay to duck out of an event
Staying in one place at a party rather than working the room
Spending one's lunch hour alone rather than joining co-workers
Becoming uncomfortable when one is singled out
Having strong focus and attention
Letting others make the first move rather than approaching them first
Patience
Thoughtfulness
Being a good observer and listener (when the conversation is meaningful)
Thinking before reacting
Enjoying peace and quiet
Being in touch with one's emotions yet not feeling pressured to express or share them
Avoiding dangerous or risky activities
Making excuses to not attend group events or large family gatherings
Being non-competitive with others
Forming a small number of deep relationships rather than many casual ones
Choosing friends carefully
Being an avid reader
Choosing interests and sports that are solitary (hiking, knitting, bird-watching, etc.)
Being creative in some way

Becoming irritable when one is overstimulated

Practicality

Appreciating structure, organization, and time limits

Choosing clothing that is uniform rather than unique or colorful

Listening to music at a low volume rather than a high volume

ASSOCIATED THOUGHTS:

I'll stay an hour, but no more. That should make Marcy happy.

I can't listen to any more office chatter. Tomorrow, I'm eating lunch in the park.

It's so noisy here. Maybe I can convince Lucas to try a different restaurant.

If I offer to work next weekend, I'll have an excuse to miss the family reunion.

ASSOCIATED EMOTIONS: anxiety, conflicted, curiosity, defensiveness, nostalgia, peacefulness, relief

POSITIVE ASPECTS: Introverted characters are good listeners and make thoughtful friends who connect on a deeper level. They think before speaking and acting, which keeps them from making silly mistakes due to rushing or high emotion. Characters with this attribute obtain their energy from peace and quiet and enjoy contemplation and reflection. They are able to keep their cool and maintain perspective in situations where extroverts become impatient or emotionally volatile.

NEGATIVE ASPECTS: While introverts can navigate social situations, being around too many people for too long will drain their energy. This often leads to them making excuses to leave early or avoid group events and gatherings. Others may not understand their need to be alone and assume that introverts are shy, unfriendly, or snobby. This misunderstanding may also cause well-intentioned friends to try and "cure" introverted characters by forcing them to attend social events, causing unhappiness and friction in the relationship.

EXAMPLE FROM FILM: Adrian Pennino (*Rocky*) is a typical wallflower, hiding in the shadows and preferring to keep to herself. Since her mother once told her that she didn't have much of a body and should develop her brain, Adrian took the advice to heart, dismissing her outward appearance and turning inward. It's not until Rocky draws her out that she fully comes into her own and is empowered to open up, gain confidence, and make herself emotionally available to someone else. **Other Examples from Literature:** Lena Karigalis (*The Sisterhood of the Traveling Pants*), Lisbeth Salander (*The Girl with the Dragon Tattoo*)

TRAITS IN SUPPORTING CHARACTERS THAT MAY CAUSE CONFLICT: adaptable, adventurous, fanatical, flamboyant, flirtatious, melodramatic, nervous, sleazy, timid

CHALLENGING SCENARIOS FOR THE INTROVERTED CHARACTER:

Being interested in someone who likes to play hard to get

Being part of a highly social and extroverted family

Being forced into a leadership role

Living in an environment that offers little privacy or time to oneself

Experiencing fame or acclaim that thrusts one into the public eye

Having to share a room with one's siblings

JUST

DEFINITION: having a strong sense of fairness

CATEGORIES: identity, interactive, moral

SIMILAR ATTRIBUTES: fair-minded

POSSIBLE CAUSES:
Having strong beliefs about right and wrong
Being a victim of unfairness growing up (having parents who favored a sibling over oneself)
Being a victim of prejudice or unjust treatment
Espousing a religion that focuses on right vs. wrong
Growing up in an environment where fairness was emphasized

ASSOCIATED BEHAVIORS:
Rejecting unfair or biased advantages
Sharing
Showing respect for others
Believing that the law should apply to everyone
Rejecting caste systems and ideals that promote inequality
Following the rules
Respecting boundaries that reinforce good relationships and fairness
Being confrontational when an injustice has occurred
Altruism
Showing disdain for cheating or short cuts
Thinking objectively
Thinking before acting
Doing the right thing even if it isn't popular
Behaving ethically
Treating people the same, regardless of age, sex, or race
Demanding justice where it's lacking
Refusing to gossip about others
Being empathetic
Not asking others to do something one would not do oneself
Not taking advantage of loopholes or omissions
Having strong leadership capabilities
Choosing what's right rather than what's easy
Feeling terrible when one makes a mistake
Understanding all the facts before offering judgment
Being an agent for change (joining a board, running for office, etc.)
Standing up for the vulnerable
Judging people by how they treat others
Identifying with victims and working to bring about justice
Not wanting to hear excuses for bad behavior

Expecting to pay for services and be paid for one's service to others
Keeping one's word
Becoming emotional (grief-stricken, enraged, etc.) when an injustice is discovered
Calling people out for perceived dishonesty
Striving to prove someone wrong if doing so will bring inequality to light
Becoming obsessed with righting a wrong

ASSOCIATED THOUGHTS:
I told the kids they couldn't have more cookies, so I guess I shouldn't eat more either.
Ben has worked here the longest. If anyone deserves a raise, it's him.
Poor Jerry. His brothers treat him terribly and his parents don't notice. It isn't right.
I have no problem taking the weekend off. I worked the last three, after all.

ASSOCIATED EMOTIONS: agitation, contempt, determination

POSITIVE ASPECTS: Just characters view the world in black and white and long for wrongs to be righted. Fair-minded, they rail against injustice and are quick to stand up for the oppressed. They aren't afraid to do the right thing, even when their convictions bring them into conflict with powerful or influential people. Because their beliefs are often challenged by those in opposition, just characters are usually well-spoken and are able to intelligently defend their point of view.

NEGATIVE ASPECTS: It's easy for just characters to seem removed emotionally from the events around them. They can easily slip into judgmental thinking and turn vigilante in their desire for justice. If they believe that the rules have ceased to promote fairness for all, they may break them, ironically contributing to the inequality. If just characters accept misinformation for truth, flawed thinking may lead them to believe that they're balancing the scales when in reality they are creating more turmoil or harm.

EXAMPLE FROM LITERATURE: The government of Robin Hood's time is greedy and cruel, requiring poverty-inducing taxes from its constituents in order to line its own pockets. When Robin runs afoul of this system and experiences its coldheartedness firsthand, he gathers a band of like-minded men and sets about robbing corrupt royalty as they pass through Sherwood Forest. He then redistributes the wealth to the country's poor, giving it back, in essence, to its original owners. **Other Examples from Literature and Film:** Paul Edgecombe (*The Green Mile*), Superman, Batman

TRAITS IN SUPPORTING CHARACTERS THAT MAY CAUSE CONFLICT: gentle, greedy, hostile, irrational, obsessive, rebellious, reckless, unintelligent, weak-willed

CHALLENGING SCENARIOS FOR THE JUST CHARACTER:
Discovering that a relative has committed a crime
Catching a mentor or trusted friend in a lie
Learning that a loved one has broken the law, but with pure motivations
Unwittingly breaking the law and having to face the consequences
Facing a situation where what is fair opposes what one believes to be right

KIND

DEFINITION: having a benevolent nature and an attitude of goodwill

CATEGORIES: identity, interactive, moral

SIMILAR ATTRIBUTES: benevolent, good-hearted

POSSIBLE CAUSES:
Growing up in a loving home
Sharing a strong sense of kinship with others
Having an appreciation for and connectedness with the world and its inhabitants
The belief that being kind is the right way to treat others
Experiencing euphoria at serving others and wanting to repeat the experience
Being influenced by kindness in one's past
Being highly empathetic

ASSOCIATED BEHAVIORS:
Going out of one's way to help someone in need
Being generous with one's money, time, and resources
Listening intently to others to show interest in what they're saying
Taking action when someone is in need (cooking a meal, sending a card, etc.)
Using uplifting and positive words
Rallying others to come to someone's aid
Showing kindness even when there is no benefit to oneself
Putting the needs of others above one's own needs
Expressing true happiness over someone else's good news
Mourning with those who have suffered loss
Responding graciously when unpleasantness occurs
Patience
Bestowing gifts
Wholeheartedly supporting someone's dream
Holding doors open for others
Smiling frequently
Having a pleasant expression and approachable bearing
Making oneself available to others at any hour of the day
Befriending the friendless
Phrasing things as nicely as possible
Going out of one's way to keep from offending others
Building people up rather than tearing them down
Being a good listener
Proactively helping
Brightening someone's day for no reason
Excusing the behavior of others
Expressing sadness or anger when seeing others treated unkindly

Using peaceful means to resolve conflict

Being content with what one has

Not sharing one's opinion if it will hurt someone else

Noticing positives and commenting on them (offering compliments, noting nice weather)

ASSOCIATED THOUGHTS:

Looks like raccoons got into Gran's trash again. I'll sweep the mess up right away.

I may as well do Stan's lawn while I'm mowing my own.

I'll ask Molly if she needs someone to collect her mail while she's away.

Everyone's so grumpy at work lately. Brownies should cheer them up.

ASSOCIATED EMOTIONS: eagerness, gratitude, happiness, love, peacefulness

POSITIVE ASPECTS: Kind characters are genuine and forthright, drawing people in with their giving natures and positive attitudes. Observant and often great listeners, they provide uplifting words or gestures when others need them most. Many kindhearted people see it as their duty to help when and where they can, even if it requires a sacrifice of some sort.

NEGATIVE ASPECTS: Kind characters know how to bestow acts of generosity but often grow flustered when kindness is returned to them. They may feel compelled to refuse a gift or repay the kindness, which can leave the giver feeling dissatisfied. They also commonly decline help or won't admit when it's needed, denying others the chance to experience the feel-good rush that comes from giving. Because they are givers and not takers, kind characters can be easily manipulated and abused by those who would take advantage of them.

EXAMPLE FROM LITERATURE: Peeta, the male tribute from District Twelve in *The Hunger Games*, shows kindness and compassion for others, even when everyone is out for themselves. As a child, he gives burnt bread to a starving Katniss and suffers a beating for it. In the Capitol, Peeta does everything in his power to make Katniss appear likable to benefactors, then continues to protect her as she is hunted by other tributes throughout the course of the games. **Other Examples from Literature and Film:** Wendy Beamish (*St. Elmo's Fire*), Fezzik (*The Princess Bride*)

TRAITS IN SUPPORTING CHARACTERS THAT MAY CAUSE CONFLICT: ambitious, dishonest, independent, self-centered, wounded

CHALLENGING SCENARIOS FOR THE KIND CHARACTER:

Living in an environment where kindness is rare and cause for suspicion

Facing a situation where one's motives are questioned

Teaming up with someone who openly takes advantage of one's kindness

Dealing with selfish people

Being kind to someone who only seems to make trouble

Finding out that one's kindness is not wanted or needed

LOYAL

DEFINITION: unswervingly devoted
NOTE: The object of one's loyalty can be a person, institution, or ideal

CATEGORIES: interactive, moral

SIMILAR ATTRIBUTES: committed, dedicated, devoted, faithful, staunch, steadfast, true

POSSIBLE CAUSES:
Experiencing loyalty in the past and valuing it
Experiencing betrayal in the past and wanting no part of it
Love
Coming from a strict military or religious background where loyalty was expected
Believing that the object of one's loyalty is more important than oneself
Fear of retribution
Being highly appreciative and desiring to show one's gratitude

ASSOCIATED BEHAVIORS:
Showing extreme devotion to rock bands, celebrities, sports figures, etc.
Proselytizing; trying to win over more fans
Seeking out others who share one's affection for the object
Talking incessantly about the object
Striving to make oneself more visible or noticeable to the object
Not tolerating any negative words spoken about the object
Taking interest in the object's hobbies and activities
Protecting the object at all costs (ignoring misbehaviors, lying to cover things up, etc.)
Putting the object's needs and desires above one's own
Spending a great deal of time with the object
Believing the best of the object
Taking steps to further the object's dreams or goals
Dismissing or shunning anyone who speaks badly of the object
Supporting the object even when one privately disagrees
Encouraging others to be loyal to the object
Sacrificing or going without if it helps the object
Maintaining friendships over long periods of time and distance
Developing deep relationships, as opposed to superficial ones
Changing one's plans to accommodate the object
Expressing empathy for the object (mourning, celebrating, worrying, etc.)
Feeling great pride at the object's achievements
Seeking out ways to serve or help the object
Craving the object's affirmation or attention
Maneuvering conversations so the object can be discussed
Not being able to be objective about the object
Rearranging one's schedule in order to accommodate the object
Often giving more than one receives

ASSOCIATED THOUGHTS:

How dare he say that about her?

This isn't convenient for me, but if it's what she needs, of course I'll do it.

Ahhhh. I get to see Juliette this weekend!

Dominic sure loves baseball. I should try and get into it, too.

Lucas is such a great man. I would follow him anywhere.

ASSOCIATED EMOTIONS: adoration, anticipation, defensiveness, eagerness, gratitude, happiness

POSITIVE ASPECTS: Loyalty is a valued quality, so characters who embody this trait will gain respect from the reader. This kind of devotion will lead people to do things they normally wouldn't do and provides a means through which to advance your plot. The beauty of loyalty as a trait is that it can be paired with so many other qualities, giving you an endless array of choices for your character.

NEGATIVE ASPECTS: Blind loyalty can lead characters to back someone even when they don't agree with them. When truth is on the line, this can damage their credibility. Their desire to support the object of their loyalty can lead them to sacrifice their own desires, needs, ideals, and beliefs. In extreme cases, these characters can become obsessive and unhealthy and lose the ability to think for themselves.

EXAMPLE FROM LITERATURE: Sam Gamgee (*The Lord of the Rings*) has one driving desire: to serve and protect Frodo—whether that means putting his own life in danger, standing up to Aragorn, spying on Frodo himself, or taking up the ring's burden when his friend is unable to do so. His loyalty is so ingrained that even when it requires sacrifice and pain, Sam remains faithful.

Other Examples from Literature and Film: Forrest Gump (*Forrest Gump*), Chuckie Sullivan (*Good Will Hunting*), Rubeus Hagrid (*Harry Potter* series)

TRAITS IN SUPPORTING CHARACTERS THAT MAY CAUSE CONFLICT: antisocial, disloyal, flaky, greedy, hypocritical, indecisive, selfish

CHALLENGING SCENARIOS FOR THE LOYAL CHARACTER:

Being loyal to someone who does or says something that goes against one's moral beliefs

Being loyal to people or organizations with opposing needs or desires

Experiencing betrayal

Watching the core principles and beliefs of an organization change to something less noble

Witnessing the object of one's loyalty behave with corruption or malice

MATURE

DEFINITION: showing strong mental development or wisdom

CATEGORIES: achievement, identity, interactive

SIMILAR ATTRIBUTES: seasoned

POSSIBLE CAUSES:
Being a firstborn child
Being forced into responsibility at an early age
Being taught the importance of wisdom and being encouraged to think for oneself
Being highly self-aware
Having a strong interest in the outer world and how it relates to oneself
Experiencing a traumatic or life-altering event
Living in an environment of day-to-day survival
Having adults as one's peers

ASSOCIATED BEHAVIORS:
Taking responsibility for one's actions
Seeing the natural consequences of one's choices and acting accordingly
Thinking things through
Seeking out wise counsel
Not being overly affected by peer pressure
Having a serious or somber manner
Planning ahead
Worrying
Taking on responsibility for others
Not engaging in age-appropriate activities
Focusing more on work than on having fun or relaxing
Difficulty properly relating to people one's age
Expressing disdain for those who lack one's level of maturity
Attempting to lead one's peers
Bossiness: *I don't care if you don't want to do it. It's not a choice!*
Taking risks
Taking on responsibilities that should be beyond one's capability or skill level
Boldness
Independent thinking
Confidence
Patience
Treating one's elders as one's equals
Exhibiting self-control
Listening more and talking less
Speaking in an inoffensive way
Being observant

Sizing up a situation or conversation before joining in
Decisiveness
Identifying and solving problems in a sensible fashion
Not engaging in behavior that is deliberately inconsiderate or disrespectful
Setting goals
Being willing to delay gratification

ASSOCIATED THOUGHTS:
They're depending on me. I can't let them down.
A vacation would be nice, but I can't afford it right now.
I wish I could have Monday off, but there's nothing I can do about it.
Girls my age are so silly. All they care about are clothes and boys.

ASSOCIATED EMOTIONS: confidence, determination, happiness, pride, resentment, satisfaction, worry

POSITIVE ASPECTS: Mature characters are responsible, trustworthy, thoughtful, and tend to be more consistent in behavior than their peers. Often viewed as deep thinkers, they can articulate their thoughts at a level beyond their years or offer wisdom that seems greater than average. Mature characters are moralistic and have strong reasoning skills. They understand the cause-effect relationship and base decisions and actions on their perceptions of right and wrong.

NEGATIVE ASPECTS: Mature characters can be critical of others, making judgments based on their own accelerated development and advanced outlook. Others may view these individuals as bossy, being too serious, or lacking a sense of fun or spontaneity. Characters who are forced into maturity before their time may feel resentment and anger for having to be responsible, while siblings may be made to feel less than adequate when adults uphold the mature character as someone to be emulated.

EXAMPLE FROM LITERATURE: Katniss Everdeen (*The Hunger Games*) is forced to grow up prematurely when her father dies and her mother sinks into depression. She becomes the provider for her mother and younger sister and also feels a lesser responsibility for many of the people in District 12. Hardworking, independent, and somber, she has survival as an end goal and bases most of her decisions on achieving that end. **Other Examples from Literature:** Darry Curtis (*The Outsiders*), Dicey Tillerman (*Homecoming*)

TRAITS IN SUPPORTING CHARACTERS THAT MAY CAUSE CONFLICT:
charismatic, excitable, foolish, indecisive, insecure, manipulative, reckless, witty

CHALLENGING SCENARIOS FOR THE MATURE CHARACTER:
Pursuing a goal for which an immature trait (impulsivity, playfulness, etc.) would be beneficial
Being forced to conform to or interact equally with one's less mature peers
Experiencing disastrous consequences when one does cut loose and have some fun
Becoming mature out of necessity and greatly resenting it

MERCIFUL

DEFINITION: displaying leniency from one's position of power; showing compassion

CATEGORIES: identity, interactive, moral

SIMILAR ATTRIBUTES: compassionate, gracious, humane

POSSIBLE CAUSES:
Being naturally empathetic
Being vulnerable and helpless in the past
Having a strong sense of right and wrong
Wanting to alleviate suffering
Having mentors or teachers who displayed compassion
Valuing others
Having a strong sense of justice

ASSOCIATED BEHAVIORS:
Forgiveness
Meting out justice with compassion
Being able to put oneself in another's shoes
Treating others with respect and fairness
Helping those who are in need
Choosing to instruct rather than punish
Encouraging others to grow, learn, and better themselves
Being unbiased
Leading by example
Patience
Not holding grudges
Offering comfort through understanding
Being a strong listener
Reflecting on the big picture instead of being caught up in the little details
Offering grace to those in need
Being hopeful for change in every case
Open-mindedness
Treating others the way one wishes to be treated
Speaking truth from the heart
Lifting people up rather than tearing them down
Recognizing opportunities to make a difference
Not being afraid to show compassion
Looking past people's actions to their motives
Empathizing with others
Being able to set aside ego and personal feelings
Acting out of a desire to help people rather than a desire to enact justice or punish

ASSOCIATED THOUGHTS:

Andy already feels bad about what happened. Why punish him further?
I know what Carla's dealing with at home, so I'm going to overlook her rudeness.
I'm giving Sarah another chance. If I don't give up on her, maybe she won't either.
Liam gave me a hard time when I lost, but I won't do the same to him. Failing hurts.

ASSOCIATED EMOTIONS: conflicted, embarrassment, gratitude, guilt, hopefulness, remorse, satisfaction, somberness, sympathy

POSITIVE ASPECTS: Characters who embody mercy have a level of understanding and compassion that elevates them above petty jealousy, bitterness, or spite. They feel no need to make an example of others or rejoice in their defeat. Instead, they feel a sense of sadness when things end badly and prefer to embrace the belief that that while mistakes happen and poor choices are made, grace and forgiveness are the actions that will bring about peace.

NEGATIVE ASPECTS: Those who value achievement and success may view merciful characters as weak, mistaking their graciousness for reluctance or fear to do what needs to be done. Those who have been wronged may grow angry and resentful when the character shows compassion to a wrongdoer. Accusations of favoritism may arise, damaging the merciful one's standing with allies.

EXAMPLE FROM FILM: In *Les Misérables*, Bishop Myriel of Digne offers shelter to a recently paroled convict, who then steals the bishop's silver and flees. When the authorities find the convict, they bring him back so charges can be pressed. Instead of punishing him, the bishop claims to have given him the silver and then adds a matching set of candlesticks to the gift. His generosity and words of mercy encourage Jean Valjean to make an honest living for himself and rise above his past, which in turn gives him the opportunity to show mercy to many others down the road. **Other Examples from Literature:** Frodo (*The Lord of the Rings*)

TRAITS IN SUPPORTING CHARACTERS THAT MAY CAUSE CONFLICT: controlling, cruel, judgmental, opinionated, paranoid, repressed, suspicious, vindictive

CHALLENGING SCENARIOS FOR THE MERCIFUL CHARACTER:
Showing mercy even when one suspects the person may be beyond redemption
Facing a situation where showing mercy now will mean pain for all later
Offering a merciful judgment that one knows will upset others
Knowing that others are judging one's actions and questioning one's ability to lead

METICULOUS

DEFINITION: taking great care with minute details

CATEGORIES: achievement

SIMILAR ATTRIBUTES: exact, fastidious, precise, scrupulous, thorough

POSSIBLE CAUSES:
Being a perfectionist
Being raised by fastidious parents in a strict environment
Mental disabilities (OCD, anorexia, etc.)
Phobias (fear of germs, failure, etc.)
Having high standards for oneself and others
Fear of letting others down or of retribution for not meeting a certain standard
A need for approval

ASSOCIATED BEHAVIORS:
Paying close attention to the tiniest details of a project
Taking one's responsibilities seriously
Always doing one's best
Taking pride in one's work
Obsessively cleaning and tidying
Micromanaging others
Going over and over the details in one's mind, looking for things that were missed
Expressing aggravation when people don't strive for the same standard
Checking the quality of other people's work
Maintaining a neat appearance
Being inefficient due to the need to get things just right
Planning ahead
Making lists
Becoming easily frustrated by change or unexpected circumstances
Double-checking to make sure a task has been done right
Frequent fine-tuning or fiddling
Being a loner
Having a hard time working with others
Having high expectations
Offering guidance and advice even when it isn't wanted or needed
Thriving in a job or role that others may find monotonous
Finding comfort in repetition and structure
Being good at organizing events and keeping track of projects
Having a good memory
Following up and checking in
Staying up-to-date with the latest news or research in one's field
Perfectionism

Preferring to work within deadlines
Keeping concise and complete notes
Thriving under pressure

ASSOCIATED THOUGHTS:
This is good, but it could be better.
What else needs to be done here?
I should make sure everyone knows what they're supposed to be doing.
Why do I have to work with these people? All they want to do is socialize.

ASSOCIATED EMOTIONS: annoyance, determination, frustration, impatience, satisfaction, smugness

POSITIVE ASPECTS: Meticulous characters strive for a certain standard in everything they do. Their determination to achieve that standard often translates into a strong work ethic. These characters are reliable and their resistance to change makes them fairly predictable. They're strong planners, are detail oriented, and are dedicated to seeing a project through to the end despite setbacks.

NEGATIVE ASPECTS: While their focus on projects is admirable, it can become all-consuming, to the point where meticulous characters neglect other areas of life. The bar that they set for themselves and others can be so high as to become unrealistic. Many of these characters expect others to be as fastidious as they are and express frustration or disdain when the people around them fall short of their expectation. This, combined with their need to micromanage and their mistrust of the quality of other people's work, can make it difficult for them to work as part of a team.

EXAMPLE FROM TV: Felix Ungar (*The Odd Couple*) is a notorious neat freak and compulsive cleaner. He shows meticulousness in other areas, too, such as cooking, personal hygiene, and punctuality. He's fastidious in his care for his children and ex-wife, loving them so intensely that his attention becomes somewhat smothering. After his divorce, it's this need to care for others that drives him to move in with his slovenly friend, Oscar. **Other Examples from Film and TV:** Colonel Jessup (*A Few Good Men*), Adrian Monk (*Monk*)

TRAITS IN SUPPORTING CHARACTERS THAT MAY CAUSE CONFLICT: disorganized, easygoing, extravagant, flaky, forgetful, impulsive, quirky

CHALLENGING SCENARIOS FOR THE METICULOUS CHARACTER:
Living with a messy roommate
Working on a project with a fly-by-the-seat-of-the-pants co-worker
Having to stay in an unclean hotel room
Being unable to bathe or change one's clothes for an extended period of time
Having to answer to a careless project manager

NATURE-FOCUSED

DEFINITION: preferring natural resources over artificial ones; being strongly attuned to nature

CATEGORIES: identity, interactive

SIMILAR ATTRIBUTES: environmentally conscious

POSSIBLE CAUSES:
Growing up on a farm or living off the land
Having parents or role models who were conservationists or environmentalists
Having strong religious or spiritual beliefs that focus on nature
Feeling whole when surrounded by nature
Growing up within a nature-focused culture (Native American, etc.)

ASSOCIATED BEHAVIORS:
Keeping a garden
Recycling
Placing a high value on life
Buying natural products (shopping at farmer's markets, etc.)
Hunting and fishing only to provide for one's family
Living in nature or close to it
Farming or ranching; living off the land
Respecting all living creatures
Being fascinated with the life cycle
Feeling spiritually tied to the earth and its creatures
Eating natural foods
Being knowledgeable about nutrition
Avoiding wastefulness (reusing, repurposing, only taking what one needs, etc.)
Canning and preserving one's food
Engaging in hiking, climbing, canoeing, and other outdoor pursuits
Avoiding pollutants and chemicals
Farming with heirloom seeds rather than altered ones
Embracing natural remedies rather than manmade ones
Meditating
Having a hearty appetite
Being highly curious
Being highly energetic
Choosing environmentally friendly modes of transportation
Feeling energized when one is outdoors
Deeply appreciating the beauty of nature
Wanting to be alone to experience the outdoors in a meaningful way
Being hyper aware of what goes into one's body
Picking up after oneself to decrease one's carbon footprint
Bird-watching

Focusing on sensory details (smells, sounds, textures, etc.) when outdoors
Happiness and satisfaction
Seeing wisdom in nature
Appreciating the different seasons and their uniqueness
Feeling protective of nature
Gaining joy from growing a garden

ASSOCIATED THOUGHTS:
I'm going to brew some lavender and fresh oregano tea for Natalie's headache.
Is it five o'clock yet? I've been waiting all week to see the mountains!
I am so glad we moved out of the city. Out here, I can hear myself think.
Tomatoes from the garden are so much better than ones from the grocery store.
I can't believe Nathan refuses to recycle. Has he seen the size of our landfill?
Look at that sunrise. It's lighting up the whole valley.

ASSOCIATED EMOTIONS: amazement, anticipation, curiosity, excitement, gratitude, happiness, peacefulness

POSITIVE ASPECTS: Nature-focused characters are strongly attuned to nature. When outdoors, they are energized, experience mental clarity, and gain a higher sense of purpose. Their respect for the land and the creatures in it leads them to make choices that impact the natural world as little as possible. They are usually active and health-conscious and are very aware of what they put into their bodies, many times choosing a vegetarian or vegan lifestyle due to their beliefs.

NEGATIVE ASPECTS: Characters with a high respect for nature may experience a disconnect with friends and family who are more urban-focused—especially if these loved ones see the character as being flaky for their views. Some nature-centric characters choose to oppose industry and government to protect the environment, thereby crossing the line from being advocates to becoming vigilantes. Others take natural living to an extreme, refusing to bathe, shave, or use deodorant. The resulting poor hygiene puts a strain on relationships.

EXAMPLE FROM FILM: In *Avatar*, the Na'vi race is highly attuned to Pandora. They are part of a biological neural network connecting all life forms and so have the greatest respect and care for their world. They live with, interact with, and take wisdom from the nature around them. When threatened by human industry seeking out a rare mineral, the Na'vi fight to save not only their lives but nature itself. **Other Examples from Literature and Film:** the Ents (*Lord of the Rings*), Pocahontas (*Pocahontas*), Perrin Aybara (*The Wheel of Time*)

TRAITS IN SUPPORTING CHARACTERS THAT MAY CAUSE CONFLICT: destructive, industrious, insensitive, pretentious, superficial, workaholic

CHALLENGING SCENARIOS FOR THE NATURE-FOCUSED CHARACTER:
Losing one's property to a natural disaster or financial ruin
Having family or neighbors who are destructive and wasteful in ways that impact nature
Being forced to move to the city where one cannot easily access nature
Conditions that prevent one from enjoying the outdoors (severe allergies, etc.)
Facing a situation where saving a natural resource is bad for the public at large

NURTURING

DEFINITION: having the desire and ability to nourish and further the development of others

CATEGORIES: identity, interactive

SIMILAR ATTRIBUTES: caring, maternal

POSSIBLE CAUSES:
Being responsible in the past as a nurturer of others (children, the infirm, etc.)
Being the recipient of great love and kindness
Wanting to be needed
Having an abundance of love
Gratitude; caring for someone out of appreciation for the kindness they have shown
Having an innate tendency to nurture others

ASSOCIATED BEHAVIORS:
Using kind, encouraging words
Speaking in a calm tone
Patience
Taking advantage of gentle teaching opportunities
Anticipating a need and meeting it
Actively listening, to show that one cares
Providing for someone's basic needs
Being protective
Jumping to someone's defense
Encouraging someone to pursue a talent or area of giftedness
Showing support
Keeping mementos in the hopes of passing them down to loved ones some day
Treating strangers like family; being a good host
Worrying over setbacks or poor choices that may happen to those in one's care
Being present for important events
Showing affection
Having the best interests of others at heart
Spotting an emotional need and seeking to fill it
Doing what's best for someone, even if it's not what the other person wants
Providing wisdom when decisions must be made
Self-sacrifice; going without so someone else can have what is lacking
Constantly assessing what a person needs
Steering someone away from dangerous situations
Expressing joy over the little things one's charge might do
Seeing the best in people and believing that anyone can change when shown love
Feeling pride and satisfaction when the one being nurtured shows growth
Doing whatever it takes to make sure someone feels safe and loved
Loyalty

Difficulty being objective when it comes to one's charges
Showing mercy; giving second chances
Forgiving easily
Being a natural caregiver, even with other people's charges
Showing confidence in others to encourage them to be more confident in themselves

ASSOCIATED THOUGHTS:
She's a good girl. She just needs a little guidance.
I've been there; maybe she can benefit from my experience.
It's supposed to get cold later. I'll make sure Richard takes his coat.
I've been shown so much love; how can I not pass that on?

ASSOCIATED EMOTIONS: adoration, amusement, happiness, hopefulness, love, nostalgia, satisfaction, worry

POSITIVE ASPECTS: Nurturing characters are generally loving, kind, and compassionate. They have a long-term focus, wanting their charges to not just survive but to thrive and succeed in life. When they see someone in need or in pain, they can't help but reach out, even if it means sacrificing their own time, money, and resources. While others may be quick to judge or stereotype, nurturers are open-minded, seeing only the need and their own ability to meet it.

NEGATIVE ASPECTS: Sometimes, the nurturing instinct can be so strong that characters with this trait are unable or unwilling to see the truth about their charges. Their unselfishness can make them the target of manipulators who would take advantage of their kindness. Nurturers are often so focused on caring for others that they don't take care of themselves. Their desire to serve can also make it difficult for them to seek help for themselves when it's needed.

EXAMPLE FROM LITERATURE: Aibilene Clark (*The Help*) has spent her career raising other women's children. She feeds them, potty trains them, puts them to bed, and cares for them when they're sick. Her capacity for love and empathy is deep, as is shown with her final charge, Mae Mobley. Aibilene does her best to make up for the indifference and neglect of Mae's mother by creating a positive mantra for the child to live by, repeating it until the love-starved little girl can say it for herself. **Other Examples from Film:** Carol Connelly (*As Good as it Gets*), Molly Weasley (*Harry Potter* series)

TRAITS IN SUPPORTING CHARACTERS THAT MAY CAUSE CONFLICT: grumpy, independent, mischievous, needy, selfish, ungrateful

CHALLENGING SCENARIOS FOR THE NURTURING CHARACTER:
Encountering someone who needs love but is unable to accept or return it
Experiencing criticism and judgment for taking someone in
Finding someone in need of help whose needs are beyond one's ability to meet
Recognizing a need for nurturing in someone who is likely damaged beyond repair
Wanting to care for someone whom the authorities say should not be nurtured

OBEDIENT

DEFINITION: submissive to authority

CATEGORIES: achievement, interactive, moral

SIMILAR ATTRIBUTES: biddable, compliant, dutiful, submissive, tame, well-behaved

POSSIBLE CAUSES:
A subservient nature
Having been taught the importance of respecting authority
Seeing the value of authority in society
Fear of retribution
A desire to please
The belief that following the rules leads to reward
A strong sense of fairness
Seeing others be punished for asking questions or displaying independent thinking
Coming from a strict religious or military background that required obedience
Gratitude and loyalty; obeying someone because of what they did in the past

ASSOCIATED BEHAVIORS:
Following orders immediately
Reading the manual before assembling an item
Seeking out the advice of people in authority
Trusting that those in authority have one's best interests at heart
Obeying an order or rule despite private misgivings
Proactively getting approval before acting
Understanding that everyone has a part to play for society to function
Being a team player
Carrying out tasks efficiently
Believing that something greater is at work and feeling appreciation for it
Respecting order (keeping a neat room, being organized, etc.)
Obeying rules even if it's inconvenient (driving the speed limit, making curfew, etc.)
Encouraging others to follow the rules
Feeling relief to not be the one making the tough decisions
Tattling when others fail to comply
Expressing resentment when those who don't follow the rules escape punishment
Wanting to know the expectations of those in charge
Feeling safe and protected
Being a law-abiding citizen
Following through on responsibilities at work or school; being dependable
Joining organizations or clubs that have a clear hierarchy
Loyalty
Respectfully speaking to and about those in authority
Becoming uncomfortable when others question those in authority

Experiencing confusion when those in authority do something unusual or untrustworthy
Consistency
Seeking the approval of authority figures rather than the approval of one's peers
Being easily cowed
Feeling trepidation when breaking even an innocent rule
Feeling shame when one breaks a rule and is discovered
Choosing to hang out with other obedient people

ASSOCIATED THOUGHTS:
It's a dumb rule but I'll follow it anyway.
Mom said to do it, so I will.
If everyone just followed the rules, we wouldn't have all these problems in the world.
I did such a good job on this project. Good thing Emily gave me an outline to follow.

ASSOCIATED EMOTIONS: happiness, indifference, resignation, satisfaction

POSITIVE ASPECTS: Obedient characters are loyal and trusting. Reliable, responsible, and fairly predictable, they will usually do what they're told without causing trouble. Their belief in upholding the social order makes them upstanding citizens.

NEGATIVE ASPECTS: Whatever the reason for their compliance, obedient characters may have trouble thinking for themselves; this can be used for ill as well as for good. If asked, the devoutly obedient character might find himself doing things he never would have done, simply because someone he trusts asked him to. Having pledged his allegiance to those in charge, he might have trouble believing or even suspecting that those same people might be untrustworthy.

EXAMPLE FROM LITERATURE: Despite his impoverished and difficult life, Charlie Bucket (*Charlie and the Chocolate Factory*) is a hopeful and obedient boy. His tour of the Wonka factory involves some strange rules that the other ticket winners unhesitatingly flout. But Charlie does what he's told and is eventually rewarded for his good behavior. **Other Examples from Literature and Film:** Darth Vader (*Star Wars Episode IV: A New Hope*), Grace Van Pelt (*The Mentalist*), Ofelia (*Pan's Labyrinth*)

TRAITS IN SUPPORTING CHARACTERS THAT MAY CAUSE CONFLICT: adventurous, controlling, free-spirited, intelligent, mischievous, observant, rebellious, resentful, rowdy, selfish, silly, suspicious

CHALLENGING SCENARIOS FOR THE OBEDIENT CHARACTER:
Being asked to do something that goes against one's moral code
Learning that the motives or character of those in authority may be questionable
Conflicting interests, such as wanting to obey a teacher while wanting to conform to one's peers
Being paired with an independent thinker who enjoys flouting authority
Having two authority figures who make conflicting requests

OBJECTIVE

DEFINITION: having a viewpoint devoid of bias or personal preference; clear-thinking

CATEGORIES: achievement, interactive

SIMILAR ATTRIBUTES: impartial, unbiased

POSSIBLE CAUSES:
A deep sense of fairness and equality
Having a strong appreciation for knowledge in its various forms
Respecting the value of experience
Being a truth-seeker

ASSOCIATED BEHAVIORS:
Having control over one's emotions
Wanting to see a problem from all sides before making a decision
Being able to identify bias, then stripping it from the equation
Seeking to get to the root of the matter
Strong listening skills
Asking questions to ensure that one fully understands
Not jumping to conclusions or making assumptions
Diplomacy; speaking in a way that has a calming effect on others
Being highly logical and rational
Setting emotions aside to allow for a neutral viewpoint
Waiting to make decisions until one can do so without emotion
Setting friendships aside as needed or establishing boundaries with people to avoid bias
Strong observation skills
Avoiding situations that may lead to personal bias (not having clients who are family, etc.)
Always seeking to find the best solution
Sometimes preferring to observe rather than participate
Taking time to investigate and gather information
Being able to see and acknowledge one's own weaknesses
Not acting reactively; maintaining a calm demeanor
Reporting the facts from all sides
Being able to put oneself in the "shoes" of everyone involved
Suppressing opinions and only reporting facts
Being able to articulate the perspective of opposing sides to show understanding
Refusing to invest in labels or stereotypes
Viewing a situation with fresh eyes despite what might have led up to it
Not omitting certain facts
Describing what happened exactly as it occurred, without interpreting it
Not relying on intuition or gut feelings
Being non-judgmental
Dealing with small disappointments with minimal upset or stress

Mental clarity
Avoiding people who try to curry favor
Being honest and valuing honesty in others
Not openly displaying emotions in day-to-day life as much as others might
Having a reserved nature
Being difficult to irritate or anger
Taking time to contemplate
Not being ruled by fear or volatile emotions

ASSOCIATED THOUGHTS:
I think I'll give everyone a few minutes to calm down before asking questions.
Because Allan's sister is involved, someone else should mediate.
I don't know a lot about eco farming, so I should find out more before weighing in.
I'll draw a diagram of the accident to help the police officers understand what happened.
I'm sure we can find a logical solution if we concentrate on facts instead of opinions.

ASSOCIATED EMOTIONS: determination, satisfaction, sympathy, uncertainty

POSITIVE ASPECTS: Objective characters do well in an advisor's role because they are able to separate emotions from a volatile situation and proceed logically. When problems arise, they will go to great lengths to come up with a solution that is fair, based on the facts presented. Others respect that these characters take the time to investigate and gather information when making decisions. By being impartial, even when family or friends are involved, the advice of an objective character usually holds a lot of weight.

NEGATIVE ASPECTS: Objectivity can be a blessing and a curse, especially when family is involved; while an impartial character has no trouble separating his feelings from the situation, loved ones may take things personally or feel betrayed by the objective character. Some situations are not ideal for characters with this trait, especially when they must act quickly. Because of their need to know all the facts, opportunities may be lost by the time a decision is reached.

EXAMPLE FROM TV: Amy Farrah Fowler from *The Big Bang Theory* is naturally objective, which suits her as a neurobiologist. She has a strong handle on her emotions and asks questions to get to the root of the issue at hand. Highly observant, she acts based on information and proven truth rather than being swayed by intuition or emotion. Even when personally involved, she is often able to pull herself out of emotional entanglements and take a logical approach to problem solving. **Other Examples from Film:** Lucius Fox (*Batman series*), Buster (*Misery*)

TRAITS IN SUPPORTING CHARACTERS THAT MAY CAUSE CONFLICT: forgetful, inhibited, manipulative, melodramatic, private, scatterbrained, uncommunicative, untruthful, withdrawn

CHALLENGING SCENARIOS FOR THE OBJECTIVE CHARACTER:
Being victimized and trying to recount the events impartially
Knowing instinctively that something is wrong but being unable to prove it
Being involved in a situation where the facts and laws result in justice not being served
Trying to protect others while keeping one's emotions in check

OBSERVANT

DEFINITION: paying careful attention

*NOTE: Being observant refers to one's ability to notice things, while being **perceptive** involves the ability to understand and draw conclusions from things that have been observed. While closely related, the two traits aren't synonymous, nor do they always go hand in hand.*

CATEGORIES: achievement, interactive

SIMILAR ATTRIBUTES: attentive, keen, sharp-eyed

POSSIBLE CAUSES:
Nosiness
Shyness; involving oneself through observation rather than participation
Curiosity
Being highly intelligent and easily bored
A fear of missing something important
Paranoia

ASSOCIATED BEHAVIORS:
Noticing when someone's mood has changed
Commenting when someone has gotten a haircut or is wearing new clothes
Listening in on multiple conversations
People watching
Picking up on someone's nervous tics or habits and asking them what's wrong
Accurately reporting what fellow students or co-workers have done all day long
Noticing details that others might miss
Seeing potential dangers before they occur
Instantly sizing up a room upon entering
Having excellent recall
Having heightened senses
Being cautious
Accurately repeating things that were said at a much earlier time
Taking safety and precaution seriously
Watching for certain details (whether someone is armed or looks suspicious, etc.)
Taking note of internal warnings and acting on them
Having a focused mind that isn't prone to wandering or daydreaming
Observing instead of busying oneself with other things (reading, surfing the net, etc.)
Avoiding distractions while driving
Noting the exit points upon entering a building
Not being in a rush
Looking people in the eye
Being mindful of body language and expressions
Reading into someone's tone, vocal hesitations, or word choices
Being nosy

Watching for cause and effect so one always knows what's happening
Taking care to place items where they will not be tipped over or tripped on
Knowing where one's personal items are at all times
Noticing pattern breaks (a co-worker's frequent absences, keys going missing, etc.)
Sitting with one's back to the wall so one can watch the whole room
Being aware of one's body and noticing changes that might indicate illness

ASSOCIATED THOUGHTS:
Denise got a new haircut. It looks great!
Why is that guy hanging out by my car?
Oh, Aunt Kathy rearranged the furniture.
Maggie looks sad today. I'll have to try and figure out why.

ASSOCIATED EMOTIONS: amusement, curiosity, unease, wariness, worry

POSITIVE ASPECTS: Observant characters notice things that others miss. By and large, people want to be seen, so the attentiveness of these characters makes others feel good. They also provide the author with a dependable observer through whom to relay important details. Those who sit back and watch are less likely to be caught in a dangerous situation or surprised by someone intent on doing harm. Due to their clear-sightedness, they can often identify threats before they happen and save themselves and others from danger.

NEGATIVE ASPECTS: Observant characters are often nosy—eavesdropping and spying in situations where their attention isn't wanted. It's also easy to draw the wrong conclusions when one is only getting part of the story, so these characters run the risk of passing erroneous judgment with the information they gather. Although many observers are subtle in their technique, some are not, and their attention can make others uncomfortable.

EXAMPLE FROM LITERATURE: Sherlock Holmes seems to have prescience about everyone and everything, but on closer examination, it becomes clear that the detective is simply a brilliant observer. Not only does he take meticulous note of his surroundings, he's able to put those details together to make discoveries that evade others. **Other Examples from Literature and Film:** Amelia Donaghy (*The Bone Collector*), The Terminator (The *Terminator* franchise)

TRAITS IN SUPPORTING CHARACTERS THAT MAY CAUSE CONFLICT: excitable, inattentive, lazy, paranoid, scatterbrained, sentimental, withdrawn

CHALLENGING SCENARIOS FOR THE OBSERVANT CHARACTER:
Being hindered by something that inhibits one's observation skills (medication, lack of sleep, etc.)
Living in a chaotic, ever-changing environment that makes it difficult to track changes
Being a keen observer who lacks perceptiveness (making no conclusions from one's observations)
Having a terrible memory; being unable to recall one's observations

OPTIMISTIC

DEFINITION: anticipating the best possible outcome; seeing events in the most positive light

CATEGORIES: identity, interactive, moral

SIMILAR ATTRIBUTES: hopeful, positive, sanguine

POSSIBLE CAUSES:
Believing that people are basically good and well-intentioned
Living by the philosophy that if one believes things to be a certain way, they will be
Naïveté
Growing up sheltered
Not wanting to acknowledge or give credence to anything unpleasant
Focusing on a greater purpose that makes life's troubles inconsequential by comparison

ASSOCIATED BEHAVIORS:
Assuming the best of people
Waking up happy and going to bed contented
Smiling and laughing
Having an uplifted countenance
Approaching new tasks with eagerness
Seeing a difficult job as an opportunity to learn and grow
Thinking positively
Trusting others
Finding something good to say even in a bad situation
Generosity
Refusing to acknowledge any possibility but a good outcome
Using kind, encouraging words
Being a peacekeeper
Looking forward to the future and whatever may come
Moving in a purposeful way; not moving in a lazy or reluctant fashion
Not letting oneself be bored or idle; finding meaningful ways to occupy one's time
Not complaining
Finding joy in the little things
Choosing not to dwell on the negative
Recognizing a difficult situation as being temporary
Having a sense of humor
Accepting things the way they are
Not sweating the small stuff
Believing that life is precious
Avoiding people who are chronically negative
Choosing not to worry
Enjoying books and movies that have happy outcomes
Viewing mistakes as learning opportunities

Playing matchmaker; wanting others to share in one's happiness
Being supportive; encouraging people in the pursuit of their goals and dreams
Believing that occasional setbacks make success more meaningful and satisfying

ASSOCIATED THOUGHTS:
This is only temporary. Things will be better soon.
I'm so excited to get to babysit the grandkids again!
Too bad Angel didn't pass the bar exam. I'm sure she'll ace it the second time around.
What wonderful opportunities are coming my way today?
It really is a beautiful world.

ASSOCIATED EMOTIONS: amusement, anticipation, eagerness, elation, excitement, gratitude, hopefulness, peacefulness

POSITIVE ASPECTS: Optimistic characters are usually pleasant to be around. As peacemakers, they strive to maintain happiness and good relations, so they're not often the cause of conflict. Their positive vibes rub off on others and beget more positivity. They often have other admirable qualities as well, such as respectfulness, compassion, and diplomacy. In a world full of naysayers, optimists bring light and hope and can be a safe haven for your hero in a difficult time.

NEGATIVE ASPECTS: Some optimists choose positivity over reality, refusing to accept things the way they really are. This can render them unrealistic and impractical. In serious situations, their die-hard hope in the face of impossible circumstances can become frustrating. At times like these, they lose credibility for being naïve and illogical. These extreme optimists are completely unprepared to cope with the worst-case scenario; in such a situation, they may become a burden to those around them instead of a support.

EXAMPLE FROM LITERATURE: Pollyanna Whittier's (*Pollyanna*) life as an orphan living with a crusty aunt is far from easy. But through her employment of The Glad Game, which she once played with her father, she's able to find the good in every situation. This is what it means to be an optimist, and Pollyanna's example is so authentic that her name has come to be synonymous with the trait. **Other Examples from Film and Literature:** Giselle (*Enchanted*), Anne Shirley (*Anne of Green Gables*)

TRAITS IN SUPPORTING CHARACTERS THAT MAY CAUSE CONFLICT: honest, confrontational, pessimistic, pushy, resentful, rowdy, superstitious

CHALLENGING SCENARIOS FOR THE OPTIMISTIC CHARACTER:
Facing a situation where there is no good outcome
Being paired with an overly intelligent or suspicious character who questions everything
Suffering a disillusionment that causes doubt (betrayal by a loved one, etc.)
Being faced with a scenario where one must temper optimism with practicality
Being surrounded by cynics who believe it to be their duty to open the optimist's eyes to reality
Developing a mental illness that steals one's optimism (depression, for example)

ORGANIZED

DEFINITION: being orderly and systematic in one's handling of matters

CATEGORIES: achievement

SIMILAR ATTRIBUTES: methodical, orderly, structured, systematic

POSSIBLE CAUSES:
A need for efficiency
Compensating for being easily overwhelmed
Being highly responsible; not wanting to let others down
Growing up in a very structured environment
OCD and similar disorders

ASSOCIATED BEHAVIORS:
Scheduling events well in advance
Being detail oriented
Keeping a neat workspace
Implementing systems for managing projects or a schedule
Frequently checking emails and messages
Having good time management
Communicating clearly and frequently with associates
Over-communicating with others
Anticipating setbacks and difficulties
Micromanaging others
Delegating tasks to others
Keeping lists
Knowing one's capabilities and scheduling accordingly
Arriving at one's destination early or on time
Keeping to a schedule
Keeping a calendar of events (birthdays, anniversaries, holidays, etc.)
Having a place for everything and keeping everything in its place
Expressing frustration when others don't put things where they belong
Expecting others to also be neat and orderly
Obsessively picking up and putting things away
Having multiple to-do lists
Investing in organizational tools (software, bins, containers, organizers, etc.)
Becoming agitated when things are in disarray
Organizing even obscure things and places (archived files, basements, attics, etc.)
Noticing and feeling satisfied when things are running smoothly
Thinking sequentially, in terms of steps
Gaining satisfaction from checking items off of a list
Making efforts to organize events and gatherings that lack order
Being very aware of the time

Frequently checking email and one's phone for messages
Impatience when one's questions aren't answered in a timely manner

ASSOCIATED THOUGHTS:
I need a system for this.
Why can't people put things where they belong?
Ahhh, the container store. My favorite place on the planet.
Time to knock some things off my to-do list!

ASSOCIATED EMOTIONS: irritation, peacefulness, pride, satisfaction

POSITIVE ASPECTS: Organized characters are adept at making things run smoothly. They're meticulous with details and plan well in advance, so nothing becomes overlooked. They like to be dependable, and feel personally responsible when they let others down. Hardworking, nose-to-the-grindstone individuals, they take care of the important daily details that allow other characters to be less organized. As such, they make great support characters.

NEGATIVE ASPECTS: Organized characters can be so focused on the minutia that their priorities become skewed and they lose sight of the big picture. Their need for order makes it difficult for them to focus in an unruly environment, limiting their efficiency under less-than-ideal circumstances. They can also struggle when working with others who lack their passion for order or who like to arrange things differently.

EXAMPLE FROM FILM: Squadron Leader Roger Bartlett (*The Great Escape*) is the organizational genius behind an ambitious escape plan that took place at Stalag Luft III, one of the highest security prisoner-of-war camps ever built. Bartlett, also known as The Big X, is determined to initiate the biggest POW breakout in history. With the help of his team, he furtively arranges for the digging of numerous tunnels, the redistribution of vast amounts of dirt, and the manufacture of civilian clothing and false documents for two hundred men, all under the noses of the guards. **Other Examples from Film:** Itzhak Stern (*Schindler's List*), Jack Byrnes (*Meet the Parents*), Jackie Harrison (*Stepmom*)

TRAITS IN SUPPORTING CHARACTERS THAT MAY CAUSE CONFLICT: artistic, disorganized, easygoing, flaky, foolish, forgetful, impulsive

CHALLENGING SCENARIOS FOR THE ORGANIZED CHARACTER:
Being grouped with disorganized people
Having to organize without the tools and implements one is used to utilizing
Living in an environment where personal space isn't valued
Becoming so overcommitted that organization of everything is virtually impossible

PASSIONATE

DEFINITION: being capable of or expressing deep feeling

CATEGORIES: achievement, identity, interactive

SIMILAR ATTRIBUTES: earnest, fervent, zealous

POSSIBLE CAUSES:
Feeling things on a deep emotional level
Being in touch with and embracing one's emotions
Being deeply loyal to a person, relationship, ideal, or organization
Mood, personality, and impulse control disorders
Drug or alcohol use
Believing on a moral level that one should stand up for what's right
Having an ingrained sense of responsibility

ASSOCIATED BEHAVIORS:
Expressing a wide range of emotions
Becoming easily angered, saddened, or excited
Using big, excited gestures
Speaking in a loud voice
Talking incessantly about the object of one's passion
Working around obstacles to get what one wants
Obsessing about the focus of one's passion
Standing up for what one believes
Expressing what one feels without thought for propriety or appropriateness
Being confrontational
Involving oneself in social or political activism
Arguing in favor of one's cause
Aligning with like-minded people
Intense loyalty
Dedicating oneself wholeheartedly to a person or cause
Showing support through the giving of money and time
Remaining loyal despite opposition
Needing to connect with people on a higher level
Taking risks
Stubbornness and determination
Working steadily toward a goal until it has been achieved
Expressing oneself in a creative or meaningful way
Being goal oriented
Courage
Emotional sensitivity
Having a single-minded focus
Researching one's passion to be as informed as possible

Thinking independently; not being swayed by others
Exhibiting passion in many areas of one's life
Being self-motivated

ASSOCIATED THOUGHTS:
What can I do to make this right?
I can't believe this is happening. Why can't people see how wrong this is?
With enough support, we can do something about this.
I hate John so much for what he did to Elise. He's going to be sorry.

ASSOCIATED EMOTIONS: adoration, determination, eagerness, excitement, frustration, hatred, impatience, love, sadness

POSITIVE ASPECTS: Passionate characters have a highly developed sense of right and wrong. They make decisions based on these values, to which they have unswerving loyalty. Once they've settled on a course of action in regards to their passions, they will stick to it despite obstacles. When opposition does occur, these characters face it head-on and work to figure out ways to continue moving forward. Passion is contagious, energizing others and encouraging them to get on the bandwagon and become excited, too.

NEGATIVE ASPECTS: Passionate characters are very focused, to the point where they may ignore or minimize other people and ideas. Their dedication to their ideal may make it difficult for them to tolerate others with opposing opinions. Passionate characters feel things deeply, which can make them oversensitive and easily offended. They tend to be demonstrative with their feelings, making others uncomfortable. Because they do act on their emotions, their mood swings may be wide and unpredictable.

EXAMPLE FROM LITERATURE: A fitting example of passion in action is the hero of the world's most famous love story. At his first glimpse of Juliet, Romeo falls head over heels for her. The odds, and most of their family and society, are against the two of them making a match, but because Romeo believes they belong together, he risks everything to gain Juliet's love. **Other Examples from Film:** Remy (*Ratatouille*), John Keating (*Dead Poets Society*), JoAnne Galloway (*A Few Good Men*)

TRAITS IN SUPPORTING CHARACTERS THAT MAY CAUSE CONFLICT: cowardly, easygoing, inhibited, nervous, thrifty, withdrawn

CHALLENGING SCENARIOS FOR THE PASSIONATE CHARACTER:
Living in a culture where it is considered unseemly or unacceptable to express one's feelings
Being faced with having to choose one passion over another
Being passionate about someone or something that puts one at odds with family or society
Becoming passionate about someone who cannot return the feeling
Wanting to avenge oneself but being morally conflicted about doing so

PATIENT

DEFINITION: exhibiting self-control and composure under trial or strain

CATEGORIES: achievement, interactive, moral

SIMILAR ATTRIBUTES: long-suffering

POSSIBLE CAUSES:
Believing that everything will work out in the end
Having an unhurried, easygoing demeanor
Maturity; understanding that it does no good to push or complain
Being other-focused rather than self-focused
Overcoming adversity (poverty, abuse, etc.) and recognizing that success takes time

ASSOCIATED BEHAVIORS:
Having a laid-back approach to life
Driving carefully; taking one's time
Speaking in an unrushed, leisurely fashion
Not worrying when things take longer than expected
Calmly waiting (not fidgeting or pacing)
Being able to amuse or entertain oneself while waiting
Not complaining when things are taking too long
Thinking positively instead of focusing on the negative
Enjoying the moment rather than always thinking about what's coming next
Sleeping well
Not worrying over factors that are out of one's control
Having the proper perspective about one's problems
Treating others kindly
Friendliness
Letting others go first (in the checkout line, at a four-way stop, etc.)
Perseverance
Bouncing back quickly from setbacks
Focusing on the end goal with calmness, believing that things will work out eventually
Biding one's time
Not being surprised by the unexpected
Being able to relax without feeling guilty
Taking time to make decisions
Giving one's full attention to others
Being content with what one has
Managing one's time wisely
Passivity; letting things happen instead of doing one's due diligence
Having faith in people and their ability to eventually do what is right
Having a relaxed mind that doesn't constantly jump from one thought to the next
Walking at an unhurried pace

Being able to delay gratification; not needing things right this minute
Expressing disappointment at delays but quickly returning to a positive viewpoint
Allowing one's mind to wander to pass the time
Turning to a different task while waiting on something else

ASSOCIATED THOUGHTS:
This is taking longer than I thought; at least I'm getting a lot done in the meantime.
I'm in no rush.
Worrying won't make the time go faster.
There must be a reason that Al didn't get that job.
I'm so blessed; how can I complain about one area of my life that's not perfect?

ASSOCIATED EMOTIONS: confidence, disappointment, gratitude, happiness, hopefulness, peacefulness, resignation, satisfaction

POSITIVE ASPECTS: Patient characters are in no rush. They realize that circumstances may take longer than anticipated, and since worrying and complaining do no good, they choose to take delays in stride. The act of practicing patience requires a plethora of other positive traits: perseverance, contentment, optimism, and peacefulness. In a world where most people suffer from overcommitment, poor time management, and a chronic need to rush, the patient person is a source of well-needed calm.

NEGATIVE ASPECTS: Sometimes, the patient character can be so easygoing that he has no sense of urgency. This presents a problem when deadlines and teamwork are involved. Patience can easily lead to carelessness and laziness, with the character becoming passive and avoiding any effort to make things happen.

EXAMPLE FROM FILM: Andy Dufresne (*The Shawshank Redemption*) is a lesson in patience. It took 19 years for him to chisel his way to freedom with only a succession of tiny rock picks. In the meantime, he took on meaningful projects, like expanding the prison library, mentoring and educating a fellow convict, and filing taxes for the prison employees. Despite many disappointments and a generally horrific existence, he stayed focused and, for the most part, remained positive and confident that he would succeed in the end. **Other Examples from Literature and Film:** Edmond Dantès (*The Count of Monte Cristo*), Keyser Söze (*The Usual Suspects*)

TRAITS IN SUPPORTING CHARACTERS THAT MAY CAUSE CONFLICT: cocky, compulsive, efficient, extravagant, impatient, impulsive, paranoid, pushy, spoiled, whiny

CHALLENGING SCENARIOS FOR THE PATIENT CHARACTER:
Being paired with people who purposely create circumstances that work against one's goal
Having to work within an unforgiving deadline
Working in a hurried environment where speed of completion is valued over quality
Having to placate those with volatile personalities to keep the peace
Working for someone who is demanding or who has unrealistic expectations

PATRIOTIC

DEFINITION: having love for or loyalty to one's country

CATEGORIES: identity, interactive

SIMILAR ATTRIBUTES: nationalistic

POSSIBLE CAUSES:
Growing up in a military family
Being a history buff; having studied one's country
Fighting in the armed services
Seeing the injustice in other countries and being grateful for where one lives
Escaping a dictatorial country to live in a place of freedom and equality
Being taught the importance of nationalism by one's family
Being forced to leave a country that one sorely misses
Being brainwashed by one's government

ASSOCIATED BEHAVIORS:
Serving in the armed forces
Wearing the country's colors
Attending parades and rallies
Displaying the nation's flag
Being loyal to one's country, people, and founding principles
Making sacrifices for one's country
Celebrating the country's holidays
Singing the national anthem
Becoming emotional during political events
Placing others before oneself
Becoming defensive or angry when someone speaks out against one's country
Deriding the practices of other nations
Teaching one's children to love their country
Buying goods that were produced in one's country
Visiting a nation's historical places
Honoring those who have died in service to the nation
Learning about the nation's beginnings; studying its roots
Believing that the needs of the many outweigh the needs of a few
Voting
Following the laws
Giving money to support a candidate or party
Holding grudges against past global enemies
Engaging in debates about the nation's politics and current events
Seeking to silence dissidents
Cheering for national sports teams
Taking an interest in national pastimes

Resisting change to the way things have always been in one's country
Supporting the protection of the homeland
Worrying about where the country is headed
Expressing grief over how much one's country has changed
Respecting those in service to the nation (military personnel, police officers, etc.)

ASSOCIATED THOUGHTS:
There's no better place to live on Earth.
I love this country.
If they don't like it here, they should go live somewhere else!
Look at that guy, sitting down during the national anthem. What a jerk!

ASSOCIATED EMOTIONS: adoration, contempt, defensiveness, excitement, love, nostalgia, smugness

POSITIVE ASPECTS: Patriotic characters are fiercely loyal, not only to their country, but also to the organizations and people in their lives. Patriotism is a passion of theirs; they educate themselves on the country's beginnings, study historical figures, learn about the governmental process, and stay informed about current events. Armed with their passion and knowledge, these characters can and will fiercely contend with anyone expressing criticism of the homeland.

NEGATIVE ASPECTS: As in the case of any fiercely loyal person, these characters can become blind to their country's faults. Their intolerance and belligerence in the face of opposition can damage their credibility and reputation. Extreme patriotism can lead a person to harm those who criticize one's country. Their blind loyalty can make them susceptible to propaganda and may lead them to extreme measures in an attempt to blot out real or perceived enemies.

EXAMPLE FROM FILM: As the movie *Braveheart* aptly shows, living conditions were far from ideal in thirteenth-century Scotland. The serfs were kept under the thumb of their nobles, living in poverty and unable to speak out against injustice. The nobles abused this system through deliberate attempts to subdue the serfs with customs like *ius primae noctis*, which gave them the right to sleep with any bride on her wedding night. William Wallace's fierce love for Scotland and what it could be for everyone—not just for the nobles—spurred him to lead an uprising. The result was a bloody and drawn-out war that resulted in Wallace's own death but also in the birth of a newly emancipated Scotland. **Other Examples from Film and Comics:** Benjamin Martin (*The Patriot*), G.I. Joe, Captain America

TRAITS IN SUPPORTING CHARACTERS THAT MAY CAUSE CONFLICT: cynical, disloyal, flaky, frivolous, greedy, nervous, rebellious, ungrateful, vindictive, whiny

CHALLENGING SCENARIOS FOR THE PATRIOTIC CHARACTER:
Seeing changes to one's country that challenge one's loyalty
Having to live or work in a country that is ambivalent toward one's nation of citizenship
Discovering that loved ones are secretly and violently opposing one's country
Learning that one's government is controlling, corrupt, or manipulative
Being on the receiving end of injustice that the government refuses to do anything about

PENSIVE

DEFINITION: musingly thoughtful

CATEGORIES: achievement, identity

SIMILAR ATTRIBUTES: contemplative, meditative, reflective, speculative, thoughtful

POSSIBLE CAUSES:
Having a mind that tends to wander or daydream
Shyness
Having a brooding or worrying nature
Being interested in issues that require deep thought (politics, religion, social issues, etc.)
Being the kind of person who needs introspection in order to process things
Desiring to escape reality
Being an intellectual

ASSOCIATED BEHAVIORS:
Staring off into space
Sitting still for long periods of time
Wandering off by oneself
Going for isolated walks or drives
Thinking carefully before speaking
Speaking in circles; talking through one's thoughts
Multitasking
Showing an appreciation for knowledge and education
Asking a lot of questions
Bringing up heady issues in order to discuss them with others
Valuing other points of view
Expressing annoyance when one's thought process is interrupted
Becoming frustrated when one is unable to satisfactorily work through a problem
Being easily bored by topics that aren't of interest
Going long periods of time without engaging with others
Seeking out knowledgeable people with whom to discuss issues
Being easily distracted
Reading and researching to further one's perspective
Forgetting appointments and meetings
Taking a job that doesn't require much thought so one can live inside one's head
Losing the thread of conversations
Taking notes or keeping journals to keep track of one's thoughts and ideas
Being reclusive
Getting overdue notices because one has forgotten to pay bills
Letting one's untended yard go to seed
Becoming stiff from sitting in one position for too long while processing ideas
Forgetting run-of-the-mill activities (eating, showering, feeding the dog, etc.)

Difficulty interacting with people if one has been introspective for too long
Insulting others by not being able to pay attention when they're speaking
Losing track of time
Blurting out thoughts that have nothing to do with the current conversation
Playing devil's advocate in an effort to see things from another viewpoint
Adding to a conversation only to discover that the topic has changed

ASSOCIATED THOUGHTS:
That's an idea that deserves serious thought.
Good grief. Is it midnight already?
What an interesting question. There are innumerable possibilities...
If the politicians thought more and fought less, they'd come up with better solutions.

ASSOCIATED EMOTIONS: amazement, amusement, annoyance, curiosity, eagerness

POSITIVE ASPECTS: Pensive characters are big thinkers. They like to ponder issues, and as such, are likely to come up with innovative answers. They're not daunted by seeming impossibilities but tackle them directly in their own quiet and thoughtful way. So much time spent in deep thought leads to a naturally philosophical attitude, well-formed opinions, and an interest in an array of topics.

NEGATIVE ASPECTS: Pensive characters tend to live in their own heads; as such, they can turn reclusive and lose touch with what's happening around them. Their inward focus may make it difficult for them to pay attention and listen; this can lead people to perceive them as arrogant, dismissive, or rude. Some pensive characters may actively avoid others, being more comfortable with their thoughts than with people, which could add to their difficulty forming meaningful relationships.

EXAMPLE FROM LITERATURE: Ponyboy Curtis (*The Outsiders*) isn't like most of the other greasers in his neighborhood. Unlike his thuggish counterparts, he likes to read and watch movies and think about things. Instead of hanging out with the gang and rumbling, he prefers to be alone, thinking about the characters he's seen on screen or the stories he's read. He's perfectly happy living in his head, which makes him kind of an oddball among his peers. **Other Examples from Literature and TV:** Jonas (*The Giver*), Wilson (*Home Improvement*)

TRAITS IN SUPPORTING CHARACTERS THAT MAY CAUSE CONFLICT:
courteous, frivolous, ignorant, playful, scatterbrained, suspicious

CHALLENGING SCENARIOS FOR THE PENSIVE CHARACTER:
Developing a mental handicap that affects one's ability to focus or analyze
Facing distractions that make it difficult to spend prolonged time in thought
Teaming up with someone whose traits (chattiness, etc.) make focused thought difficult
Working in an environment where logical thought isn't common or valued
Being forced to speak on an issue before one has had time to consider it

PERCEPTIVE

DEFINITION: showing intuitive observation and insight

CATEGORIES: achievement, interactive

SIMILAR ATTRIBUTES: discerning, insightful, intuitive

POSSIBLE CAUSES:
Having a "sixth sense" that enables one to notice or feel things that others don't
Being deeply attuned to others
Being highly empathetic
Being attuned to patterns and other data that enables one to make accurate predictions

ASSOCIATED BEHAVIORS:
Accurately assessing what one is observing
Making predictions based on incoming data
Noticing things that other people don't see
Making connections that other people miss
Noticing changes and patterns
Reading people well
Predicting outcomes that seem outrageous but turn out to be correct
Sensing that something is wrong
Having highly attuned senses
Being compelled to share the truth even when it makes things difficult
Sharing knowledge in the hopes that others will be warned or danger will be averted
Expressing confidence, pride, or haughtiness at one's ability to see what others don't
Quickly assessing problems
Finding solutions
Seeing solutions as black-and-white
Being able to read people's moods
Gleaning a great deal of information from a short period of time spent observing
Caring about others
Being observant
Knowing oneself accurately and intimately
Gaining insight into others by observing actions or seeing their possessions
Expressing frustration when one's perceptions are brushed off or dismissed
Evaluating people on a number of levels (analyzing behaviors, emotions, motives, etc.)
Being logical yet having good intuition
Being good with people by reading them while interacting
Picking up on secrets without necessarily meaning to
Being able to put oneself in another's shoes
Seeing how things fit together in a bigger picture
Preparing for the future, even when others are not

Proactively making changes to protect oneself and loved ones
Quickly and accurately sizing up a situation

ASSOCIATED THOUGHTS:
Am I the only one seeing this?
I have to tell them what's coming.
I don't like the way he phrased this on his résumé. Sounds fishy to me.
Alice has a thing for Barry? And look, he's clueless about it. This should be interesting.

ASSOCIATED EMOTIONS: confidence, eagerness, elation, frustration, impatience, reluctance, smugness

POSITIVE ASPECTS: Perceptive characters are beneficial in that they have great observation skills, are able to accurately assess what they're observing, and can put the pieces together to see what's coming down the road. Astute problem solvers, they quickly and easily arrive at solutions. This helpful capability isn't all that common, and as such, is an enviable trait.

NEGATIVE ASPECTS: Perceptive characters can become impatient when others miss what they so obviously see. This impatience can lead to scorn and disdain, which doesn't endear them to others. Sometimes, although their predictions or solutions might make sense, people reject both the information and the messenger out of fear or anxiety. Despite their insight, these characters have blind spots like anyone else and may not be able to easily see and solve their own problems. Others may also become embarrassed or mistrustful when they realize the perceptive character has caught on to their secrets.

EXAMPLE FROM LITERATURE: As the runt of the litter, Fiver (*Watership Down*) is small and timid. But he also bears a gift for reading his environment and knowing when something is wrong. Due to his perception, Fiver predicts that disaster is coming to his warren and he's able to save a handful of his mates. His intuition also warns him of danger along their journey to find a new home. Although his fellow travelers at first are put off by his strangeness, they eventually come to respect his insight and rely on his input. **Other Examples from Film, Literature, and TV:** Dick Hallorann (*The Shining*), the precogs (*Minority Report*), Sherlock Holmes, Patrick Jane (*The Mentalist*)

TRAITS IN SUPPORTING CHARACTERS THAT MAY CAUSE CONFLICT:
empathetic, flaky, hostile, inattentive, indecisive, paranoid, private, shy, superstitious

CHALLENGING SCENARIOS FOR THE PERCEPTIVE CHARACTER:
Being able to put pieces together but lacking the attentiveness to notice the pieces to begin with
Perceiving negative outcomes that no one will accept or want to hear
Living in a deceptive environment where it's difficult to accurately assess what's going on
Interacting with other perceptive people and wondering if they can be trusted

PERSISTENT

DEFINITION: stubbornly continuing on despite opposition, difficulty, or danger

CATEGORIES: achievement, moral

SIMILAR ATTRIBUTES: determined, perseverant, relentless, tenacious

POSSIBLE CAUSES:
Desperation
The belief that one's goal is the only thing worth pursuing
Ambition
Having something to prove, either to others or to oneself
Stubbornness
Having an obsessive personality
Learning through experience that persistence pays off in the end

ASSOCIATED BEHAVIORS:
Having an end goal in mind
Learning from past mistakes
Breaking a big goal into bite-sized pieces that are less intimidating
Trying new methods when an old one fails to produce results
Assessing problems and coming up with possible solutions
Asking others for their support and encouragement
Making oneself accountable by sharing one's goal and timeline with others
Patience
Accepting that the journey will be long and that setbacks will occur
Making plans
Training and gathering knowledge that will help
Replacing bad habits with good ones
Avoiding people or events that could impede one's progress
Making immediate sacrifices to attain the long-term goal
Growing excited when small milestones are reached
Investing large amounts of money, time, and energy to achieve one's goal
Becoming obsessed
Spending a lot of time thinking about how to get results
Being temporarily crushed by setbacks but eventually bouncing back
Enlisting the help of others
Becoming so involved in achieving one's goal that relationships falter
Not taking care of one's health (having poor nutrition, stress headaches, etc.)
Never giving up, even in the face of seeming impossibility
Basing decisions on how they can help achieve the goal
Giving up former hobbies and interests; cutting back on other commitments
Performing poorly at work or school due to a lack of focus
Strongly believing in oneself
Offering encouragement to others who are working toward their own goals

Poor hygiene (not shaving, not showering, wearing the same clothes, etc.)
Becoming defensive when others express doubt, particularly as time passes
Experiencing mood swings about a project, from confidence to confusion to despair
Shutting out anything that counts as a distraction
Never giving up hope

ASSOCIATED THOUGHTS:
It'll happen eventually. I just have to keep working.
On to Plan B.
They're laughing now, but just wait. Someday, I'll be the one laughing.
There has to be a way to make this happen. If I keep thinking about it, it'll come to me.
This is too important to give up on. Deep down I know Mary understands that.

ASSOCIATED EMOTIONS: anticipation, confidence, denial, determination, disappointment, eagerness, excitement, frustration, worry

POSITIVE ASPECTS: Persistent characters have great will power. They will do whatever it takes to achieve their goals. While discomfort, inconvenience, or pain would sidetrack some, persistent characters aren't distracted from their purpose. They have incredible focus, always keeping the prize in their sights. In this way, persistence as a character trait is admired and envied; we can't help but be impressed by someone who overcomes circumstances that would defeat the average person.

NEGATIVE ASPECTS: Because of their single-mindedness, persistent characters often become consumed by their desires. Everything else is peripheral: career, relationships, even morals. They can become so focused on the goal that everything else falls to the wayside. These characters are often stubborn to a fault, refusing to give up even when the pursuit of their goal becomes destructive. They don't heed the advice of others and may sacrifice common sense for obsession. Although the goal might be noble, their way of pursuing it can become less than honorable.

EXAMPLE FROM TV: Wile E. Coyote has only ever had one goal: to catch Road Runner. His entire existence centers around how to catch, entrap, disable, and outsmart his opponent. When one idea doesn't work, he moves on to another, and another, completely disregarding his own injuries and inconveniences along the way. It doesn't matter that Road Runner is faster; through his own intelligence, resources, and his invaluable connections at the Acme Company, Wile E. Coyote is confident that if he just sticks with it, one day he will achieve his goal. **Other Examples from Film:** Maya (*Zero Dark Thirty*), Richard Kimble (*The Fugitive*), Rudy Ruettiger (*Rudy*)

TRAITS IN SUPPORTING CHARACTERS THAT MAY CAUSE CONFLICT:
easygoing, empathetic, flaky, irrational, lazy, pushy, needy, timid, unselfish, weak-willed

CHALLENGING SCENARIOS FOR THE PERSISTENT CHARACTER:
Facing an illness or decline that threatens one's physical or mental ability to carry on
Having access to limited or insufficient resources
Working within an impossible deadline
Having to choose between one's goal and the other important things in one's life
Being pitted against an equally persistent villain

PERSUASIVE

DEFINITION: able to influence others by argument, entreaty, counsel, or protest

CATEGORIES: achievement, identity, interactive

SIMILAR ATTRIBUTES: compelling, convincing, eloquent, influential

POSSIBLE CAUSES:
Being naturally charismatic
Being passionate about a certain subject
Confidence
Desiring to enlighten or educate others
Having a knack for reading people and influencing them
Knowing how to speak, write, or otherwise present matter in the most appealing way

ASSOCIATED BEHAVIORS:
Being charming
Inspiring trust in others
Instinctively knowing the right thing to say
Paying close attention to others
Being a charismatic speaker
Listening actively
Reading others well
Carefully tailoring one's approach to the audience
Being confident
Having a reputation as someone who knows one's stuff
Being passionate
Showing vulnerability in order to gain empathy
Persuading others through results; doing what one says one will accomplish
Knowing what concerns people care about and having answers ready
Showing extreme dedication to one's cause
Being diplomatic
Staying focused on the end result
Relating to people; finding common ground
Sticking to one's beliefs
Saying the same thing in many different ways
Using different methods to persuade different kinds of people
Speaking and acting with authority and confidence
Voicing one's opinion as fact
Remaining calm in the face of opposition
Expressing empathy for others
Using humor to disarm others and put them at ease
Anticipating objections and providing solutions that address concerns
Viewing opposition as an opportunity to win someone over
Being a skilled debater

Speaking of one's weaknesses so they look like strengths
Studying the art of persuasion
Thanking people for listening and weighing in
Showing respect for others
Treating each concern seriously
Promising to follow up or look into areas one was unable to address
Encouraging people to have an open mind
Proving credibility through one's knowledge rather than citing one's résumé

ASSOCIATED THOUGHTS:
How can I win this guy over?
What's the best approach with this group?
I'm right about this; now I just have to convince everyone else.
If I emphasize the positives, they'll forget about the negatives.

ASSOCIATED EMOTIONS: confidence, determination, excitement

POSITIVE ASPECTS: Persuasive characters are passionate. It is often their zeal and devotion, as much as their eloquence, that convinces people to jump on the bandwagon. Characters with the gift of persuasion are charismatic and charming, drawing others to themselves. Their successes often occur due to their ability to read people and relate to different people groups. This trait can enable these characters to elicit change and make a difference in their communities and the world at large.

NEGATIVE ASPECTS: Persuasive characters are charming. Due to the ease with which they read people, it can be easy for them to slip into a manipulative role, telling others what they want to hear and faking concern in an effort to win them over. Because of their passion and the belief that their cause is just, they can also become frustrated or angry when people don't come around to their way of thinking.

EXAMPLE FROM HISTORY: Many words have been used to describe Winston Churchill, but most would agree that *persuasive* is entirely appropriate. He was a student of rhetoric and public speaking. His speeches were motivational, inspirational, and carefully crafted weapons of persuasion, winning over a lukewarm parliament and encouraging his people to never give up hope, even in the midst of defeat. To this day, he is believed to be a master of persuasive speaking, and his techniques are studied by those wishing to motivate and inspire others. **Other Examples from Literature and Film:** Sherlock Holmes, Harvey Dent (*The Dark Knight*), Dr. King Schultz (*Django Unchained*)

TRAITS IN SUPPORTING CHARACTERS THAT MAY CAUSE CONFLICT:
confrontational, disrespectful, inflexible, pretentious, sleazy, stubborn, timid

CHALLENGING SCENARIOS FOR THE PERSUASIVE CHARACTER:
Having to persuade others about something that goes against one's moral code
Having to choose whether or not to use immoral means to persuade one's audience
Facing an actively hostile audience
Being reluctantly persuasive; being good at influencing but not wanting a leadership role

PHILOSOPHICAL

DEFINITION: inclined to the reflective study of beliefs, attitudes, values, and concepts connected with our existence; deep-thinking

CATEGORIES: identity, interactive

SIMILAR ATTRIBUTES: deep

POSSIBLE CAUSES:
Being highly intelligent
Having a love of wisdom
A desire for enlightenment and truth
Growing up in a family of scholars

ASSOCIATED BEHAVIORS:
Being widely read and educated
Seeking out higher education
Educating oneself on history and other cultures
Researching the evolution of mythology or religious beliefs
Sitting in deep thought
Having an inward focus; losing track of conversations or peripheral events
Asking deep questions
Watching documentaries
Seeking answers to the big questions about God, morality, life and death, etc.
Learning a second language that aids in one's studies (Latin, etc.)
Having a large collection of books pertaining to subjects of philosophical interest
Seeking out experts in an effort to learn more
Being inwardly reflective and interested in knowing why we exist
Being preoccupied with one's thoughts rather than what's happening externally
Overanalyzing
Being highly logical
Isolation
Questioning everything
Taking a long time to express an opinion; being unable to give a quick answer
Feeling like life is passing too quickly or things are happening too fast
Ascribing to highbrow humor
Difficulty making superficial small talk
Being impatient with illogical people
Continually making comparisons and evaluating
Thinking obsessively
Writing and journaling
Reading books in a foreign language
Socializing with other intellectuals
Categorizing

Having a diverse and complex vocabulary

Showing frustration at interruptions when one is lost in thought

Having a difficult time relating to less cerebral people

ASSOCIATED THOUGHTS:
What is real? What is truth?
What is my purpose?
How can I evolve?
Is free will an illusion?
What happens after death, and is there a God?

ASSOCIATED EMOTIONS: amazement, conflicted, curiosity, depression, desire, frustration. hopefulness, loneliness, overwhelmed, uncertainty

POSITIVE ASPECTS: Philosophical characters read deeply into situations and aren't afraid of intellectual heavy lifting in order to find answers. Well-educated and thoughtful, when they share what is on their minds, they can provoke curiosity in others and encourage them to probe harder to resolve their own unanswered questions. These characters have a lot of wisdom, and while they won't dole it out quickly, they are excellent sounding boards for friends or family who need to work through problems.

NEGATIVE ASPECTS: These characters can sometimes find themselves alienated from life itself, for as they quest for answers, they can forget to experience the world firsthand. Friends and family may view them as silent, brooding types, or feel that they overthink everything. Philosophical characters can have hobbies that most people don't get or aren't interested in, and they tend to have fewer relationships because of the importance solitude plays in puzzling out life's big mysteries. They can also be long-winded when imparting ideas, causing impatience or boredom.

EXAMPLE FROM TV: Wilson, the wise yet odd neighbor to Tim Taylor in *Home Improvement*, is a storehouse of interesting facts and deep insight. Whenever Tim is wrestling with relationships or difficult decisions, Wilson peeks over the fence to provide his own philosophical views on the subject. Often he asks a thought-provoking question or two to steer Tim toward an epiphany. **Other Examples from Literature and TV:** Hamlet (*The Tragedy of Hamlet, Prince of Denmark*), Spock (*Star Trek series*)

TRAITS IN SUPPORTING CHARACTERS THAT MAY CAUSE CONFLICT: decisive, frivolous, inflexible, irrational, melodramatic, obedient, paranoid, playful, scatterbrained, worrywart

CHALLENGING SCENARIOS FOR THE PHILOSOPHICAL CHARACTER:
Experiencing a debilitating mental disability that makes logic and linear thinking difficult
Losing one's life work of journals, study materials, or computer files to a disaster
Educating oneself on a belief only for new information to surface and prove it inaccurate
Discovering something about oneself that leads to feelings of shame or disappointment

PLAYFUL

DEFINITION: fond of playing and fun

CATEGORIES: identity, interactive

SIMILAR ATTRIBUTES: coltish, frisky, frolicsome, fun-loving

POSSIBLE CAUSES:
Immaturity
Wanting to have fun
Having a short attention span
A desire to avoid work, responsibility, conflict, etc.
Laziness

ASSOCIATED BEHAVIORS:
Laughing often
Using fidgety, impatient movements
Teasing, cajoling, or making jokes
Turning work into a game
Mimicking others in an effort to lighten a serious mood
Encouraging others to sneak out of work to have fun
Enjoying adventure
Procrastinating on work projects
Not giving one's all when it comes to work
Turning a mundane object into a toy
Speaking in a loud voice
Focusing on the here and now
Not thinking too far ahead
Being open-minded
Acting spontaneously
Collecting action figures or toys and displaying them around one's workspace
Being silly
Dressing colorfully or with flair
Running instead of walking
Standing instead of sitting
Doing anything to get a laugh
Speaking without thinking
Avoiding serious activities (meetings, boring family dinners, etc.)
Acting impulsively
Creating ditties and rhymes that get everyone laughing
Watching and playing sports
Choosing fun with friends over quiet time at home
Competitiveness for fun
Being easily bored

Making do with what one has
Laziness
Irresponsibility
Being passionate about one's hobbies or interests
Focusing on the positive and ignoring unpleasantness

ASSOCIATED THOUGHTS:
Is it Friday yet?
This is BORING!
I wish I didn't have to work today.
How can we make this fun?
Bob is such a killjoy. Dude, lighten up!

ASSOCIATED EMOTIONS: amusement, curiosity, denial, excitement, happiness, hopefulness, impatience

POSITIVE ASPECTS: Playful characters are always looking for a good time. They make even the most boring and uninspiring projects fun, so people like to have them around. Unlike mischievous people, playful characters have good intentions and don't willfully hurt others or make them uncomfortable. Childlike in attitude, these characters love to laugh, naturally lifting the spirits of those around them.

NEGATIVE ASPECTS: Because of their pursuit of fun, playful characters often have a hard time buckling down and getting to work. They can be lazy, prone to procrastination, and may not give 100% to a project. These tendencies may not endear them to peers with a high sense of responsibility, and they can rub serious people the wrong way. Their lighthearted attitudes may convince others that playful characters can't be trusted with important projects, which may keep them from progressing in their careers.

EXAMPLE FROM FILM: Josh Baskin (*Big*) may look like an adult but he's actually just a kid. As such, he gravitates towards toys and games. He enjoys being with friends and having fun. His approach to work involves curiosity and play. Oblivious to verbal sparring and office politics in the workplace, his easygoing attitude is refreshing and even inspiring to his co-workers. **Other Examples from Film:** Fraulein Maria (*The Sound of Music*), Tommy Callahan III (*Tommy Boy*)

TRAITS IN SUPPORTING CHARACTERS THAT MAY CAUSE CONFLICT: cruel, demanding, efficient, fussy, inflexible, pensive, perfectionist, resentful, studious

CHALLENGING SCENARIOS FOR THE PLAYFUL CHARACTER:
Being surrounded by somber, work-minded people
Unwittingly contributing (through one's playfulness) to a serious problem for a loved one
Being forced to find the balance between playfulness and responsibility
Having to take charge of an important project that has far-reaching effects

PRIVATE

DEFINITION: having strong personal boundaries; preferring to keep one's affairs to oneself

CATEGORIES: interactive

POSSIBLE CAUSES:
Growing up with little privacy (having many siblings, sharing rooms with others, etc.)
Fear of rejection and being hurt
Being the victim of trauma or abuse in the past
Growing up isolated in some way (living in a monastery, etc.)
Having one's secrets exposed, resulting in embarrassment or humiliation
Trusting the wrong person and being hurt by them
Being exposed to the dark side of people and how information is misused
Living with people who tended to over share
A fear of being judged

ASSOCIATED BEHAVIORS:
Not offering up personal information
Closing curtains and locking doors in an effort to be truly alone
Deflecting questions; steering conversations to less personal topics
Keeping one's fears and desires to oneself
Avoiding gatherings and community events
Being a quiet neighbor
Reluctance letting others into one's home
Deleting one's browser history
Following the rules to keep from calling attention to oneself or standing out as odd
Keeping things light and fun in social settings
Isolation
Pretending that one's interests are boring so others won't ask questions
Being a strong listener
Being aware of one's surroundings and other people
Growing embarrassed quickly
Feeling uncomfortable when others ask too many questions or are intrusive
Avoiding situations where one might be vulnerable
Difficulty asking others for help
Independence
Enjoying solitude
Growing anxious at the thought of letting others get close
Keeping one's vacation plans to oneself
Making excuses to avoid social functions
Introversion
Using careful wording; thinking before speaking
Feeling self-conscious
Avoiding gossips and rumormongers

Respecting the privacy of others
Not asking many questions for fear of being rude or invasive
Feeling interrogated when others ask personal questions
Staying in a hotel rather than in another person's home

ASSOCIATED THOUGHTS:
Why does Jeff have to ask so many questions? Can't he take the hint?
I'll tell Janet I'll meet her at the restaurant, otherwise she'll offer to pick me up at home.
If one more person asks me how I'm doing, I'm going to scream.
Nancy just scrolled through Misha's cell phone pictures without asking. So rude!

ASSOCIATED EMOTIONS: agitation, anxiety, defensiveness, determination, dread, frustration, insecurity, nervousness, paranoia, regret, unease

POSITIVE ASPECTS: Private characters have a lot of respect for others and their personal boundaries. They avoid asking too many questions and have a strong intuitive sense for when another person is uncomfortable. They are able to work independently and stay on task and can easily separate work from personal life.

NEGATIVE ASPECTS: Private characters have a difficult time sharing personal information and often resent being asked to do so. It can be difficult for them to open up enough to establish a meaningful connection. Often misperceived as shy, these characters are very choosy about who they welcome into their lives; by the time they get around to trusting someone, it's possible that the desired friend may have moved on to someone who will more easily let them in.

EXAMPLE FROM FILM: In the movie *Highlander*, Russell Nash has good reason to keep to himself. Immortal, he has been furtively roaming the world for four hundred and fifty years, moving from place to place and adopting new identities along the way. Unable to reveal his true self and unwilling to watch another mortal wife grow old and die, he distances himself from others and is careful to reveal only what is necessary at the moment. **Other Examples from Literature:** Boo Radley (*To Kill a Mockingbird*), Laura Burney (*Sleeping with the Enemy*)

TRAITS IN SUPPORTING CHARACTERS THAT MAY CAUSE CONFLICT: cooperative, extroverted, friendly, generous, gossipy, nosy, paranoid, pushy

CHALLENGING SCENARIOS FOR THE PRIVATE CHARACTER:
Having to ask for help, especially from strangers
Developing feelings for someone who requires pursuit in order to gain their attention
Being revealed as vulnerable to co-workers (having an angry ex-boyfriend make a scene, etc.)
Being forced into a situation where one must share with others (therapy, rehab, etc.)

PROACTIVE

DEFINITION: thinking and acting ahead; anticipating difficulties or challenges that bring about change

CATEGORIES: achievement

SIMILAR ATTRIBUTES: farsighted, forward-thinking, strategic

POSSIBLE CAUSES:
Being goal-oriented and achievement-focused
Needing to be prepared
Extreme worry or paranoia
Constantly being threatened or in danger
Having a strong sense of responsibility
Growing up in a well-prepared family (survivalists, doomsday preppers, etc.)

ASSOCIATED BEHAVIORS:
Thinking before acting
Being a rational thinker
Having strong foresight; being able to see how things are connected
Broad-mindedness; seeing the forest for the trees
Researching and investigating a problem from all angles
Testing a solution before putting it into play
Watchfulness; looking for early indicators of change so one can counteract
Crowd sourcing for information; relying on teamwork
Creating checklists and questions that need answering
Thinking of the worst-case scenario so one can test out ideas
Prioritizing well
Taking one's time rather than rushing
Being able to think on one's feet
Having a strong gut instinct
Asking people how one can do something better for next time
Being hardworking and thorough
Taking advantage of opportunities
Learning skills and furthering one's education to become more proficient
Doing things without being asked
Seeing what needs to be done and doing it
Paying close attention to the emotions of others
Speaking up when needed
Never hesitating to take the lead
Spotting possible danger
Thinking about the weather, travel plans, and what might go wrong before setting out
Reliability
Not relying on luck

Identifying what is holding one back and taking action to overcome it
Remaining calm in intense situations
Taking responsibility for one's actions
Confidence
Rising to the challenge
Organization
Asking for help when one needs it
Always having a purpose

ASSOCIATED THOUGHTS:
Ben is behind on reports. While he's finishing last month's numbers, I'll start entering this month's.
If I mow the lawn without Dad having to ask, maybe he'll let me borrow the car this weekend.
That tire looks low. I should get it checked before we leave on our trip.
Lorna looks ready to murder Alana. I don't know what happened, but I better head this off.
Tim's such a great speaker. I'll ask him for tips before my next presentation.

ASSOCIATED EMOTIONS: anticipation, confidence, curiosity, determination, satisfaction, wariness

POSITIVE ASPECTS: Proactive characters think ahead, prepare, and then act, thereby taking control of their own destinies. Because they are always seeking to improve, they are often successful in business and make good leaders. These characters look at the big picture rather than only focusing on their immediate interests. By taking care of problems before they occur, they can spend more time doing activities that they find important instead of dealing with the fallout that comes from a lack of preparation and foresight.

NEGATIVE ASPECTS: Because proactive characters can usually predict trouble and avoid it in advance, they have a hard time with people who can't do the same. They tend to unfairly judge family, friends, or co-workers who procrastinate, viewing them as lazy for not being as on top of things as they themselves are. Their high standards and expectations don't differentiate between work and home; this can strain relationships, especially when priorities differ.

EXAMPLE FROM LITERATURE: When Randy Bragg (*Alas Babylon*) covertly learns of an impending nuclear war, he takes survival into his own hands and springs into action. Although unable to stop the coming apocalypse, he acts quickly and decisively. By securing cash, stocking up on groceries and water, and hoarding gasoline, he is able to save his family. **Other Examples from Film:** Colonel Sam Daniels (*Outbreak*), David Levinson (*Independence Day*)

TRAITS IN SUPPORTING CHARACTERS THAT MAY CAUSE CONFLICT: calm, controlling, easygoing, empathetic, flaky, frivolous, irrational, lazy, melodramatic, pretentious, pushy, rowdy

CHALLENGING SCENARIOS FOR THE PROACTIVE CHARACTER:
Working for a boss whose knee-jerk responses lead to shifting goals and priorities
Having insufficient resources that make it difficult to proactively get ahead
Wanting to act but not having enough knowledge or information to do so
Facing opposition in the form of an administration that doesn't trust one's instincts

PROFESSIONAL

DEFINITION: exhibiting specialized knowledge and applying it with courtesy and good judgment

CATEGORIES: achievement, interactive, moral

POSSIBLE CAUSES:
Having successful, career-focused parents
Feeling validated through one's business savvy, knowledge, or educated skill set
Being career- and success-focused
Having a desire to lead; being ambitious
Maturity
Confidence and high self-esteem
Being highly ethical

ASSOCIATED BEHAVIORS:
Being a strong team player
Having the education and knowledge required to be proficient at one's job
Being experienced in a specific field of work
Reliability, trustworthiness and honesty
Having strong people skills
Objectivity
Working well under pressure
Having a strong command of language and being able to articulate oneself well
Adaptability
Keeping one's promises
Maintaining control over one's emotions
Being proactive
Thinking before acting
Treating others with respect and courtesy
Being a strong listener
Assessing the politics of a situation and acting accordingly
Using good hygiene
Being well dressed
Acting appropriately for the situation
Having a high stress tolerance
Being able to prioritize
Politeness
Following through on commitments; providing what people need
Removing one's personal feelings from the equation
Using good judgment, especially in volatile situations
Taking responsibility for one's mistakes
Being organized and prompt
Supporting others so they can succeed

Positivity

Watching for opportunities or threats and bringing them to the attention of leaders

Being an advocate for oneself and for others

Having a good reputation with one's peers

Offering encouragement, not discouragement; being "glass half full"

ASSOCIATED THOUGHTS:

The meeting is on Monday, so that gives me two days to prepare.

Eric's been through a lot lately, so I'll let his sarcastic comment go.

When will Rick understand that spreading rumors makes people lose respect for him?

Firing Sadie will cause friction, but it's necessary. I'll handle this as discreetly as possible.

ASSOCIATED EMOTIONS: confidence, determination, eagerness, frustration, hopefulness, satisfaction, skepticism

POSITIVE ASPECTS: Characters who behave professionally are hardworking, loyal, ethical, and highly objective. They manage well under stress and can remove their emotions when making decisions, allowing them to make choices that are unbiased and best for the situation. Others tend to look up to and admire professionals, viewing them as trustworthy and capable of sound judgment.

NEGATIVE ASPECTS: Professionals are often held to a higher standard than other people, meaning that their transgressions are more noticeable. Because of their professionalism, if they are caught doing something embarrassing or unseemly, they are judged harshly for it. Bad decisions can haunt them, hampering their careers and casting doubt on their trustworthiness. These characters will have to work twice as hard as others to win back trust and esteem. Jealous co-workers, friends, or neighbors may jump on opportunities to bring them down a peg or two, hoping to prove that professional characters are as fallible as everyone else.

EXAMPLE FROM FILM: Clarice Starling, an FBI trainee in *The Silence of the Lambs*, is well-educated, highly trained, and determined to win Hannibal Lecter's trust. Although unnerved by Lecter's cannibalistic past and psychological insight, she remains professional, controlling her strained emotions while negotiating conditions for his help. Her bravery and tenacity win Lector's admiration; in reward, he provides leads for her to follow—as long as she is willing to probe her past wounds for his enjoyment. **Other Examples from Film and Pop Culture:** JoAnne Galloway (*A Few Good Men*), J.C. Wiatt (*Baby Boom*), Donald Trump

TRAITS IN SUPPORTING CHARACTERS THAT MAY CAUSE CONFLICT: bitter, cowardly, flaky, greedy, indecisive, irresponsible, jealous, lazy, unethical, unreliable, vindictive

CHALLENGING SCENARIOS FOR THE PROFESSIONAL CHARACTER:

Working for a new, inept boss who inherits his position of power rather than earning it

Experiencing a personal downfall or tragedy that cripples one professionally

Seeing an opportunity for success if one is willing to bend the rules or set aside ethics

Being told to look the other way if one wishes to keep one's job

Being falsely accused of corruption by a jealous, unscrupulous competitor

PROPER

DEFINITION: marked by appropriateness and correctness; stately

CATEGORIES: identity, interactive, moral

SIMILAR ATTRIBUTES: decorous, dignified, formal

POSSIBLE CAUSES:
Regional influences
Monetary status
Parental expectations
A desire to do the right thing
Not wanting to offend
Snootiness
Insecurity
Coming from a strict rule-following background

ASSOCIATED BEHAVIORS:
Being keenly aware of what others think
Following rules
Keeping a tidy home
Not leaving the house unless one's appearance is perfect
Speaking with proper grammar
Using a controlled voice (a soft tone, appropriate volume, etc.)
Not showing emotion in public
Loyalty
Creating many rules to keep others in line
Adhering to societal norms
Having high expectations for oneself and for others
Expressing disdain when others do things that are considered tacky
Belonging to prestigious groups or societies
Social climbing
Being strict with one's children to keep them from being an embarrassment
Adhering to a schedule or routine
Having good posture
Being meticulous about certain things
Having good hygiene
Taking one's responsibilities seriously
Being involved in the community
Supporting charities
Judging others based on how proper or improper they are
Responding to negativity with dignity
Avoiding conflict
Not liking surprises

Not doing anything that will make others feel uncomfortable
Doing anything to avoid a scene
Maintaining the status quo
Refusing to be drawn into arguments or disagreements in public
Avoiding public affection unless the gesture is socially acceptable (air kisses, etc.)
Thinking before one speaks
Having impeccable manners
Showing gratitude to one's host or hostess, even if one cannot stand them
Difficulty relaxing and letting go of propriety

ASSOCIATED THOUGHTS:
What's the proper thing to do in this situation?
What will the neighbors think?
Why does Barbara always have to make a scene?
I know Ian thinks he's doing the right thing, but can't he be more subtle about it?

ASSOCIATED EMOTIONS: amusement, annoyance, disappointment, disgust, embarrassment, scorn

POSITIVE ASPECTS: Proper characters are polite, upstanding citizens who don't intentionally cause trouble within societal norms. They respect authority, and since they can be counted on to toe the company line, they make excellent yes-men. These characters are extremely loyal, sticking to a person, group, philosophy, or belief to the bitter end.

NEGATIVE ASPECTS: Proper characters are comfortable with the way things have always been and don't respond well to change. They are often close-minded and stick to their guns even when they're wrong. Because morals and rightness are often handed down through ancient tradition or a chain of command, proper characters rely on others to tell them what is right and don't often think for themselves. Because they value propriety, they can be disdainful of those who behave inappropriately.

EXAMPLE FROM LITERATURE: Aunt Alexandra (*To Kill a Mockingbird*) is a genteel southern lady with pristine manners and a flawless appearance. She hosts society parties, bakes her own refreshments, and takes great pride in her family heritage. Although she disagrees with some of the choices her brother Atticus is making, her sense of propriety keeps her loyal to him and provides Jem and Scout with a decorous, albeit strict, caregiver. **Other Examples from Literature and Film:** Mary Poppins (*Mary Poppins*), Queen Elizabeth II (*The Queen*)

TRAITS IN SUPPORTING CHARACTERS THAT MAY CAUSE CONFLICT: confrontational, curious, disorganized, lazy, melodramatic, mischievous, reckless, rowdy, uncouth

CHALLENGING SCENARIOS FOR THE PROPER CHARACTER:
Being proper while having a compulsion for a disgusting or inappropriate habit
Being teamed with uncouth, improper characters
Lacking the resources to maintain an appropriate lifestyle
Experiencing a crisis in which society plummets into survival mode, making propriety a luxury

PROTECTIVE

DEFINITION: inclined to safeguard, shield, or carefully supervise the persons or items in one's charge

CATEGORIES: achievement, identity, interactive, moral

POSSIBLE CAUSES:
Serving in a caregiver role
Love and respect
Being responsible for others (one's younger siblings, etc.) at an early age
Exposure to "lean" times (where water, food, or shelter is scarce)
Having struggled in the past to provide for one's family
Proximity to danger or corruption where one must defend one's resources
Abuse
The belief that one cannot be too careful
Being the caregiver of a family member with a mental or physical handicap
A past failure (real or imagined) to protect a person, one's assets, or one's resources

ASSOCIATED BEHAVIORS:
Being aware of danger and risk, and avoiding them as much as possible
Carefully watching situations that could grow volatile
Asking questions; needing to know details
Researching and fact gathering
Being in close proximity to the one needing protection
Being an active listener; offering support and counsel
Wanting someone to succeed and working to help them achieve their goals
Balancing concern for safety with respecting another's independence and freedom
Lightly touching others to let them know one is there
Being proactive; thinking ahead to what might be needed
Distrust of strangers
Encouraging sound choices and decision making
Offering strength when it is needed
Understanding the risks before acting
Being vigilant when it comes to friends or influencers
Acting in someone's best interest without being overbearing, bossy, or controlling
Protecting someone for their sake, not for one's own best interests
Following rules and behavior patterns that have proven safe in the past
Needing to know where someone is, who they are with, and what they are doing
Being hyper sensitive to time; using time limits as a method of monitoring
Seeing to the needs of those in one's care
Being an advocate for someone else
Worrying, especially when one has little or no control over events
Calling, texting, and visiting as a way of checking in
Difficulty trusting others and letting go of control

Taking on more responsibility to help someone or increase one's influence with them

Seeing a possible threat in every situation

Being wary of new experiences or places

Being there when help is needed

Looking out for those who are ill-equipped to do so themselves

Providing information or advice to help someone be prepared

ASSOCIATED THOUGHTS:

She has no idea that Neal's a player. I better let her know.

I'll go to Rick's party so I can make sure he doesn't get out of hand like last time.

I can't let Peter wear that to school; the kids will rip him apart.

Bob's home situation is so awful. I'll cover this shift to get the boss off his back.

ASSOCIATED EMOTIONS: conflicted, determination, gratitude, irritation, regret, skepticism, suspicion, wariness, worry, unease

POSITIVE ASPECTS: Protective characters care deeply and have the best interest of their charges at heart. They are willing to set aside their own wants and needs to make sure the needs of their loves ones are taken care of. As their loved ones explore the world and their place within it, protectors act with vigilance to ensure that no harm comes to them. These characters are excellent at assessing possible risks and minimizing them, protecting their assets and resources from those who might take advantage, while offering help and counsel to loved ones who need it.

NEGATIVE ASPECTS: While protectors safeguard the people and things they care about, conflict arises when opinions differ as to the best course of action. Despite good intentions, power struggles can create a tug-of-war between the protector's need to keep a charge safe and the charge's desire for autonomy. When rules and precautions chafe, a charge may rebel, damaging the relationship or worse—intentionally putting himself in danger in order to prove that he can take care of himself.

EXAMPLE FROM TV: Dean Winchester from the series *Supernatural* is extremely protective of not only his brother Sam, but anyone he considers family, including his fellow hunters. He will go to any lengths to protect them from the evil they fight day-to-day, going up against demons, Leviathans, the Four Horsemen, and Death himself. Risking his life for others is in a hunter's job description, but Dean takes it a step further, selling his soul to the devil in order to save Sam's life.

Other Examples from Film and Literature: Leigh Anne Tuohy (*The Blind Side*), Korben Dallas (*The Fifth Element*), the unnamed father in *The Road*

TRAITS IN SUPPORTING CHARACTERS THAT MAY CAUSE CONFLICT: cruel, greedy, honorable, just, manipulative, self-destructive, selfish, sleazy, unethical, vindictive, violent

CHALLENGING SCENARIOS FOR THE PROTECTIVE CHARACTER:

Trying to protect those who undermine the protector's efforts out of a sense of unworthiness

Encountering a powerful force (the police, the government) that tries to take one's resources

Needing to protect someone despite not having the knowledge or resources to do so

QUIRKY

DEFINITION: exhibiting peculiarities or idiosyncrasies

CATEGORIES: identity, interactive

SIMILAR ATTRIBUTES: eccentric, offbeat, peculiar, unconventional, unusual

POSSIBLE CAUSES:
Entitlement; believing that one has earned the right to act however one wants
Being unconcerned with what others think
A desire to break free from an overly strict or regimented past
Growing up in an environment that held little respect for conventionality
Dementia
Immaturity
Insecurity
Craving attention
Having an independent streak; taking pride in one's individuality

ASSOCIATED BEHAVIORS:
Wearing unconventional clothing combinations
Not caring about one's appearance; being more interested in other things
Exhibiting peculiar habits
Not picking up on common social cues from others
Relating somewhat awkwardly to others
Embracing one's weirdness
Doing things to deliberately stand out
Doing what one wants without worrying about what others think
Flouting the rules
Making up one's own rules
Unpredictability
Confidence
Independence
Being amused when others are discomfited by one's uniqueness
Sticking to one's individuality despite opposition
Being open-minded
Enjoying life
Doing even mundane tasks a little differently than others
Defying the norm
Being annoyed when others follow trends and jump on popular bandwagons
Espousing beliefs and opinions that are different from the mainstream
Becoming defensive when one's individuality is criticized
Anger that escalates to bitterness, turning one's quirkiness into an act of defiance
Speaking in a straightforward manner; not mincing words
Isolation

Grouping with other quirky people
Expressing creativity
Adopting quirky habits in an attempt to gain attention or acceptance
Transparency; being true to oneself without worrying about the perceptions of others
Unnerving others with one's odd ways, ideas, and unpredictability

ASSOCIATED THOUGHTS:
Most people wouldn't put these clothes together, but I think they look awesome!
I don't know why everyone liked Avatar so much. I thought it was dumb.
I wonder if I can walk from Central Park to Riverside Boulevard backward.
Today, I'm not going to speak. Instead, I will sing.

ASSOCIATED EMOTIONS: amusement, anger, anxiety, confidence, defensiveness, determination, embarrassment, indifference, satisfaction, wariness

POSITIVE ASPECTS: Once quirky characters have been labeled as peculiar, no one expects them to act conventionally, so they can get away with things that others can't, which is a nice little tool for the writer's arsenal. Because they are easily stereotyped, they are often underestimated or overlooked by society at large. Their tendency to think outside the box enables them to see problems from a different angle and come up with unusual solutions.

NEGATIVE ASPECTS: While everyone has something to offer, the gifts of a quirky person are not often sought out or graciously received. These characters are easily misunderstood and viewed with suspicion, making them convenient scapegoats. Their strangeness usually ensures that they live on the outskirts of community and fellowship.

EXAMPLE FROM FILM: Willy Wonka (*Willy Wonka & the Chocolate Factory*) is a fairly weird proprietor. His clothes are outlandish, he employs a crew of Oompa-Loompas, and it's common practice for children to disappear or be otherwise disfigured while touring his factory. Through his words and his actions, it's clear that he lives outside of society's norms and does so with complete confidence. And because he's known as a quirky guy, people take it all in stride. **Other Examples from Film:** Spike (*Notting Hill*), Tish Ambrosé (*SpaceCamp*)

TRAITS IN SUPPORTING CHARACTERS THAT MAY CAUSE CONFLICT:
diplomatic, fussy, inhibited, proper, responsible, sophisticated

CHALLENGING SCENARIOS FOR THE QUIRKY CHARACTER:
Living in a strict society with zero tolerance for individuality
Experiencing a situation where one has to conform in order to achieve one's goals
Being misunderstood or wrongly judged due to one's quirkiness
Having a goal that conflicts with one's offbeat nature (wanting to be popular, etc.)

RESOURCEFUL

DEFINITION: capable of adapting to new situations by making do with what one has

CATEGORIES: achievement, interactive

SIMILAR ATTRIBUTES: clever, enterprising, ingenious

POSSIBLE CAUSES:
Experiencing a shortness of resources in the past
Being impoverished; having no other choice but to figure out new ways of surviving
A desire to live simply
Frugality or thriftiness
Independence; not wanting to rely on others
A desire to be more responsible or efficient with one's resources
Being highly imaginative or creative

ASSOCIATED BEHAVIORS:
Keeping cool in the face of difficult circumstances
Being proactive
Being a good problem solver
Assessing a situation quickly and accurately
Determination
Maintaining a positive outlook
Believing that there are always solutions if one just looks hard enough
Having a basic understanding of how things work
Taking pride in one's ability to care for oneself
Tinkering with things to better understand how they work
Thinking outside the box; ingenuity
Recycling
Repurposing discarded objects into something new and useful
Holding onto items because they might one day come in handy
Hoarding tendencies
Acquiring what one needs in a creative way
Making items instead of buying them (clothes, food products, home decor, etc.)
Keeping inventory of the items at one's disposal
Thinking ahead
Bartering or trading with others for what can't be produced
Educating oneself on areas where knowledge is lacking
Recognizing that there isn't only one solution to a given problem
Keeping an eye out for new opportunities
Being organized
Looking for ways to cut costs or save money
Having a backup plan
Viewing a tight budget as a challenge

Anticipating problems before they arise

Taking risks; not being afraid to experiment

Learning from one's mistakes

Believing that nothing is impossible

Scorning people who are wasteful or extravagant

Becoming obsessive about saving money or resources

Being a fixer who is unafraid of hard work

ASSOCIATED THOUGHTS:
I can't believe Marie threw this bottle away when there's still shampoo in the bottom.
If I think long enough, I'll figure out a solution.
It would be a shame to throw out this cracked cutting board. How else could I use it?
What resources do we have at our disposal?

ASSOCIATED EMOTIONS: annoyance, confidence, curiosity, desperation, determination, eagerness, pride, satisfaction, worry

POSITIVE ASPECTS: Resourceful characters are forward-thinking. They're able to anticipate problems and begin planning in advance. When a difficult situation does arise, the resourceful character keeps his head; instead of panicking, he chooses to focus on finding a solution to the problem—usually in the form of something unorthodox or unconventional. Determined, confident, and imaginative, the resourceful character is a handy individual to have around when everything goes south.

NEGATIVE ASPECTS: Because of their ability to work independently, resourceful characters can have difficulty depending on or working with others. Their need for self-sufficiency can lead to isolation and even paranoia as they worry about other people wanting to take away their resources or freedom. These characters can also become too frugal, choosing to live in poverty and squalor rather than part with their money or resources.

EXAMPLE FROM LITERATURE: In *The Boxcar Children*, four young siblings are forced to live on their own in an abandoned train car. To survive, they do what they have to do. The eldest gets a modest job doing lawn work. The others comb the dump to find serviceable items that can be washed and repurposed. They even dam the local lake to create a bathing area and a cool place to keep their milk from spoiling. Although young, the Alden children are able to make do by using the items at their disposal and keeping their eyes open for new opportunities to better their situation. **Other Examples from Film and Literature:** John Rambo (*First Blood*), William and Elizabeth (*The Swiss Family Robinson*), Philippe the Mouse (*Ladyhawke*)

TRAITS IN SUPPORTING CHARACTERS THAT MAY CAUSE CONFLICT:
extravagant, generous, haughty, irresponsible, lazy, selfish, spoiled, subservient

CHALLENGING SCENARIOS FOR THE RESOURCEFUL CHARACTER:
Having to be resourceful while lacking creativity or imagination

Being paired with people who are extravagant and wasteful

Facing a hindrance that makes resourcefulness difficult (an injury that affects mobility, etc.)

Having to be resourceful not just for oneself, but for a large number of needy dependents

RESPONSIBLE

DEFINITION: being accountable for one's actions and obligations

CATEGORIES: achievement, identity, interactive, moral

SIMILAR ATTRIBUTES: accountable, dependable, reliable, trustworthy

POSSIBLE CAUSES:
Being the first-born
Growing up as a caregiver for younger siblings or debilitated parents
Facing a situation in the past where survival depended on one's ability to care for oneself
Having an acute sense of right and wrong
Gratitude that compels one to take care of others
Having a patriotic sense of family, community, and country
Growing up in an environment of strict rules and expectations
Belonging to a family with built-in obligations (a family that runs its own business, etc.)
The belief that people should be held accountable for their actions

ASSOCIATED BEHAVIORS:
Having a solid work ethic
Keeping promises
Doing one's job to the best of one's ability
Taking pride in one's work
Finishing projects in a timely manner
Looking out for the people in one's charge
Taking on extra duties in order to make ends meet
Accepting responsibility when mistakes are made
Not making excuses
Feeling remorse, regret, or guilt when one's choices have let someone else down
Experiencing anxiety when complications make it difficult to fulfill one's obligations
Taking pride in one's reputation; striving to uphold it
Relating to people in a respectful manner
Knowing one's strengths and weaknesses and working within and around them
Self-discipline
Facing difficult circumstances head-on
Being organized
Learning from one's mistakes
Taking initiative
Feeling overwhelmed at times
Treating people fairly
Expressing frustration when others don't follow through on their responsibilities
Picking up the slack when someone drops the ball and feeling resentment as a result
Sacrificing to make sure one's responsibilities are met
Taking the lead in a group situation

Working within deadlines
Being intrinsically motivated
Telling one's charges what they want to hear to spare them anxiety
Finding it difficult to ask for help out of a reluctance to appear weak
Following up after the fact to make sure that others are satisfied

ASSOCIATED THOUGHTS:
I don't know how I'm going to get this done, but I'll make it work.
Why can't people just do what they say they're going to do?
This is a good opportunity but I simply don't have time. I'll tell them to ask someone else.
I'll need to get up an hour earlier than usual if I'm going to get to the meeting on time.

ASSOCIATED EMOTIONS: anticipation, anxiety, confidence, determination, overwhelmed, resentment, satisfaction

POSITIVE ASPECTS: When the chips are down, responsible characters are the go-to people. They are trustworthy and work hard to provide what's needed. This trait is strongly tied to morality, so no matter what else is going on, responsible characters will do what needs to be done in order to satisfy obligations. These characters will make sacrifices and put others before themselves if it is for the greater good. They are loyal to those within their circle, be it family, friends, a community, or the company they work for. Because they can be relied on to take their commitments seriously, they make ideal leaders, caregivers, and mates.

NEGATIVE ASPECTS: Characters with this trait take their responsibilities so seriously that it can be difficult for them to let go and have fun. Guiding, parenting, and moralizing is sometimes done without thought. This kind of involvement is not always appreciated by others, and responsible characters can find themselves excluded or even vilified by people looking to stretch boundaries and find their own way. Younger people especially may perceive others with this trait as being boring and overly serious, not seeing their value until trouble arises and help is needed.

EXAMPLE FROM FILM: In *Saving Private Ryan*, Captain John Miller has a duty to fulfill—one that he doesn't particularly believe in. But as an army captain, it's his responsibility to locate Private Ryan and send him home. The difficulties are seemingly insurmountable: Ryan's whereabouts are unknown, France is literally crawling with enemy soldiers, and most of Miller's company are not on board, to the point of attempting a mutiny after two of their members are killed. Through it all, Captain Miller not only holds to his duty but encourages his team to do the same. In the end, he completes his mission, and pays the ultimate price to do so. **Other Examples from Literature:** Frodo Baggins (*The Lord of the Rings*), Martin Brody (*Jaws*)

TRAITS IN SUPPORTING CHARACTERS THAT MAY CAUSE CONFLICT: flaky, impulsive, irresponsible, lazy, mischievous, quirky, reckless, selfish, uncooperative, uninhibited

CHALLENGING SCENARIOS FOR THE RESPONSIBLE CHARACTER:
Having goals that conflict with one's morals (being a responsible thief, a dishonest parent, etc.)
Having conflicting responsibilities that necessitate difficult choices
Having a compulsion or bad habit that makes it difficult to be responsible
Being responsible for a project or objective that one doesn't believe in

SENSIBLE

DEFINITION: characterized by sound judgment and keen awareness

CATEGORIES: achievement, interactive

SIMILAR ATTRIBUTES: levelheaded, practical, pragmatic, realistic, reasonable

POSSIBLE CAUSES:
Intelligence
Being highly logical
Having parents who encouraged one to think deeply
Being a caregiver or having responsibility for others
Being highly rational

ASSOCIATED BEHAVIORS:
Investigating one's options before reaching a decision
Weighing the pros and cons
Having realistic expectations of an outcome
Having good control over one's emotions (especially high or rash emotion)
Being rooted in the present; living based on what one sees and knows to be real
Understanding what is needed and expected, then acting accordingly
Pausing to consider; thinking before acting
Reasoning well with others
Having strong common sense
Assessing the odds and risk before committing
Dressing and acting appropriately for the situation
Being well-spoken
Offering practical insight and advice
Objectivity
Not asking or expecting more than is reasonable
Adhering to commonly held beliefs and ideas
Being respected by others
Keeping one's opinion to oneself when it's prudent to do so
Respecting the experience and wisdom of others
Speaking in a calm, soothing tone
Being the voice of reason when emotions are volatile
Protecting others from themselves (stopping friends from acting impulsively, etc.)
Swaying others through practicality and common sense
Not taking risks
Seeking out wisdom or advice
Reusing or recycling an item for practicality
Entering relationships cautiously
Admiring others who are practical
Refusing to be coerced into risky behaviors

Multitasking

Being a good decision maker (even under pressure)

Having realistic hopes and expectations

Maintaining good health

Not overindulging (drinking too much, eating too much, etc.)

Expressing impatience or frustration with dreamers and idealists

Being responsible and trustworthy

Anticipating change and adapting in order to avoid unwelcome surprises

Appreciating order and rules

Having strong leadership and organizational skills

ASSOCIATED THOUGHTS:

The clerk probably won't give me a refund without a receipt, but it never hurts to try.

Diane is excited about this investment opportunity, but I'd rather go with something less risky.

I doubt Edgar will win the election, but we need options. It's a step in the right direction.

I'm not sure what the dress code is, but business casual is usually a safe choice.

ASSOCIATED EMOTIONS: confidence, determination, gratitude, satisfaction

POSITIVE ASPECTS: A sensible character is an anchor, a life raft. When a situation turns tense or emotional, these characters are often the voice of reason and can bring things back under control. They are responsible, prepared, and can provide solid counsel for someone whose judgment is cloudy or uncertain. They can quickly assess problems and lay out options in a matter-of-fact way that avoids messy emotional ties.

NEGATIVE ASPECTS: Sensible characters are often content to settle rather than strive for improvement. Because they like to assess the odds of success and stick with what makes sense, they're not likely to chase a big dream or pursue risky goals. Their disdain for spontaneity may cause others to view them as boring.

EXAMPLE FROM FILM: Ellis "Red" Redding in *The Shawshank Redemption* is a con who smuggles contraband within the prison, providing a practical service that keeps him safe from the other inmates. He befriends wrongfully convicted Andy Dufresne and offers counsel on how to survive the brutal environment. Alert to any change in mood within the prison, Red knows which wheels to grease and when it's best to get out of the way. **Other Examples from Literature and Film:** Laura Ingalls (*The Little House on the Prairie* series), Dr. McCoy (*Star Trek* series), Sam Baldwin (*Sleepless in Seattle*)

TRAITS IN SUPPORTING CHARACTERS THAT MAY CAUSE CONFLICT: childish, compulsive, indecisive, flaky, foolish, melodramatic, playful, superstitious

CHALLENGING SCENARIOS FOR THE SENSIBLE CHARACTER:

Having to work with or be around foolish people

Being exposed to something one doesn't believe in (paranormal activity, first contact, etc.)

Being forced to act on faith instead of logic

Being compelled to pursue an impossible dream or go in a direction that doesn't make sense

SENSUAL

DEFINITION: appreciating the senses; seeking to explore one's appetites to gain sensory gratification

CATEGORIES: identity, interactive

SIMILAR ATTRIBUTES: carnal, epicurean

POSSIBLE CAUSES:
Having a deep love for all things and experiences
Being highly exploratory
Having a creative or artistic nature
Having a heightened awareness of and sensitivity to one's senses
Having a strong libido

ASSOCIATED BEHAVIORS:
Being highly curious
Having a deep appreciation for music, art, and beauty
Being highly tactile
Having a romantic nature
Wanting to share emotional or sensory experiences with others
Being sensitive to one's emotions and the emotions of others
Taking one's time while eating or drinking to fully enjoy the experience
Being hyper aware of warmth and light
Planning ahead to create the right mood (lighting candles, choosing music, etc.)
Enjoying color and its effect on one's emotional state (seeing them as more vivid, etc.)
Appreciating the play of light (how it creates shadows, softens colors, etc.)
Breathing evenly and slowly
Texture sensitivity (e.g. awareness of a fabric's softness and how it feels against skin)
Wanting to taste new foods
Enjoying textures on the tongue
Feeling physical changes associated with arousal (tingling nerves, rising body heat, etc.)
Feeling intoxicated by a pleasing scent
Boldness
Being sensitive to smells
Living for the moment
Being uninhibited
Seeking out physical gratification
Sexual teasing and bantering
Giving and receiving massages
Being attracted to another in a way that feels intoxicating
Engaging in sex
Experiencing a release in bodily tension when one's sensual desires are met
Giving oneself over to sensations; becoming less aware of everything else

Having a vivid imagination; fantasizing
Desiring to discover and explore
Intensely desiring pleasure or ecstasy
Appreciating the aesthetics of nature
Having a passion for life and what it brings
Experiencing an emotional reaction to movies, books, art, or natural beauty
Dancing or swaying as a way of expressing one's emotions
Wearing perfume or scented powders
Enjoying nudity
Publicly displaying affection
Sending suggestive notes, texts, or pictures
Being touchy-feely

ASSOCIATED THOUGHTS:
The smell of those orchids is intoxicating.
Spending the day on the window chaise and warming myself in the sun is pure bliss.
Alan's skin is so soft. I could spend hours tracing the slope of his back.
Every time I see the moonlight, I want to dance in it, be bathed in it.

ASSOCIATED EMOTIONS: adoration, curiosity, desire, excitement, love, satisfaction

POSITIVE ASPECTS: Fearless and passionate, sensual characters are explorers. They seek gratification by delving into their senses and trying everything they can imagine. Highly attuned to emotion and desire, these characters love deeply and seek bliss in every moment, wasting no opportunities.

NEGATIVE ASPECTS: In their quest for sensory stimulation and emotional gratification, these characters can sometimes take things too far. Poor judgment and an inability to make sound decisions in the heat of the moment may lead to irresponsibility, infidelity, and a greater risk of dependence on addictive substances.

EXAMPLE FROM FILM: In *9 ½ Weeks*, Elizabeth McGraw, a recent divorcée, has an affair with a man she barely knows. Throughout their experience, they explore the senses together, not only through adventurous sexual play but through food, clothing, colors, sounds, and textures.
Other Examples from TV: Charlie Harper (*Two and a Half Men*), Samantha Jones (*Sex and the City*)

TRAITS IN SUPPORTING CHARACTERS THAT MAY CAUSE CONFLICT: callous, inhibited, introverted, withdrawn

CHALLENGING SCENARIOS FOR THE SENSUAL CHARACTER:
Living where sensuality is forbidden or inaccessible (a convent, prison, etc.)
A sensory processing disorder that causes hypersensitivity to a texture, smell, noise, etc.
Family or friends who disapprove of one's choices and label one as a sexual deviant
Being caught in a vulnerable state (a nosy neighbor appearing during a skinny dip)

SENTIMENTAL

DEFINITION: being strongly influenced by feelings or emotional sentiment

CATEGORIES: identity, interactive

SIMILAR ATTRIBUTES: emotional, romantic

POSSIBLE CAUSES:
Having an overly sentimental parent
Wanting the attention that comes when excess emotion is expressed
Being unable to move beyond highly emotional events in one's past
Being deeply in tune with one's emotions and wanting to experience them frequently

ASSOCIATED BEHAVIORS:
Being deeply touched by kindness; feeling one's emotions keenly
Nostalgia
Having a clear view of one's ideal spouse, job, etc., and refusing to compromise
Making decisions based on one's feelings rather than on logic
Holding on to and cherishing keepsakes
Having clear memories of important days or occasions (a birth, a break-up, etc.)
Loyalty
Seeking out information on one's ancestry and family
Valuing the stories behind certain keepsakes
Passing down heirlooms
Buying personalized gifts for people
Valuing time spent with loved ones
Crying over sad movies or books
Freely expressing one's feelings, even in public
Becoming emotional when memories are stirred (when a song is played, etc.)
Being hurt when others don't return one's intensity of feeling
Offering the gift of one's time
Wanting to make loved ones happy and fulfilled
Thoughtfulness (sending notes with a lunch, texting a lover for no reason, etc.)
Idealizing one's memories; remembering the good parts and forgetting the bad
Feeling a sense of loss when one's keepsakes are broken or lost
Being sensitive; having one's feelings easily hurt
Discovering someone's deepest desire and finding a way to fulfill it
Tying one's happiness to other people
Giving sappy love gifts on special occasions (Valentine's Day, etc.)
Becoming emotional over tokens from the past (a poem, a ticket stub, etc.)
Sending handwritten notes instead of emails
Knowing the preferences and passions of the people in one's life
Smothering others with emotion and attention
Viewing a loved one as being especially talented or gifted

Speaking whatever emotion one is feeling at the time
Inviting people over and cooking for them instead of taking them out to dinner

ASSOCIATED THOUGHTS:
I'm going to write Laura a note so she knows how much her friendship means to me.
I should hold onto this and give it to my granddaughter one day.
I've never been so happy in my whole life!
Why would he say such a thing when I've been nothing but kind to him?

ASSOCIATED EMOTIONS: adoration, amazement, anticipation, desperation, elation, excitement, gratitude, happiness, love

POSITIVE ASPECTS: Sentimental characters are in touch with their feelings; they don't see the need to hide their emotions and are usually transparent and honest in their expressions. Unselfish and other-focused, they can be highly loyal and their emotions are often wrapped up in the people who share their lives. Romanticism appeals to them, making them thoughtful and generous characters.

NEGATIVE ASPECTS: Because of their tendency toward emotionality, sentimental characters often clash with people who are more practical and are often viewed as being melodramatic, unrealistic, and unstable. Their demonstrative nature may make others uncomfortable or even drive them away. Sentimental characters can often get so caught up in their feelings for others that they forget who they are or how to be independent. Their sentimentality can taint their perceptions, leading them to see events how they want to see them instead of how they actually are.

EXAMPLE FROM LITERATURE: Marianne Dashwood (*Sense and Sensibility*) is the sentimental Dashwood daughter. Her emotions are easily stirred by poetry, nature, and romantic gestures. When John Willoughby comes to her aid, she falls deeply in love with him, refusing to hear any of the warnings from the practical people in her life. **Other Examples from Film and Literature:** Allie Hamilton (*The Notebook*), Anne Shirley (*Anne of Green Gables*)

TRAITS IN SUPPORTING CHARACTERS THAT MAY CAUSE CONFLICT: analytical, cruel, humorless, just, meticulous, proper, uncommunicative

CHALLENGING SCENARIOS FOR THE SENTIMENTAL CHARACTER:
Being forced into a practical or logical career field (accounting, computer technology, etc.)
Being surrounded by people who encourage high emotion that reinforces a lack of balance
Having to sell or get rid of one's heirlooms in a non-romantic way
Being paired with a very practical, no-nonsense spouse who is not a romantic
Being sentimental but also craving logic and reason

SIMPLE

DEFINITION: not fancy; plain

CATEGORIES: identity, interactive

SIMILAR ATTRIBUTES: down-to-earth, low maintenance, plain, unassuming

POSSIBLE CAUSES:
Having a strong sense of self
Being able to take things at face value
Growing up in a tight-knit community or family
Being easily overwhelmed
Being aware of and grateful for what one has
Having an understanding nature

ASSOCIATED BEHAVIORS:
Transparency in relationships
Not judging others
Being content with what one has
Not needing to be fussed over
Honesty
Practicality
Wisdom that comes from observation and listening
Being comfortable in one's own skin
Having no need for pomp or pretense
Seeing beauty in things that others miss
Being comfortable with silences in conversation
Not over-complicating things; keeping it simple
Feeling a sense of accomplishment through hard work
Being grounded in reality
Not needing accolades or recognition
Choosing comfort over style
Being adaptable; taking change as it comes
Optimism
Being strongly tied to one's family and friends
Not caring about having the best or the newest things
Being unafraid of hard work or doing one's share
Avoiding the limelight
Maintaining a "natural" appearance (not wearing makeup, etc.)
Being easy to talk to and be with
Humility
Generosity
Being a strong observer
Patience
Taking one's time

Not placing high expectations on others
Enjoying the simple things
Not being interested in fashion trends
Being content to go along with others instead of leading
Having a quiet nature
Not being demanding
Being authentic; knowing who one is
Not needing material things to be happy

ASSOCIATED THOUGHTS:
Everyone will probably be dressed up, but I'm more comfortable in jeans.
I like baking with Mama, even though she hums more than she speaks.
I can't wait for our date! I hope we go star gazing like last time.
Mara deserves all the attention on her birthday, so I'll wait to mention my promotion.

ASSOCIATED EMOTIONS: gratitude, happiness, hopefulness, peacefulness, satisfaction

POSITIVE ASPECTS: The adage *what you see is what you get* applies aptly to simple characters. Open and honest, they have worthy priorities and a broad-minded perspective. They're adept at balancing their emotions, are good listeners and friends, and are generally content with what they have.

NEGATIVE ASPECTS: Simple characters are often happy to stay in the background, increasing the likelihood of their being overlooked. If they have something to say, it's usually important or insightful, although others may not listen or trust their wisdom because of their unassuming natures. Their desire to keep things simple means they're often reluctant to get involved in initiatives or try new experiences, which robs them of opportunities that could lead to greater satisfaction and happiness.

EXAMPLE FROM LITERATURE: Melanie Wilkes (*Gone with the Wind*) is a frail young woman who is more interested in discussing books than in gossiping. Her clothes—even at her engagement party—are described as plain and she doesn't complain when war creates shortages of food, clothing, and other necessities. A supporting character in the story, Melanie's simplicity and quiet demeanor provide a sharp contrast to the main character's extravagance, frivolity, and melodrama. **Other Examples from Literature:** Marcus Brewer (*About a Boy*), Elizabeth Bennet (*Pride and Prejudice*)

TRAITS IN SUPPORTING CHARACTERS THAT MAY CAUSE CONFLICT: extravagant, flamboyant, frivolous, haughty, judgmental, melodramatic, perfectionist, proper, worrywart

CHALLENGING SCENARIOS FOR THE SIMPLE CHARACTER:
Taking a job in a high-maintenance industry (being an accountant at a fashion magazine, etc.)
Constantly being drawn into unwelcome turmoil by melodramatic friends
Having to leave one's home for safety reasons (a natural disaster, for example)
Being misjudged as weak due to one's desire for simplicity and peace
Being forced to move from the town where one grew up and is comfortable

SOCIALLY AWARE

DEFINITION: being aware of the wrongs within society and desiring to correct them

CATEGORIES: interactive, moral

SIMILAR ATTRIBUTES: humanitarian, public-spirited

POSSIBLE CAUSES:
Having a deep belief in social responsibility
Being taught from a young age to respect the world and the people in it
Being exposed to abuse or cruelty
Having a strong sense of right and wrong
A life-changing experience (viewing poverty or injustice in the third world, etc.)
Personally witnessing unethical behavior and living through the fallout
High intelligence
The belief that doing right is its own reward
Utilitarianism (the idea that doing what is best for all is beneficial in the long run)
Adhering to a spiritual or religious belief (karma, etc.)
Being empathetic

ASSOCIATED BEHAVIORS:
Recognizing the effects of one's actions
Not being prejudiced
Recycling
Giving to charities that support ethical ideals
Knowing the rules and abiding by them
Trusting others until they're proven untrustworthy
Respecting the needs and opinions of others
Being deeply compassionate
Giving money to panhandlers
Having rock solid core values
Selflessness
Donating time to a social cause (building a house, digging a well, etc.)
Having a strong sense of fairness
Noticing homeless people on the street rather than averting one's gaze
Being highly attuned to the environment and everything in it
Traveling to places with the intent of improving the quality of life there
Seeing potential in those who have been written off by others
Honesty
Sticking to one's principles; choosing what's right over what's easy
Blowing the whistle on unethical treatment or inequality
Integrity
Raising awareness of social injustices
Attending fundraising events
Mentoring those less fortunate

Loyalty
Working well with others
Forging strong bonds and relationships
Judging others by one's own beliefs and ideals
Becoming a vegan or vegetarian
Being highly empathetic
Fostering or adopting children
Starting a charity organization

ASSOCIATED THOUGHTS:
How can Steve do that and still look himself in the mirror?
That poor dog barks all day long. Why have a pet if you leave it tied up outside?
People are lazy. If everyone recycled, it would make such a difference.
Why would I want to travel to a country where they treat women like property?
Buy shoes from them? No way. They use child labor to manufacture them.

ASSOCIATED EMOTIONS: anger, anguish, conflicted, determination, eagerness, love, skepticism

POSITIVE ASPECTS: Characters who are socially aware are willing to examine things that most people find uncomfortable or repugnant. While others may see a difficult situation and turn away out of grief or shock, the socially aware character will internalize the emotion, feeling it along with the sufferer. This ability to empathize leads these characters to action, however great the odds or opponents. Often inspirational, they're adept at mobilizing people to work toward a common goal that, in the end, benefits many.

NEGATIVE ASPECTS: Socially aware characters are zealous in their beliefs. They see most issues as black or white and have a hard time accepting opposing opinions. In their effort to win others over, they can be pushy or tactless, and end up turning people off. While their intentions are to help others and they can clearly see the big-picture goal, socially aware characters tend to over-simplify matters, which can make finding an effective and efficient solution difficult.

EXAMPLE FROM LITERATURE: In *A Time to Kill,* Ellen Roark is a law student with a strong social conscience. A member of the ACLU, she's an avid opponent of the death penalty and has actively fought against it. When a young African-American girl is raped and her father is put on trial for the murder of her attackers, Ellen makes the trip to Mississippi on her own dime to assist in his case on a pro bono basis. **Other Examples from Film and Pop Culture:** Lucy Kelson (*Two Weeks Notice)*, Bono

TRAITS IN SUPPORTING CHARACTERS THAT MAY CAUSE CONFLICT: callous, cowardly, extravagant, greedy, obedient, selfish, timid, traditional

CHALLENGING SCENARIOS FOR THE SOCIALLY AWARE:
Facing seemingly overwhelming odds and opponents in order to right a wrong
Wishing to help many causes but only having the resources to save one
Choosing whether or not to sacrifice one's time, money, relationships, etc., to help others
Being asked to compromise one's beliefs

SOPHISTICATED

DEFINITION: having worldly knowledge and wisdom

CATEGORIES: identity, interactive

SIMILAR ATTRIBUTES: cultivated, debonair, polished, refined, urbane, worldly

POSSIBLE CAUSES:
Having parents who were world travelers
Being exposed to different cultures growing up (educational travel, etc.)
Attending a finishing school
Having a family pedigree that demands sophistication (royalty, upper class, etc.)
A desire to learn and experience
Growing up with power or wealth that offered exposure to high society

ASSOCIATED BEHAVIORS:
Dressing appropriately and neatly
Having knowledge of world issues and being able to converse about them
Being self-assured
Carrying oneself with confidence; having good posture
Elegance
Being conscious of what's fashionable and current
Speaking more than one language
Being educated in regards to quality (knowing good wine from bad, etc.)
Having good manners (opening doors for others, standing so someone else can sit, etc.)
Being socially adept
Having a strong sense of personal style
Engaging in conversation
Showing an interest in the arts (music, paintings, etc.)
Being highly social
Being well-read
Speaking in a controlled tone of voice
Having a knowledge of relevant historical events
Having worldly experience; being exposed to other cultures and ideas
Understanding the rules of popular sports or activities
Being apt at small talk
Seeking ways to increase one's knowledge and personal growth
Being polished (being graceful, tucking in the edges of one's skirt when sitting, etc.)
Independence
Eating and enjoying food from different cultures
Having a working knowledge of current politics and players
Smiling
Avoiding gossip or snarky judgments
Being well-groomed and neat

Exhibiting control in public (not eating or drinking too much, etc.)
Being willing to try new things
Wanting to learn
Having a good command of vocabulary
Sipping a drink instead of chugging it
Participating in events for enrichment (attending the opera or ballet, etc.)
Being socially aware (raising awareness of injustices, supporting a charity, etc.)
Networking with others to obtain information or help

ASSOCIATED THOUGHTS:
Alex didn't help his wife out of the car? She's six months pregnant!
I can't wait to see The King and I with Lucy.
I wonder if Emma and I have read any of the same Italian books?
Prague is so beautiful this time of year. I wish I could be there.

ASSOCIATED EMOTIONS: confidence, curiosity, gratitude, happiness

POSITIVE ASPECTS: Sophisticated characters have knowledge of different cultures and ways of living. They often adopt some of the aspects of these foreign cultures, which gives them a unique flair. Their exposure to different people groups can make them tolerant and open-minded.

NEGATIVE ASPECTS: Sophisticated characters are not all snobby socialites drinking wine while snarking over society gossip and dropping names; yet, some are, and they can give a bad name to others. Members of this more superficial subset wear the right designer brands and go to all the important events. Wielding their power and wealth like a club to remind others of their status, these characters are often feared or disliked by their peers.

EXAMPLE FROM FILM: The lead character in the film *Sabrina* grows up as the shy, uncertain daughter of the chauffeur to a wealthy family. Although she has lived all her life on the Larrabee property, watching the Larrabee boys from afar, she remains unnoticed until she makes a trip abroad to Paris. She returns as a stylish, self-assured, worldly young woman who suddenly attracts the notice of both David and Linus and finds herself in the position of having to choose between them. **Other Examples from Pop Culture:** Audrey Hepburn, Princess Diana, Grace Kelly

TRAITS IN SUPPORTING CHARACTERS THAT MAY CAUSE CONFLICT: abrasive, inflexible, rowdy, sleazy, timid, traditional, uncouth, violent

CHALLENGING SCENARIOS FOR THE SOPHISTICATED CHARACTER:
Dealing with people of power and influence who are crass and disrespectful
Losing one's wealth or influence due to a family member's mismanagement
An experience that changes one for the worse (haughtiness after traveling the world, etc.)
Receiving criticism from loved ones when one changes as a result of one's experiences

SPIRITUAL

DEFINITION: focusing on one's higher self; being interested in religious or sacred matters

CATEGORIES: identity, interactive, moral

SIMILAR ATTRIBUTES: pious, religious, reverent

POSSIBLE CAUSES:
Growing up in a religious environment
A near-death experience that shines a spotlight on one's mortality
Being grateful for the blessings in one's life
Having a pivotal religious experience
Embracing the humble belief that there are things greater than oneself

ASSOCIATED BEHAVIORS:
Crediting God, the universe, or another source for one's accomplishments
Praying or seeking spiritual counsel before making important decisions
Feeling one with nature and having a respect for all life
Believing that all living creatures have a soul
Studying passages from holy books (the Quran, the Bible, Śhruti, etc.)
Aligning one's moral code with a spiritual belief system and acting accordingly
Attending services at a church, synagogue, shrine, etc.
Feeling connected to those who share similar beliefs
Proselytizing
Praying or meditating
Believing in miracles and signs
Seeking knowledge about the world, life, and things that cannot be seen
Accepting ideas or beliefs that have been passed down from others
Having a deep faith, even when doing so goes against common sense
Seeking to learn from those more knowledgeable in spiritual matters
Participating in sacred rituals
Wearing specific garments associated with one's religion
Doing charity work
Searching for spiritual enlightenment via fasting, dream quests, a walkabout, etc.
Raising one's children according to one's spiritual beliefs
Abstaining from certain things (sex, alcohol, meat, etc.) as part of one's beliefs
Experiencing guilt when one falls short of the spiritual ideal
Believing in an afterlife
Trusting in something that is greater than oneself
Thinking deeply about spiritual matters
Being open-minded to things that are impossible to explain
Striving to improve oneself
Sacrificially giving of one's money, time, and resources
Devoting oneself to serving others rather than serving oneself

Working towards a spiritual end goal (enlightenment, entering the afterlife, etc.)
Depending on religion or an aspect of religion to save one's soul
Communing with nature
Reacting to tragedy in a grace-filled manner
Seeking self-actualization
Forgiving others

ASSOCIATED THOUGHTS:
What is the right thing to do in this situation?
How can I serve others?
In the grand scheme of things, I'm so insignificant.
Is this right for me? Am I on the right path? If only there was a sign.

ASSOCIATED EMOTIONS: adoration, anticipation, contempt, desire, determination, fear, gratitude, guilt, happiness, love, peacefulness, worry

POSITIVE ASPECTS: Spiritual characters are loyal and often hold themselves to a high moral standard. In the face of criticism and doubt, they remain true to their beliefs. Their outward focus gives them a different perspective on tragedy and setbacks, allowing them to learn from negative experiences and grow in character.

NEGATIVE ASPECTS: Highly spiritual characters can become so focused on their religion that they lose touch with real life and become marginalized in modern culture. Their dedication to upholding what they believe to be right can also make them critical and inclined to disapprove of others when they fall short of the spiritual character's standard. People who are not spiritual may struggle to understand those who are, believing them to be gullible or weak.

EXAMPLE FROM HISTORY: Mother Teresa of Calcutta selflessly devoted her life and all of her resources to God and the sharing of his love to the poorest of the poor. Profoundly prayerful and with an enormous capacity to love, she served those in poverty for 69 years, with little concern for her own needs. So great was her focus on others that when she was granted the Nobel Peace Prize in 1979, she received it "for the glory of God and in the name of the poor." **Other Examples from Literature, Film, and TV:** the Jedi (*Star Wars* series), the native Aborigines in *Quigley Down Under,* Kwai Chang Caine (*Kung Fu*)

TRAITS IN SUPPORTING CHARACTERS THAT MAY CAUSE CONFLICT: controlling, cruel, evil, inflexible, selfish, self-destructive, unethical, violent

CHALLENGING SCENARIOS FOR THE SPIRITUAL CHARACTER:
Being in a situation where one's spiritual beliefs clash with social norms
Needing to defy one's spiritual beliefs in order to achieve one's goal
Having another strong trait (greed, laziness, etc.) that makes following one's beliefs difficult
Experiencing conflict when a family member or close friend opposes one's spirituality
Having a family member leave one faith for another

SPONTANEOUS

DEFINITION: enjoying what naturally occurs; given to acting on healthy impulses

CATEGORIES: identity, interactive

POSSIBLE CAUSES:
Growing up in a strict environment and wishing to be free of such structure
Growing up in a spontaneous and impulsive family
Being free-spirited
Having a short attention span
Wanting to live for the moment without considering the consequences
Being a naturally adventurous person who likes the adrenaline rush
Being extroverted; changing one's plans when an opportunity arises to hang out with others

ASSOCIATED BEHAVIORS:
Embracing change
Making do with what one has
Dropping in at a friend's house instead of calling ahead
Seeing opportunities for fun in every situation
Living by a very loose schedule or not having one at all
Being content; not stressing when the situation is less than ideal
Not understanding when others can't proceed without a plan or preparation
Disorganization
Taking impromptu trips and vacations
Deliberately altering one's routine in an effort to keep things fresh
Making plans but changing them when a better option presents itself
Tasting new foods and trying new experiences
Being a risk-taker
Not thinking things through to their logical conclusion
Living in the moment without worrying about the future
Encouraging others to make the most of life
Being unconcerned with details
Unpredictability
Frequently changing one's mind
Being highly unique; expressing one's individuality
Creativity
Choosing an untraditional job that allows for spontaneity (acting, writing, art, etc.)
Having an easygoing, go-with-the-flow attitude
Letting other people make decisions
Working toward short-term goals rather than long-term ones
Being enthusiastic
Being open-minded
Feeling stifled when life becomes too predictable
Experimenting with different hobbies, activities, and pastimes

Being silly
Staying calm and even-keeled when things don't go according to plan
Enjoying surprises
Not being ruled or overly affected by fear or worry

ASSOCIATED THOUGHTS:
I've never been down this road before. Let's see where it goes.
Time to make dinner. I wonder what we've got in the pantry.
I'm so bored. I'll just pop over to Tim and Julie's and see what they're doing.
For my next vacation, I want to just show up at the airport and pick a destination!

ASSOCIATED EMOTIONS: amusement, anticipation, curiosity, elation, excitement, impatience, surprise

POSITIVE ASPECTS: Spontaneous characters take life as it happens. Many of them feel confined by structure and rules and seek to live life moment to moment, doing whatever suits their fancy. While most people are intimidated by change, spontaneous characters see it as an opportunity to stretch themselves and broaden their horizons. Free-spirited and untraditional, these characters do things that others wouldn't do and jump quickly when swift action is required.

NEGATIVE ASPECTS: These characters don't often think things through and end up taking action without considering all the risks. Their reluctance to plan can result in them showing up unprepared (if at all), which can make them a detriment when they're expected to work as part of a group. Often enthusiastic about a new endeavor, their reliability and productivity may wane when their interest starts to drift. This tendency makes it difficult for others to trust them with important duties.

EXAMPLE FROM TV: Phoebe Buffay (*Friends*) is a free spirit who flies by the seat of her pants. Uninhibited by other people's rules, she often strays from the traditional path, such as running like a child instead of in a dignified fashion, crossing professional lines with her massage clients, and periodically acting as her alter ego, Regina Phalange. She doesn't seem to have any long-term goals and is content to live life as it comes, taking the good with the bad and making the best of every situation. **Other Examples from TV and Film:** Michael Scott (*The Office*), Adele August (*Anywhere But Here*)

TRAITS IN SUPPORTING CHARACTERS THAT MAY CAUSE CONFLICT: ambitious, analytical, cautious, controlling, disciplined, industrious, inhibited, nervous, nosy, organized, proper, responsible, sensible

CHALLENGING SCENARIOS FOR THE SPONTANEOUS CHARACTER:
Having to work a structured, predictable job with no freedom of self-expression
Lacking the time or money needed to enjoy spontaneous pursuits
Having conflicting goals (wanting to be spontaneous while also wanting to please others, etc.)
Pursuing a goal that requires strict discipline, organization, and planning
Living or working with someone who craves discipline and order

SPUNKY

DEFINITION: an inclination toward liveliness and high energy

CATEGORIES: interactive

SIMILAR ATTRIBUTES: animated, bubbly, energetic, lively, peppy, spirited

POSSIBLE CAUSES:
Being free-spirited
Having an excess of energy
Being fun-loving
Having encouraging or permissive parents

ASSOCIATED BEHAVIORS:
Enthusiasm
Wanting to make people smile
Excitability
Curiosity
Having a cheerful outlook
Speaking quickly with lots of gesturing and touching
Enjoying surprises and making new discoveries
Waking up energized and looking forward to the day
Desiring to learn by experience
Seeing the magical in the everyday
Trying new things just for fun
Enjoying new challenges
Friendliness
Interrupting out of excitability rather than from intentional rudeness
Skipping or moving with a bouncing step
Positivity
Assertiveness
Enjoying music, crowds, and events
Not complaining
Letting go of things that are beyond one's control
Committing random acts of kindness
Spontaneity
Making suggestions for fun activities: *I know...let's go to the circus!*
Making silly faces and being goofy to raise people's spirits
Being active; enjoying exercise
Not worrying about what others think
Not wasting opportunities
Being determined; never giving up
Encouraging others
Being happy

Speaking one's mind
Making decisions that are driven by emotion
Wearing colorful clothing
Having a strong sense of identity
Unpredictability
Not being afraid to show one's exuberance
Difficulty going slowly, taking one's time, or just lazing around

ASSOCIATED THOUGHTS:
I love Emma's red hair. I think I'll color mine, too!
I'm going to freak everyone out and start dancing on the table.
They say only boys can try out, but who cares? I want to play rugby, too.
Everyone's worrying too much about winning. This is supposed to be fun!

ASSOCIATED EMOTIONS: anticipation, confidence, excitement, happiness, satisfaction

POSITIVE ASPECTS: Spunky characters are bubbly and optimistic and know what makes them happy. They can bring up the mood in a room and can often be found encouraging people to try new things and chase their dreams. Leading by example, they help others to let go of their fears and be themselves.

NEGATIVE ASPECTS: Spunky characters are so energetic and unpredictable that it can be exhausting to be around them. They don't always read situations well and may not know when to try and cheer someone up or when to step back and give them space. Others may believe them to be naïve or irresponsible because they live in the moment and don't think too far ahead.

EXAMPLE FROM FILM: Camp counselors Gary and Becky in the film *Addams Family Values* are spunky and enthusiastic, spreading good cheer and encouragement among all the campers at Camp Chippewa. Their can-do attitude and refusal to be put off by rudeness or antisocial behavior make them worthy adversaries for Wednesday and Pugsley, who are determined to break out and save their uncle Fester. **Other Examples from TV:** Becky Rosen (*Supernatural*), Kenneth Parcell (*30 Rock*)

TRAITS IN SUPPORTING CHARACTERS THAT MAY CAUSE CONFLICT: abrasive, confrontational, proper, pretentious, stingy, traditional

CHALLENGING SCENARIOS FOR THE SPUNKY CHARACTER:
Working through a relationship break up
Being in a social situation where one must be composed or reserved
Working within a tight deadline
Having to follow rules that one does not agree with
Feeling torn between being oneself and making a loved one proud

STUDIOUS

DEFINITION: diligent in the pursuit of learning

CATEGORIES: achievement

SIMILAR ATTRIBUTES: academic, bookish, learned, scholarly, well-read

POSSIBLE CAUSES:
Growing up in an academic family
Having a great respect for truth and knowledge
The desire to escape an ignorant upbringing
The need to escape one's limiting environment

ASSOCIATED BEHAVIORS:
Frequenting the library
Being widely read
Reading the classics
Taking on a heavy workload of classes
Not accepting *I don't know* for an answer; consulting resources to educate oneself
Being knowledgeable about many different subjects
Having an extensive library
Feeling impatience and scorn for those who choose to remain uninformed
Engaging in debates and discussions with other scholarly types
Being open-minded
Using big words
Getting so caught up in studying that one forgets other matters
Neglecting one's appearance
Showing partiality to one's preferred academics (Aristotle, Newton, Hawking, etc.)
Enjoying homework and schoolwork
Happily sharing one's knowledge with others
Becoming frustrated when answers don't present themselves
Haughtiness
Doing more than the required coursework
Taking great pride in one's academic achievements
Being philosophical about lofty ideas and issues
Being more comfortable with books than with people
Speaking over people's heads
Having a serious manner
Taking advanced classes
Choosing one's words carefully
Protecting one's reputation as an academic
Verifying one's information before sharing
Exhibiting perfectionist tendencies with one's schoolwork
Expressing anger when one's reputation is questioned
Preferring solitude and quiet

ASSOCIATED THOUGHTS:
I need more information before I can make an informed opinion.
Who can I talk to who knows about this subject?
What can I learn from this situation?
This blog post on ancient Egypt is interesting. I'll share it with the History Club.

ASSOCIATED EMOTIONS: confidence, curiosity, determination, impatience, satisfaction, scorn, smugness

POSITIVE ASPECTS: Studious characters are valuable due to their vast knowledge and love of learning. If a problem arises and information is lacking, they know where to go to find answers. When it comes to seeking knowledge, they are hardworking, uncompromising, and driven. Studious characters know things that others don't and are eager to share what they've learned; as such, they can be very helpful advisors to your hero.

NEGATIVE ASPECTS: Studious characters are dedicated to seeking truth and learning new things—so dedicated that other things, like relationships and important issues, can take a back seat. Their vast knowledge can make them proud and haughty, leading them to scorn those who don't know as much as they do. Studious characters know a lot of things, but an education based solely on book knowledge rather than real world experience can make for an impractical person who is out of touch with reality and incapable of helping anyone.

EXAMPLE FROM TV: Lisa Simpson (*The Simpsons*) is something of a misfit in her family due to her studious nature and intellectual bent. She has a wide range of knowledge covering many important topics that reach far beyond her hometown of Springfield. As a member of MENSA, her intellectual capabilities sometimes make her a little self-righteous. But overall, she is kindhearted and seeks to help others with her knowledge. **Other Examples from Literature and Film:** Hermione Granger (*Harry Potter* series), Brian Johnson (*The Breakfast Club*)

TRAITS IN SUPPORTING CHARACTERS THAT MAY CAUSE CONFLICT: foolish, frivolous, indecisive, irrational, lazy, paranoid, scatterbrained, superstitious

CHALLENGING SCENARIOS FOR THE STUDIOUS CHARACTER:
Experiencing a situation where one's sources become unreliable
Having a tight deadline that makes extensive research impossible
Working with distractions that make study difficult
Losing access to one's resources; having to rely solely on one's current knowledge
Desiring answers in areas that are not well documented or easily understood

SUPPORTIVE

DEFINITION: providing encouragement and assistance to others

CATEGORIES: interactive, moral

SIMILAR ATTRIBUTES: encouraging, sympathetic

POSSIBLE CAUSES:
Having a helpful, generous nature
Being highly empathetic and intuitive
Having a caring nature
Having a nurturing disposition
Experiencing past help during a difficult time and knowing the necessity of support

ASSOCIATED BEHAVIORS:
Being an attentive listener
Encouraging the dreams and aspirations of others
Using positivity to boost other people's moods
Offering feedback or advice if asked
Smiling and making strong eye contact
Offering supporting gestures (touching an arm, hugging, squeezing a shoulder, etc.)
Making people feel valued and important by commenting on their best qualities
Donating time to others (charity work, doing favors, helping out, etc.)
Offering kind words to those in need: *You always make good choices, Tim.*
Integrity
Setting aside one's own plans when someone is in need
Infusing one's actions with a sense of peace
Trustworthiness
Being non-judgmental
Calling a friend just to check in
Bestowing pick-me-up gifts (bringing flowers to a sick friend, etc.)
Seeking opportunities to help (scouring work ads when a friend loses her job)
Putting the needs of a friend before one's own needs
Telling people why they're special
Avoiding criticism
Cheering for other people, no matter how small their successes
Introducing shy friends to others so they don't have to reach out on their own
Offering gentle honesty when one's opinion is requested
Speaking in a soft or encouraging tone
Focusing on what one can offer rather than how one can benefit
Trusting others
Sharing one's experiences with others to show solidarity
Forgiveness
Being sensitive to the feelings of others
Protectiveness

Showing compassion

Validating another's feelings: *Of course you're upset. Anyone in your position would be.*

Providing tough love when needed

Saying *I'm sorry* in an effort to acknowledge someone's pain

Asking what one can do to help

Handling smaller issues that crop up while a friend is incapacitated

Crying out of sympathy

Caring unconditionally

ASSOCIATED THOUGHTS:

Melinda is trying so hard. I'll bake some cookies as a special after-school snack.

Justin was snappy today. Poor guy—his boss must be on the warpath again.

If Lisanne asks for the truth, I'll tell her, but in a way that won't hurt her feelings.

Poor Mom. Three dates and three guys who didn't work out. Time for a girl's night.

ASSOCIATED EMOTIONS: anguish, determination, disappointment, disbelief, love, sympathy

POSITIVE ASPECTS: Supportive characters make good partners and friends. They are there for the people around them, listening without judgment and doing whatever is needed. Natural cheerleaders, they encourage their loved ones to reach for their dreams and succeed. Supportive characters have caring natures and are trustworthy, making it possible for friends and co-workers to be vulnerable with them.

NEGATIVE ASPECTS: Sometimes supportive characters are weighed down by their friends' collective need for a listening ear. This can make it difficult for them to remain positive. If others are always looking for help due to one calamity or another, there is no give-and-take, which can make supportive characters feel unappreciated and resentful—neither of which are good for relationships.

EXAMPLE FROM FILM: When her long-term fiancé accepts his first case as a lawyer, Mona Lisa Vito (*My Cousin Vinny*) accompanies him to the deep South. As he bumbles his way through the murder case, Lisa supports him by reading his law books and sharing important bits of legal advice, snapping pictures of the crime scene, and making sure he's suitably attired for court. She's out of her element, both in the courtroom and in Alabama, but she sticks with her man and ends up as the star witness, providing the key piece of evidence that breaks the case in their favor. **Other Examples from Film:** Lynn Sear (*The Sixth Sense*), George (*Erin Brockovich*), Scott Pritchard (*No Way Out*), Goose Bradshaw (*Top Gun*)

TRAITS IN SUPPORTING CHARACTERS THAT MAY CAUSE CONFLICT: disloyal, pessimistic, reckless, selfish, uncooperative, ungrateful

CHALLENGING SCENARIOS FOR THE SUPPORTIVE CHARACTER:

Having a friend who is always on the verge of one disaster or another

Needing the support of others who are too busy or distracted to help

Being partially responsible for a friend's hurt and having to confess

Finding oneself stuck in a situation fraught with drama and needing a way out

TALENTED

DEFINITION: having a marked (often innate) ability, usually in a creative, athletic, or artistic field

CATEGORIES: achievement, identity

SIMILAR ATTRIBUTES: accomplished, adept, expert, gifted, proficient, skilled

POSSIBLE CAUSES:
Having a natural aptitude in a given area
Being exposed to many different experiences and activities
Dedication and perseverance
A deep, passionate love of a sport, type of music, art form, etc.

ASSOCIATED BEHAVIORS:
Gravitating towards activities that emphasize one's skill
Pushing oneself to always improve
Perfectionism
Exhibiting a strong work ethic
Associating with people who can further one's career or increase one's advantage
Learning everything possible about one's area of giftedness
Trying new tricks and techniques to increase one's ability
Competitiveness
Being goal oriented
Not being satisfied with the status quo
Worrying about the motives of others: *Do they like me for me or for what I have to offer?*
Growing up too fast
Seeking out successful mentors and coaches
Comparing oneself to others
Worrying about one's image
Idolizing and studying successful icons in one's field of giftedness
Quickly outpacing other same-age athletes or artists
Having difficulty accepting a loss gracefully
Perseverance
Becoming cocky or haughty
Losing one's love for the talent; feeling like practice or training is a job
Fearing failure because one's family is invested in one's success
Making one's talent the highest priority in one's life
Setting aside anything or anyone that would be a distraction from one's talent
Becoming devastated by a loss or setback
Demanding to be treated like an accomplished talent
Taking pride in one's skill
Experiencing burnout
Feeling defined by one's talent and wanting something more

ASSOCIATED THOUGHTS:

This is what I was made to do.
I want to be the best.
If I don't make first chair, I don't know what I'll do.
No one can beat me at this.
Great, another recital. I wish Mom and Dad would let me quit piano lessons.

ASSOCIATED EMOTIONS: anticipation, anxiety, confidence, disappointment, doubt, eagerness, elation, envy, insecurity, nervousness, pride, smugness

POSITIVE ASPECTS: Talents make characters well-rounded; they add dimension. With so many skills to choose from, they provide innumerable opportunities for creating unique characters. Talents, along with their other attributes, can make our characters valuable in group and social settings by giving them something to offer, whether it be practical (cooking, sewing, carpentry) or entertaining (singing, painting, acting) in nature.

NEGATIVE ASPECTS: Talented characters can come across as smug, disdainful, and overconfident. They are often envied for their abilities and can easily become targets. Those with talents might wonder whether people are showing true interest in them for who they are or only because of their abilities. As such, it's not uncommon for very talented people to be insecure, untrusting, and lonely.

EXAMPLE FROM POP CULTURE: Questions about his personal life aside, no one can contest Michael Jackson's giftedness. His vocal abilities and natural stage presence at age five were nothing short of amazing. He was an accomplished songwriter, penning the lyrics to many of his #1 hits, and could dance in a way that few could or can to this day. Unfortunately, talented people are as flawed as everyone else, and his personal life was marred by legal difficulties, questionable medical procedures, and other strangeness. But even after his death, his undeniable talent remains. **Other Examples from Pop Culture:** Michael Jordan, Michael Phelps, Fred Astaire, Aretha Franklin, John Williams, Steven Spielberg

TRAITS IN SUPPORTING CHARACTERS THAT MAY CAUSE CONFLICT: easygoing, gullible, jealous, lazy, prejudiced, vindictive

CHALLENGING SCENARIOS FOR THE TALENTED CHARACTER:
Meeting another talented person who has no work ethic
Discovering that one's talent is an impediment to achieving one's goal
Rejecting one's talent to pursue a passion in an area where one is unskilled
Facing criticism from parents or caregivers who don't appreciate one's talent
Dealing with pushy parents trying to live out their unfulfilled dreams through one's gift

THRIFTY

DEFINITION: marked by sensible management and economy

CATEGORIES: achievement, moral

SIMILAR ATTRIBUTES: economical, frugal

POSSIBLE CAUSES:
Having economical or penny-pinching parents
Growing up in an environment of need
A desire for efficiency
A fear of going without
Fearing what the future may hold
Feeling a responsibility to be a good steward of one's resources and possessions

ASSOCIATED BEHAVIORS:
Saving money rather than spending it
Making a budget and sticking to it
Showing disdain for waste and extravagance
Keeping a close eye on one's accounts
Using coupons
Using only what one needs
Shopping at thrift stores or buying on consignment
Making purchases when things go on sale
Participating in hobbies and activities that are inexpensive
Eating all the food on one's plate at mealtimes
Saving up for large purchases rather than buying right away
Fixing broken items in an effort to get more use out of them
Living within one's means
Repurposing old items (turning a bald tire into a swing, etc.)
Wearing hand-me-downs
Adopting items that others are throwing away
Making sacrifices in one area to be able to afford things in another area
Being economical with one's resources (water, electricity, air conditioning, etc.)
Buying used items (cars, textbooks, clothing, furniture, etc.)
Being jealous of those who don't have to worry about money
Fixing things oneself instead of hiring someone else to do it
Selling outgrown items instead of throwing them out or giving them away
Holding onto old items in case they can be used later
Taking pride in the amount of money one is able to save
Obsessive bookkeeping (balancing checkbooks, keeping all receipts, etc.)
Teaching one's children to be responsible and to take care of their things
Becoming upset when something is broken out of carelessness and must be replaced
Expressing a lack of tolerance for those who live above their means

Paying down one's mortgage as quickly as possible
Asking for cash for one's birthday so it can be used to pay the bills
Being reluctant to borrow money
Looking for small ways to bring in money (doing odd jobs, babysitting, etc.)

ASSOCIATED THOUGHTS:
Have I budgeted for this?
I wonder when the vacuum cleaners will be going on sale.
I hate to throw out Jack's old tools. Maybe there's some way I can salvage them.
No wonder they're in debt; look at the money they waste!
I'm low on gas. Maybe I'll walk to the store.

ASSOCIATED EMOTIONS: agitation, contempt, determination, jealousy, pride, satisfaction, scorn, worry

POSITIVE ASPECTS: Thrifty characters aren't wasteful; they make the most of what they have. Their financial practicality may cause them to be economical in other areas, too—with their time and materials, for example. While others get into trouble because they've been irresponsible with their resources, thrifty characters usually don't have to go without and they may be in a position to help others or further themselves. Their penchant for saving rather than spending makes it easier to buckle down during difficult times.

NEGATIVE ASPECTS: Because thrifty characters are so used to saving, they often have trouble spending; this tendency can turn them miserly or stingy. Other people may view them as tightfisted because of their self-discipline and grow frustrated when they refuse to reciprocate in traditional gift-giving situations (birthdays, Christmas, etc.). On the other hand, thrifty characters may look down on others as being wasteful or extravagant. They may view money, resources, or results as being more important than people, which can make it difficult for them to relate properly to others.

EXAMPLE FROM LITERATURE: Having lived with her brother for most of her adult life, Marilla Cuthbert (*Anne of Green Gables*) finds it hard to change her thrifty ways when Anne comes along. Anne's dresses are made from serviceable materials bought on sale, and they don't contain a frill, tuck, or puff that isn't absolutely necessary. Marilla's hair is always pulled into a tidy knot with two pins stuck through it, as if to do anything more or different would be a waste of time and energy. Poor Anne has a hard time at first, being far from economical, but over time, the two rub off on each other, and Marilla's thriftiness is made less severe. **Other Examples from Film and TV:** Thomas Fairchild (*Sabrina*), Olivia Walton (*The Waltons*)

TRAITS IN SUPPORTING CHARACTERS THAT MAY CAUSE CONFLICT: childish, extravagant, foolish, generous, irresponsible, rowdy

CHALLENGING SCENARIOS FOR THE THRIFTY CHARACTER:
Being paired with an extravagant or flamboyant character
Living in a culture where thriftiness is frowned upon rather than a trait to be emulated
Facing a situation where one must masquerade as someone of wealth and extravagance
Working in a job where there is constant waste (a hotel kitchen, restaurant, etc.)

TOLERANT

DEFINITION: accepting of the beliefs, ideas, and behavior of others, even when they oppose one's own

CATEGORIES: interactive, moral

SIMILAR ATTRIBUTES: accepting, broad-minded, liberal, open-minded, permissive

POSSIBLE CAUSES:
Living in a multicultural society
Having parents who encouraged open-mindedness
Being exposed as a child to many different ideas and beliefs
Having a respect for people, freedoms, and human rights
Understanding that what makes us different also makes us unique and interesting
Being highly patient

ASSOCIATED BEHAVIORS:
Patience
Being able to compromise
Working well with others
Being willing to explain or teach others
Respecting the views of others
Forgiveness
Understanding how one's past will affect one's beliefs and behavior
Being non-judgmental
Avoiding intolerant people
Reflecting on what others have said; seeing things from their perspective
Being objective
Not seeking to sway or change someone else's mind
Being considerate of others
Friendliness
Agreeing to disagree
Accepting others for who they are
Respecting the right for all religions to exist and for people to pick their own paths
Focusing on the positives in relationships and situations
Thinking before reacting
Refusing to hold a grudge
Controlling one's emotions
Being diplomatic
Not needing to be in control of everything
Putting oneself in another's shoes
Altering one's ideas as one gains insight
Recognizing that opinions conflicting with one's own are still valid
Not becoming defensive or taking things personally

Attempting to find common ground with others
Traveling outside of one's culture and country
Being willing to listen and learn
Being at ease with oneself
Going with the flow
Being a good communicator
Having an inherent sense of fairness

ASSOCIATED THOUGHTS:
I wish kids wouldn't carve their names into trees, but I guess that's how they express themselves.
Lorna's new boyfriend isn't my type, but if he makes her happy, that's all that matters.
I wish my sister would discipline her kids, but they're hers to raise, not mine.
Alan speaks Swahili and English at home. His kids will benefit from knowing two languages.

ASSOCIATED EMOTIONS: happiness, peacefulness

POSITIVE ASPECTS: Tolerant characters are broad-minded, believing that everyone can and should make their own choices and decisions. Rather than push their agendas on others, these characters are willing to listen to alternate ideas and beliefs. In the face of disagreement, they can appreciate the fact that everyone has a right to their own viewpoints. Tolerant characters are good mediators and can be objective in situations where passions get in the way. They understand that compromise and patience are often the tools needed to move forward.

NEGATIVE ASPECTS: These characters can appear to be passionless if, in their fervor to make sure others are heard, their own voices are lost. This may cause them to miss out on opportunities to be seen as unique individuals and encourage others to assume they are too passive. Others may also take advantage of the patience and understanding of a tolerant character and run right over them in an effort to seize control or do as they want.

EXAMPLE FROM FILM: When Charles S. Howard (*Seabiscuit*) decides to get into the horse racing game, he finds himself needing a knowledgeable staff to aid him. The experts he chooses—and the horse, as well—would have been dismissed by others as unqualified, irrelevant, and incorrigible. But he is able to see past their flaws to their potential. Even when they let him down, he shows them mercy, reminding them that you shouldn't throw away a life just because it's a little messed up. **Other Examples from Film:** Herman Moore (*Remember the Titans*), Alex Goran (*Up in the Air*)

TRAITS IN SUPPORTING CHARACTERS THAT MAY CAUSE CONFLICT:
controlling, cruel, just, inflexible, manipulative, spoiled, vain

CHALLENGING SCENARIOS FOR THE TOLERANT CHARACTER:
Living within a policed state where one's freedoms are limited
Teaching a class where the students see tolerance as a weakness to exploit
Encountering someone whose beliefs or actions one cannot tolerate
Dealing with people who cite tolerance to further their agenda of doing whatever they want

TRADITIONAL

DEFINITION: acting and thinking in accordance with established beliefs and practices

CATEGORIES: identity, interactive

SIMILAR ATTRIBUTES: conservative, conventional, orthodox

POSSIBLE CAUSES:
Being brought up with a respect for one's heritage and past
Identifying strongly with one's ancestors
Taking pride in one's family history
Belonging to an "old family" with deeply embedded traditions
Having a romanticized view or interest in the past and old traditions

ASSOCIATED BEHAVIORS:
Placing old beliefs and practices above innovation and new ideas
Holding to simplistic beliefs and values that do not change
Dressing and acting in ways that adhere to an established code
Finding comfort in patterns, routines, and old customs
Doing something a certain way because that's how it's always been done
Being happy with the status quo; not seeking changes
Passing on ideas to one's children (marriage or gender roles, superstitions, etc.)
Clinging to a long-standing family career (raising cattle on a family ranch, etc.)
Participating in old-fashioned customary events (coming of age dances, etc.)
Celebrating ceremonies and holidays that remain unchanged throughout the years
Having strong ties to one's family, community, and culture
Mistrusting outsiders or people with different ideas and beliefs
Respecting the wisdom of one's elders
Openly disapproving of modern ways and technology
Being community-minded or family-focused
Wearing special clothing to denote a position of respect (priest robes, etc.)
Understanding and using the language of one's ancestors
Aligning oneself politically and religiously with the family's beliefs
Creating art or music in a traditional style (using tribal drums, sculpting wood, etc.)
Participating in long-standing rituals (baptisms, pilgrimages, parades, etc.)
Adapting to change only when forced to do so
Rarely questioning old beliefs or traditions
Inheriting responsibilities due to family ties
Retelling folklore and old stories from one's past
Living in a family home or on property that has been passed down for generations
Using the same recipes and healing remedies as one's ancestors
Using greetings and responses that have been in place for generations
Offering a customary gift (giving silver for a 25th wedding anniversary, etc.)
Singing customary songs to promote unity (national anthems, hymns, etc.)

Feeling a bond with others who share the same history, lineage, and customs
Marrying within one's culture
Attaining a position of power because of age or lineage rather than competence
Choosing relationships with others who share the same views and values
Actively seeking to preserve old ways and institutions for future generations

ASSOCIATED THOUGHTS:
Fishing is the family business. Always has been, always will be.
I can't believe Sarah didn't wear black to the funeral.
A cut onion is the best cure for a bee sting. Everyone knows that.
Of course Alexa will go to Cambridge. Everyone in our family has gone there.
I hope Rena was kidding when she said she wasn't planning on baptizing her baby.

ASSOCIATED EMOTIONS: defensiveness, determination, gratitude, nostalgia, peacefulness

POSITIVE ASPECTS: Traditional characters are comfortable in their own skin. Soothed by the past, they survive tumultuous times by drawing on the strength of those who came before them. They respect their ancestors and their wisdom and carry on traditions and values, ensuring that future generations will be familiar with their roots. People know where they stand with traditional characters—as long as they respect their beliefs and don't try to force change on them. These characters feel a great kinship with those who are like-minded and enjoy socializing with others who have the same customs and values.

NEGATIVE ASPECTS: These characters are not generally accepting of changes that depart from their traditions and structures. Unwilling to compromise if doing so goes against tradition, they can be difficult to talk to or reason with. They can sometimes harbor suspicion and bias toward those who differ in thought or behavior; as a result, they close themselves off from new ideas and innovation. This can limit their opportunities for personal growth, a better quality of life, and enlightenment.

EXAMPLE FROM FILM: In *Brave*, Queen Elinor is so loyal to the customs of her people that she tries to force her daughter to marry someone allied with their clan. This leads her rebellious daughter to bargain with a witch for a spell that unintentionally turns Elinor into a wild black bear and puts the entire kingdom in jeopardy. **Other Examples from TV and Film:** Sherman Potter (*M*A*S*H**), Michael P. Keaton (*Family Ties*), Comte Paul de Reynaud (*Chocolat*), Tevye (*Fiddler on the Roof*)

TRAITS IN SUPPORTING CHARACTERS THAT MAY CAUSE CONFLICT: devious, free-spirited, imaginative, independent, lazy, quirky, rebellious, uninhibited

CHALLENGING SCENARIOS FOR THE TRADITIONAL CHARACTER:
Being forced to adapt as society changes (city expansion, people moving in, etc.)
Experiencing a shift in government that brings about new laws and regulations
Discovering that a family member plans to break with tradition and do something unorthodox
Encountering openly judgmental people who scorn one's beliefs and customs
Caring for a sick child whose condition is unimproved by traditional remedies

TRUSTING

DEFINITION: relying or depending on others based on a belief in their strength and integrity

CATEGORIES: interactive, moral

POSSIBLE CAUSES:
Having a sheltered yet loving upbringing
Being raised by parents who were supportive and reliable, yet protective
The belief that people are inherently good
Growing up in an environment where truth and honor were core values
Not having experienced crime, greed, or other negative influences

ASSOCIATED BEHAVIORS:
Trusting the judgment of someone who has earned it
Committing to causes that one believes in
Making decisions based on positive past experiences
Asking few questions; needing no more information than what one has been given
Doing as one is told
Taking people at their word
Acting honorably and assuming that others will do the same
Asking innocent questions that reflect one's limited insight into human nature
Nodding and smiling
Agreeing or committing without hesitation
Kindness
Feeling empathy for others
Being magnanimous when things don't go as planned
Honesty
Believing in one's ability to read people and their intentions
Having a cheerful demeanor
Believing that the motives of others are good
Helpfulness and thoughtfulness
Offering information freely if one believes that it will help
Giving someone the benefit of the doubt
Letting go of things that aren't important to move forward or get along with others
Having few worries
Feeling connected to people
Altruism
Straightforwardness; not having hidden agendas
Being attuned to the emotions of others
Wanting to make the world a better place
Allowing others to make decisions
Rarely jumping to conclusions
Showing one's respect of others and their privacy
Being trustworthy (keeping someone's confidence, not engaging in gossip, etc.)

Being willing to try something new
Not being brought down by the occasional error in judgment
Pursuing strong relationships where one can safely be vulnerable
Idealism
Forgiveness
Not trying to manipulate others
Learning from one's mistakes while maintaining a belief in the goodness of others

ASSOCIATED THOUGHTS:
Dee is good about returning books. Maybe she forgot about the one she borrowed.
I'm so grateful that Terry's friend is handling the renovation. He'll do a good job.
Dean's a good driver, so I don't mind loaning him my car for the weekend.
Too bad Eric's working late again. Maybe we can get together next month instead.

ASSOCIATED EMOTIONS: gratitude, happiness, peacefulness, relief

POSITIVE ASPECTS: Trusting characters are positive forces who believe that most people will prove themselves trustworthy. They open themselves up and act with honesty and integrity, expecting others to do the same. Trusting characters have strong, deep relationships that are built on mutual respect. Even if trust is broken, they can move on without it dampening their belief that people in general are good at heart and will do the right thing if given the chance.

NEGATIVE ASPECTS: These characters are transparent, even when they shouldn't be. Some of the people they encounter will not have their best interests at heart, stealing their time, money, and ability to trust. In extreme cases, they may become jaded toward others and question the motivation and intentions of all people.

EXAMPLE FROM FILM: Simon Bishop (*As Good as it Gets*) is a friendly, kindhearted person who wants to believe the best of people. When his dog briefly disappears, he questions his neighbor and believes his claimed innocence, although it's later revealed that the neighbor tossed his dog down the garbage chute. He also trusts his agent to hire a legitimate model for Simon's latest art project. When the model turns out to be a homeless boy who robs and nearly beats Simon to death, he suffers a period of self-doubt and depression. But he doesn't let it get him down for long. By the end of the story, Simon is back to his optimistic self, befriending his crusty neighbor and regaining the joy and inspiration he had briefly lost. **Other Examples from Literature and Film:** Cindy Lou Who (*How the Grinch Stole Christmas*), King Arthur (*The Once and Future King*), Forrest Gump (*Forrest Gump*), Buddy the Elf (*Elf*)

TRAITS IN SUPPORTING CHARACTERS THAT MAY CAUSE CONFLICT: cowardly, devious, disloyal, dishonest, jaded, manipulative, pessimistic, suspicious

CHALLENGING SCENARIOS FOR THE TRUSTING CHARACTER:
Entering into a relationship with someone who admits to cheating in the past
Experiencing fallout for trusting the wrong person
Trying to earn the trust of someone who is naturally suspicious
Being criticized by pessimistic people for being "too trusting"

UNINHIBITED

DEFINITION: not restricted or restrained by societal or psychological norms

CATEGORIES: identity, interactive

SIMILAR ATTRIBUTES: free, liberated, unrestrained

POSSIBLE CAUSES:
Being content with oneself
Being free-spirited
A history of not fitting in
Self-confidence
Being hurt by society or authorities in the past and choosing to defy them in the present

ASSOCIATED BEHAVIORS:
Flouting laws and rules
Going against the flow
Using a loud voice
Asking questions of those in authority
Wanting to know the reasoning behind rules or judgments
Not being a blind follower
Resisting peer or parental pressure (picking one's own path, opting not to have kids, etc.)
Freely expressing one's feelings in front of others
Laughing boisterously
Using big motions
Not being easily embarrassed
Walking with the head held high and a bounce in one's step
Ignoring criticism and scorn
Wearing unconventional clothing and hairstyles
Not being overly concerned with what others think
Talking freely about subjects that some consider taboo (sex, drug use, religion, etc.)
Having a carefree, easygoing attitude
Associating with those who live on the edge of society
Changing one's interests, one's look, and one's path to find the right fit
Participating in activities that one enjoys but may not be good at
Supporting others in loud, public ways (singing karaoke with a friend to afraid to go up alone)
Happily doing things alone if no one else will join in
Encouraging others to be free and unrestrained
Participating in activities that are frowned upon (skinny dipping, etc.)
Freely speaking one's mind
Making fun of those who are uptight or reserved
Deliberately doing things to embarrass others
Avoiding toxic or needy relationships
Being willing to move, travel, and try new things

Intentionally pushing the boundary of what's acceptable
Taking pride in one's uniqueness
Confidence
Having artistic or creative hobbies
Being overtly sexual or flirtatious
Adventurousness and a willingness to explore everything

ASSOCIATED THOUGHTS:
Oh, it's a stupid rule anyway.
People probably won't approve, but I don't care.
I don't understand why people get so uncomfortable talking about sex.
Why isn't anyone dancing? I'll get things started.
I like Bill, and he's attracted to me. I'm going to plant one on him to see if sparks fly.

ASSOCIATED EMOTIONS: amusement, confidence, happiness, indifference, pride

POSITIVE ASPECTS: Uninhibited characters are unconcerned with social norms and the opinions of others; therefore they are free to be themselves. The strictures that keep others from expressing themselves in public have no hold on someone with an uninhibited nature. The self-confidence of these characters is appealing and admirable, especially to those who wish they could let go of their inhibitions.

NEGATIVE ASPECTS: Uninhibited characters can take their individuality so far that they don't consider the feelings and sensitivities of others and can make them uncomfortable. Their disdain for the rules can cause trouble for them and their more responsible friends. Because they value individuality and freedom, these characters may express scorn for those who are more reserved, labeling them as uptight and in need of "loosening up". Others may make snap judgments about an uninhibited person and assume wrong things about them.

EXAMPLE FROM FILM: As a prostitute, it makes sense that Vivian Ward (*Pretty Woman*) is unconcerned with conforming to society's norms, but it's as much her personality as her profession that defines her as uninhibited. She sits on tables instead of chairs and eats pancakes with her fingers. At a polo match, she hoots and hollers and doesn't mind that she's the only one doing it. Walking down Rodeo Drive in her thigh boots and safety-pinned shirt, she's completely at ease despite the looks she gets. While capable of getting her feelings hurt, she mostly ignores the haters and is content to be herself. **Other Examples from Film and Pop Culture:** Rod Tidwell (*Jerry Maguire*), Dennis Rodman, Marilyn Manson

TRAITS IN SUPPORTING CHARACTERS THAT MAY CAUSE CONFLICT: devious, fussy, haughty, humorless, inhibited, introverted, nervous, proper, worrywart

CHALLENGING SCENARIOS FOR THE UNINHIBITED CHARACTER:
Being thrust into an atmosphere of structure and predictability
Losing one's freedoms
Suddenly becoming aware of and concerned with what others think
Experiencing drastic, unforeseen consequences for one's uninhibited behavior
Forced responsibility (having to raise a sister's kids when their mother dies, etc.)

UNSELFISH

DEFINITION: thinking of others and acting on their behalf rather than being concerned with oneself

CATEGORIES: interactive, moral

SIMILAR ATTRIBUTES: selfless

POSSIBLE CAUSES:
Having an altruistic nature
A religious upbringing that emphasized serving others
The belief that what goes around comes around
Appreciating the joy that comes from helping others
The belief that every person's value is equal to one's own
Having a strong sense of right and wrong
Gratitude for the blessings one has received

ASSOCIATED BEHAVIORS:
Observing others to learn what they want
Letting others make decisions (where to dine, where to go on vacation, etc.)
Letting others go first (in the grocery line, at stop signs, etc.)
Buying thoughtful gifts to make someone happy
Willingness to share what one has
Instinctively knowing what someone needs
Interpreting the meaning behind people's words
Giving sacrificially of one's resources to help someone else
Making donations to charities
Empathy
Attentive listening
Speaking thoughtfully, so as not to hurt other people's feelings
Humility
Thinking of others more than oneself
Looking for ways to help others
Flexibility; being willing to change one's plans if someone needs help
Patience
Sharing emotions with others (crying, laughing, etc.)
Being more concerned about the person in need than with what others may think
Forgiving others
Helping others when there is no benefit for oneself
Giving something up to help another overcome a weakness (dieting with a friend, etc.)
Gently telling someone the truth, even if it won't make them happy
Having a great capacity to love others
Not judging others
Making oneself emotionally available to others

Inconveniencing oneself in order to help someone
Thinking positively, particularly about people
Befriending the unpopular or rejected

ASSOCIATED THOUGHTS:
My plans aren't as important as helping Joan today.
The TV volume doesn't sound loud to me, but it bothers Will so I'll turn it down.
I'm glad Sean feels comfortable calling any time. He knows I'd do anything for him.
Oh boy, Gini looks upset. I'll put on the coffee and finish this crossword later.

ASSOCIATED EMOTIONS: anticipation, eagerness, gratitude, happiness, love, peacefulness, satisfaction, sympathy

POSITIVE ASPECTS: Unselfish characters put others before themselves. They are adept at reading people and interpreting their words to determine what they really want or need. These characters aren't tied to material items and often see their possessions as resources to be shared with others. Those who are truly unselfish don't seek to benefit themselves but act out of a desire to make others happy and help them achieve their goals.

NEGATIVE ASPECTS: Unselfish characters run the risk of having their own needs neglected and their resources depleted because they are so focused on giving. Their desire to help can make them an easy mark for people who would take advantage of their kindness; it is also easy for them to land in financial trouble because they are so willing to use their resources to benefit others. The truly selfless character is rare; oftentimes, seemingly unselfish people will serve others with an ulterior motive of gaining friendships, approval, or kindness in return.

EXAMPLE FROM FILM: Mulan (Disney's *Mulan*) is devoted to her family and worries about disappointing both them and her ancestors. Knowing that she lacks the grace and polish to win a suitable marriage match, she tries her best anyway, since it's what her family and culture expect. When her elderly, disabled father is drafted into the Chinese army, she gives up her freedom and even her identity to save him, disguising herself as a boy to take his place. On her own for the first time and ill-equipped to fight, she risks everything so that he can live. **Other Examples from Literature:** Melanie Wilkes (*Gone with the Wind*), Beth March (*Little Women*)

TRAITS IN SUPPORTING CHARACTERS THAT MAY CAUSE CONFLICT:
dishonest, flaky, impatient, manipulative, pushy, spoiled, stingy

CHALLENGING SCENARIOS FOR THE UNSELFISH CHARACTER:
Being persecuted or in some way punished for acting unselfishly
Being surrounded by takers and negative thinkers
Having one's unselfish motives questioned

WHIMSICAL

DEFINITION: fancifully spontaneous; giving in to humorous or imaginative impulsiveness

CATEGORIES: identity, interactive

SIMILAR ATTRIBUTES: fanciful, free-spirited, quaint

POSSIBLE CAUSES:
Growing up in an artistic or creative environment
Having parents who encouraged exploration and expression over structure and rules
Being a free spirit
Being highly playful and fun-loving
Having a strong sense of curiosity

ASSOCIATED BEHAVIORS:
Embracing a unique and often comical outlook
Feeling unrestrained by rules or society
Unpredictability
Happiness
Seeking out new and different experiences
Encouraging others to explore their sense of fun
Having a strong sense of humor
Spontaneity
Flamboyancy
Seeing beauty in things most others do not
Attempting to shake things up
Breaking minor rules or going against the norm for innocent fun
Giving over to laughter
Asking unusual questions: *Are leprechauns related to gnomes, do you think?*
Voicing funny thoughts to encourage laughter
Being strongly imaginative
Daydreaming about fantastical or impossible things
Showing cleverness
Being in tune with one's moods and emotions
Having a fun and vibrant attitude
Silliness
Embracing creativity
Making random choices to see what will happen
Kidding around with friends
Enjoying make-believe and storytelling
Thinking in a nonlinear fashion
Embracing one's inner child
Joining fantasy role-playing groups online or in real life
Enjoying surprises and unexpected results

Having an unusual perspective
A desire to dress up and role-play
Appreciating the unusual
Taking an interest in strange or obscure music and art
Expressing oneself in odd or unusual ways
Making faces to express one's emotions
Impulsiveness
Not caring or worrying about what others think
Getting a crazy or unusual idea and running with it

ASSOCIATED THOUGHTS:
That hill is huge! I should roll down it to see how dizzy I get.
So, what happens if a genie rubs a magic lamp? Does he get three wishes too?
Janie's mom looks like a unicorn. You know, without the horn. Hey, I should tell her that!
I think I'll wear only green from now on and see how long it takes people to notice.

ASSOCIATED EMOTIONS: amazement, anticipation, curiosity, desire, happiness, satisfaction

POSITIVE ASPECTS: Whimsical characters always make things interesting. Their offbeat and open-minded way of looking at life can inspire others to let go, laugh, and embrace their inner child. Having a strong sense of humor and enjoying both fantasy and fun, whimsical characters embrace imagination and can liven up stuffy, serious moments with good-natured levity.

NEGATIVE ASPECTS: These characters' lack of seriousness can make them appear irresponsible, landing them in trouble with others. While they are chasing fun, they might not be there for the people who need them, weakening those relationships. Some may grow frustrated at how fanciful and spontaneous these characters are when seriousness and consistency might be the better choice.

EXAMPLE FROM FILM: Fraulein Maria (*The Sound of Music*) is a grown woman and nun initiate, but she barely fits the mold. She repurposes ugly curtains into play clothes, dances on hilltops, and makes up songs while biking through Switzerland. It's simply in her nature to be lighthearted and spontaneous, which serves her well, first as a governess and later as the mother of seven. **Other Examples from Literature:** Lucy Pevensie (*The Lion, the Witch, and the Wardrobe*), Anne Shirley (*Anne of Green Gables*)

TRAITS IN SUPPORTING CHARACTERS THAT MAY CAUSE CONFLICT:
analytical, cautious, controlling, disciplined, fussy, humorless

CHALLENGING SCENARIOS FOR THE WHIMSICAL CHARACTER:
Experiencing a loss or defeat, especially when one has worked hard to achieve one's goal
Living in a somber environment (a convent or a Catholic boarding school, etc.)
Having to make small talk with someone who is stuffy and serious
Being assigned a task that requires following guidelines and focused thinking
Wanting to be seen as a professional but struggling with the regimented nature of it

WHOLESOME

DEFINITION: being of high moral fiber; having a good influence on others

CATEGORIES: identity, interactive, moral

SIMILAR ATTRIBUTES: chaste, pure, unblemished, virtuous

POSSIBLE CAUSES:
Having been sheltered from worldly things
A desire to remain pure or innocent
Being naturally naïve; not being influenced by things that negatively impact others
A religious upbringing

ASSOCIATED BEHAVIORS:
Dressing modestly
Having a lighthearted attitude
Abstaining from activities that don't seem right (drinking, swearing, etc.)
Being sheltered from or naïve about unwholesome activities
Saving oneself for marriage
Making wise decisions
Having strong willpower and being able to resist temptations
Paying attention to the important things and avoiding distractions
Not understanding people who are wicked or disobedient
Being friendly, kind, and outgoing
Feeling righteous about the choices one makes
Valuing one's innocence and purity
Being monogamous
Accepting people for who they are, without judgment
Being family-oriented
Passively influencing peers (through one's example) to make better choices
Overtly encouraging friends to do the right thing
Exhibiting good manners
Smiling and laughing
Being optimistic
Seeing the good in people
Wanting to help others
Having high standards and specific expectations for a love match
Believing in gender roles and that a man's duty is to protect a woman
Choosing a higher calling that requires lifelong service and purity (e.g. becoming a nun)
A desire to pass on one's moral beliefs to others
Offering counseling to those who have lost their way
Seeing things simply; not complicating matters
Showing respect for authority
Following the rules

Being responsible
Trusting others
Acting in an ethical manner
Exhibiting self-control and not overindulging
Taking a long-term approach to making decisions; keeping the consequences in mind
Being subservient; embracing a wholesome lifestyle out of a desire to please

ASSOCIATED THOUGHTS:
Is this a good decision?
What will other people think?
If Wanda does this, it will be bad for her. I should stop her.
Nancy's friends are walking a dark path. I don't want her to be mixed up with them.

ASSOCIATED EMOTIONS: confidence, curiosity, happiness, indifference, love, satisfaction, smugness, uncertainty, worry

POSITIVE ASPECTS: Wholesome characters aren't impulsive; they think carefully about their decisions and always try to do the right thing. Their actions often have a positive influence on others, encouraging peers to make better choices. Because their decisions are based on ethics, wholesome characters typically possess other admirable qualities like kindness, generosity, honesty, and respectfulness.

NEGATIVE ASPECTS: While parents, teachers, and other authority figures greatly admire wholesomeness as a quality trait, peers of these characters may not be so welcoming. Some can be threatened by upright people, assuming them to be self-righteous or fake, which may prompt the cynics to try and prove that these characters aren't as virtuous as everyone thinks. Scrutiny like this can create pressure for the wholesome character to always make the right choices and never fall from grace. This can lead to hidden vices and shame when they don't feel they can open up and be themselves in public.

EXAMPLE FROM POP CULTURE: Smack in the middle of the Great Depression, America found a refreshing escape in the singing, dancing, ringleted person of Shirley Temple. Her films, with their wholesome and cherubic characters, were written to inspire hope and optimism in a people living in dark times, and she quickly became America's sweetheart. **Other Examples from TV:** John Boy Walton (*The Waltons*), the Cleaver family (*Leave it to Beaver*), Mr. Rogers (*Mr. Rogers' Neighborhood*)

TRAITS IN SUPPORTING CHARACTERS THAT MAY CAUSE CONFLICT: addictive, devious, evil, impulsive, morbid, promiscuous, pushy, rebellious, sleazy, uninhibited

CHALLENGING SCENARIOS FOR THE WHOLESOME CHARACTER:
Living in a society where wholesome decisions are chastised rather than lauded
Being tempted to indulge in an unwholesome activity
Becoming confused over what is wholesome and what isn't
Having a negative impact on one's peers despite one's wholesome behavior
Having others seek to ruin one's reputation in any manner they can

WISE

DEFINITION: having deep understanding and sound judgment resulting from insight, time, or experience

CATEGORIES: achievement

SIMILAR ATTRIBUTES: knowledgeable, sage

POSSIBLE CAUSES:
Intelligence
Having a deep understanding of a specific topic
Having experienced a plethora of situations and experiences
Being well-read and contemplative
Dedicating oneself to a life-long study of a topic, people, or environment (Jane Goodall, etc.)

ASSOCIATED BEHAVIORS:
Watching and listening before speaking
Only speaking when one has something to add to the conversation
Seeing the world for how it really is
Being a good judge of character
Making time for meditation
Viewing mistakes as learning opportunities
Having an open heart; showing compassion for others
Abiding by one's unwavering moral standards
Humility
Forming strong beliefs and opinions over the course of many years
Thinking deeply before committing to a path or action
Knowing oneself intimately
Empathizing with others
Pursuing self-growth
Wanting to learn
Embracing good habits that promote health and happiness
Making balanced decisions
Seeing the bigger picture
Sharing one's knowledge with others
Constantly evaluating oneself
Patience with others, especially the young and inexperienced
Being teachable
Being widely read
Having a sense of humor
Showing kindness to others
Asking questions and seeking out answers
Taking advantage of opportunities to learn or experience new things
Respecting the world and the creatures in it
Open-mindedness

Maturity

Patience

Being able to set aside one's emotions to be objective

Seeing past what's outside (persona) to what is inside (the individual)

Understanding cause and effect

Desiring change and working toward bringing it about

Accepting oneself and one's flawed nature

ASSOCIATED THOUGHTS:

Jason's mom shouldn't worry. In time, he'll find his direction.

All this trouble could be avoided if people just took a deep breath before acting.

Some call me master, but I am only a lifelong student.

If I tell Greg what to do, he'll never learn to think for himself.

ASSOCIATED EMOTIONS: amazement, amusement, anguish, anticipation, curiosity, gratitude, happiness, hopefulness, peacefulness, satisfaction

POSITIVE ASPECTS: Wise characters have the benefit of age and experience. Open-minded and mature, they are life-long learners who look for opportunities to share what they know in a way that benefits others. Those with wisdom see the big picture and have great passion for the people around them and the world they live in. As such, people treat them with respect and reverence and often show appreciation for their unique, wide-angle view.

NEGATIVE ASPECTS: Wise characters are extremely patient and are not usually in a rush for things to happen. They may have the attitude that everything will work out as it is meant to, which can be frustrating or seem trite to others. However, sometimes acting quickly or proactively is necessary; opportunities to create change and lessen suffering may be missed if immediate action is sacrificed in favor of caution and reflection.

EXAMPLE FROM LITERATURE: Gandalf (*The Lord of the Rings* trilogy) has the benefit of age and experience, both of which have made him incredibly wise. As such, he offers guidance to the people of Middle Earth and is able to help them fight off the armies of Mordor. When he himself needs help, he does not hesitate to consult those who have greater knowledge, for Gandalf understands that the pursuit of wisdom is never-ending. **Other Examples from Film and Literature:** Ramírez (*Highlander*), Obi-Wan Kenobi (*Star Wars* series), Albus Dumbledore (*Harry Potter* series)

TRAITS IN SUPPORTING CHARACTERS THAT MAY CAUSE CONFLICT: controlling, cruel, disrespectful, gullible, impatient, paranoid, reckless, self-destructive, suspicious

CHALLENGING SCENARIOS FOR THE WISE CHARACTER:

Dealing with headstrong youth who have no respect for age, knowledge, or authority

Foreseeing something terrible in the future and being powerless to stop it from happening

Offering advice and counsel and being ignored

Discovering that one's mentors have not always had the best intentions

Offering advice and having it used for harm instead of for good

WITTY

DEFINITION: having intellectual capacity marked by clever humor

CATEGORIES: identity, interactive

SIMILAR ATTRIBUTES: droll

POSSIBLE CAUSES:
Having a strong sense of humor or dry observation that is combined with quick thought
Growing up in a home where intellectual or thoughtful humor was encouraged
A desire for acceptance or admiration
Insecurity
A desire for control; using one's intellectual prowess to put others in their place
A nervous response to being in an uncomfortable situation

ASSOCIATED BEHAVIORS:
Making jokes based on high intellect
Avoiding and disdaining the "easy laugh" (potty humor, slapstick comedy, etc.)
Always having the last word
Quick thinking
Naturally seeing the humorous side of things
Reading into what people say; naturally spotting double meanings
Having keen perception of people, particularly noting their flaws and ironies
Translating one's knowledge into comedic observations
Using one's wit to chastise or reprimand others
Passive-aggressive behavior
Taking in what others say
Using comparisons to be humorous
Indulging in exaggeration
Quoting movies, books, and pop culture in a humorous way
Speaking in a carefree tone, as if wittiness comes naturally without a lot of work
Knowing one's context; tailoring quips to one's audience
Likability
Competitiveness; engaging in a battle of wits with other witty people
Being able to read one's audience
Saying things that are unexpected
Thinking creatively
Confidence
Laughing often
Flirtatious behavior
Delivering jokes with a deadpan expression or minimal movements
Playing with words; showing an interest in vocabulary
Admiring other quick wits
Studying the masters
Making observations that are ironic and humorous that others never considered

ASSOCIATED THOUGHTS:
How can I say that in a funny way?
That went over well. I'll use that again.
I love that Taylor can laugh at himself and doesn't take things too seriously.

ASSOCIATED EMOTIONS: amusement, confidence, happiness, pride

POSITIVE ASPECTS: Witty characters make observations that can turn mundane situations or events into hilarity. These characters are often the first to make a joke and can elevate an existing quip by adding another layer of observation, carrying the humor farther. Quick-thinking, witty folks deliver one-liners which are both clever and eye-opening, allowing others to experience a situation's meaning at a different level, often through the lens of irony. Because most people like to laugh, witty characters are often well-liked by others.

NEGATIVE ASPECTS: Characters with a quick wit can sometimes let their mouths get ahead of their good sense, offering humor when it isn't wanted or needed or joking in a way that makes people uncomfortable. Some characters who are enthralled with their own wittiness can veer into caustic wit and sarcasm, which can hurt or humiliate others. There is also the chance that an observation about a group or belief could unknowingly touch on a sensitive subject and offend listeners. In addition, people can be turned off by a witty character's constant one-upmanship.

EXAMPLE FROM TV: In the television show *M*A*S*H*, Hawkeye Pierce has a comeback for everything. Intelligent, quick-witted, and a born smart aleck, he uses humor both as a means of making his unwilling presence at the Korean conflict bearable, and as a release for his cynicism and resentment. While his constant jokes grate on some members of the unit, many of his fellow soldiers and medical practitioners find it a welcome relief. **Other Examples from Film and TV:** Porthos (*The Three Musketeers*), Niles Crane (*Frasier*)

TRAITS IN SUPPORTING CHARACTERS THAT MAY CAUSE CONFLICT: devout, eccentric, humorless, insecure, introverted, proper, volatile

CHALLENGING SCENARIOS FOR THE WITTY CHARACTER:
Working in a serious environment where humor isn't appreciated
Facing a foreign audience or culture that doesn't get one's humor
A debilitation that limits one's ability to be witty (mental decline, fatigue, etc.)
Feeing burned out or blocked, and no longer achieving the big laughs

APPENDIX A

CHARACTER PROFILE QUESTIONNAIRE

Want to get to know your character better? Reflect on the questions below, which are designed to get you thinking about who your character is, what he shares about himself, what he hides, what motivates him, and what he really needs. Answer the questions that will best help you build your character, making him dynamic, memorable, and unique!

BASIC INFORMATION:

What is the character's age, sex, ethnicity? Describe his physical appearance (hair and eye color; body build; skin tone; height and weight; unique features such as glasses, scars, dimples, etc.). How does he dress? What about his clothing speaks to the kind of person he is? What one thing does he carry around with him? What item can he not live without and why?

VOICE:

Does the character speak quickly or slowly? Does he overuse any verbal tics, like *um, uh,* or *ah*? Are his sentences short and choppy or does he ramble on? How would you describe the tone? Quality? Volume? Is it pitched high or low? How does emotion come through in his voice when he is angry or nervous or happy? How does his level of education or world experience dictate his speech? If you walked blindfolded into a room where your character's voice was one of many, which element would allow you to identify your hero's from the rest? Is there something about the voice that others find particularly appealing or annoying?

EDUCATION AND FINANCES:

How educated is the character? Is he naturally intelligent, clever, witty, or perceptive? Is he book smart, self-taught, or widely experienced in a specific area? Has he earned any accolades or recognition for his knowledge? Does his education translate to a job where he barely scrapes by, or does it allow him to live a comfortable lifestyle? Does he have more than one job? Is his work personally satisfying or only a means to an end?

SPECIAL SKILLS AND TALENTS:

What skills does your character rely on day-to-day? Does he have a knack for computers, a green thumb, or the ability to inherently see how mechanical items work? What special talents does he have? Name one unique talent the character has that no one knows about, and one talent that he openly shares. Are any of his talents or skills a source of pride or embarrassment? Which and why?

FAMILY:

What are the character's family dynamics? Is he single or married? Does he have kids? If he's a child or teen, what are his parents and siblings like? Does he have close or distant relationships with them? What family values and beliefs does he hold dear? What parental "fumblings" did he experience firsthand growing up that he refuses to repeat with his own family? What parental teachings helped him become a better person?

INTERESTS:

What interests and hobbies does he have? Do other people know about these hobbies, or does he keep them to himself? If there was one thing the character could do without anyone knowing, what would it be? Does he like to do these things with others, or alone? Why is that? What activity is the character's "stress outlet"? What activities does he find entertaining? In what way does he show his creative side? What interest or hobby would he like to pursue but doesn't feel qualified to do so?

PEOPLE AND COMMUNITY:

How close is your character to the people around him? Does he know his neighbors, interact with them at the mailbox, join them for barbecues or does he not even know their names? Does he volunteer? If there was a fire or flood or disaster that affected his community, would he stay to help others or get out? If he needed help, would he ask for it, and if so, who would he ask?

MORALS AND ETHICS:

Does your character see things in black and white or shades of gray? Does he champion any causes? What issues does he feel strongly about? How does he react when those beliefs are challenged? Why are these issues so important to him? Was there a specific person or event who strongly influenced him to believe the way he does about his important issues? Which of his beliefs, opinions, or ideals does he hide from others, and why? Which moral beliefs will he hold to, no matter what?

IDENTITY VS. PERSONA:

What five words would your character use to describe himself? What five words would his best friend use? What about a co-worker, an acquaintance, and a stranger? How does the character's view of himself differ from the ways others see him? Of all the words used to describe your character, which ones are true, and which ones are not? Are other people making assumptions about your character based on how he looks and acts? Does the character intend for this to happen, or is he unaware that he is sending out these messages about himself? What is one thing that surprises him about how others view him? Does this make him upset or happy?

RELATIONSHIPS:

Who is closest to your character and why? Who would your character like to be closer to? Is he the type of person to make the first move and greet others, or does he wait for someone else to do it? Is he slow to trust, or does he open up quickly because he has a good sense about people? What type of person is he attracted to? Is he satisfied with his current relationships, or is there something he feels is lacking? What person is your character vulnerable with, or is there anyone he can show his sensitive side to? Who does your character avoid and why? What type of person turns him off? If someone from his past were to reappear in his life, who would he most want it to be and why? Who would he least want it to be?

SECRETS:

What is your character's biggest secret and who would he least like to discover it? Why is this secret so important? Does he think about it often or hardly at all? Is the secret a source of pain, humiliation, joy, or something in between? Is he a secret keeper for anyone else? What secrets does he know about the people around him that he doesn't share? Do they know he is privy to their secrets, or did they confide in him in the first place? Do people trust him with their private thoughts or is he incapable of keeping information to himself? If he can't keep a secret, why does he end up sharing the information with others?

FEARS:

What is your character afraid of that is quirky or surprising, considering the type of person he is? Does this fear cause embarrassment, or is it completely irrational? Is it a fear he is trying to overcome? Did a past event cause this fear? Regarding deeper fears—ones that he does not want to admit to—which affects him the most? How does he hide this fear from others? Does he fake it, pretending that it's not a problem for him? What persona does he show the world to keep people at a distance so they won't discover his fear?

BACKSTORY AND WOUND:

Thinking about that deeper fear, the one the character does not want to reflect on or admit to...what event in his past caused the very thing he fears to come to pass? How did this event send his life on a new path? As a result, who or what did he discard from his life, what did he lose, and what joy did he give up? How does this fear make the character feel unworthy and flawed? How can this wound be introduced into the character's present story? How can you make the character face a similar situation and wound again, yet this time overcome it?

WANTS, NEEDS, AND DESIRES:

What surface wants does your character have at the start of the story—to get a new job, to be recognized for his hard work, to pull off a surprise party for his wife? What does he think will make him happy? Then, going deeper: what is lacking in the character's life? What needs are not being met? What are his hopes and dreams, the very things he dare not wish for, the things that seem too big or too hard to pursue? If he could wave a magic wand and make one thing appear, what would he pick for himself? What would build his self-esteem, make him feel whole, and allow him to face any hardship or challenge life could throw his way? What are his life goals?

FLAW-CENTRIC:

Thinking on the character's wants and needs and his biggest wish and desire: what flaws would be detrimental to achieving his goal? What flaws mask his insecurities about himself, yet also make it hard for him to reach his goal? What flaws get in the way of his relationships, causing friction? What flaws reinforce the character's belief that he doesn't need to change, or that change is too hard, so why bother? What flaws surface when he suffers a failure or setback or he becomes stressed or upset?

ATTRIBUTE-CENTRIC:

Again, thinking on your character's deepest need and the goal that will make him feel complete, confident, and happy: what strengths will help him achieve success? What strengths must he develop in order to overcome his flaws? Which strength seems like a weakness—something undesirable—but turns out to be the key to achieving his goal?

STRESS AND PRESSURE:

How does your character handle challenges? Does he embrace them, or avoid them? If he's under pressure, does he rise to the moment or falter, making mistakes and showing poor judgment? Does emotional strain cause him to lash out or show anger and frustration? Does he snap when stressed, or does he take a deep breath and do what needs to be done? What is your character's breaking point? What failures is he sensitive to? What kind of ticking clock scenario might make him emotionally reactive?

EMOTIONAL RANGE:

How expressive is your character? Does he use big gestures to show his feelings, or does he show them through small shifts in body language and action? Is your character outwardly emotional, or does he hide what he feels? If he's stoic, how does emotion leak out despite his best efforts? What would it take for your character to show his anger? His desire? Happiness or anxiety? When he lies or is upset, does a specific tic give his emotions away?

PUT IT ALL TOGETHER:

Having deep, intimate knowledge of your hero is what leads to successful character creation. Brainstorming the answers to some of these questions should help you get a better handle on your character so he can behave according to who he is. Not everything you discover should end up in the story, but knowing for yourself gives you the confidence to write the character in a compelling and realistic way.

APPENDIX B

CHARACTER ATTRIBUTE TARGET TOOL

T hink of the your character's attributes as a target made of concentric circles. At his heart lies **morality**, the foundation that determines his sense of right and wrong and determines the rest of his attributes. **Achievement-focused** traits aid the character in reaching professional and personal goals. **Interactive** attributes help with communication, encouraging meaningful connections with other people and the world. **Identity** attributes contribute to self-discovery and satisfy his need for creative and personal expression. Choosing attributes from all four areas will greatly contribute to creating a complex and relatable hero.

CHARACTER ATTRIBUTE TARGET TOOL

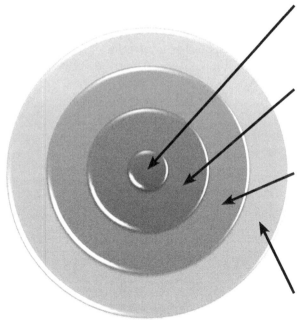

MORAL: positive traits are tied to the character's moral center. Right and wrong, ethics and deeply embedded beliefs determine attributes.

ACHIEVEMENT: attributes align with morals, but are goal-focused. Traits assist the character in achieving important life milestones.

INTERACTIVE: strengths form through interaction with people and the environment. These traits help the character work with others, handle conflict, convey ideas and forge healthy relationships.

IDENTITY: attributes are tied to a personal sense of identity, leading to satisfaction and contentment with who one is. Traits emerge to allow the character to explore and better understand what makes them unique.

We've created an example below of how this works by profiling the attributes of Aragorn from *The Lord of the Rings*. Once you're ready to try this tool on your own character, visit Writers Helping Writers at http://writershelpingwriters.net/writing-tools for a printable blank target.

CHARACTER ATTRIBUTE TARGET TOOL EXAMPLE

Character: Aragorn (*The Lord of the Rings*)

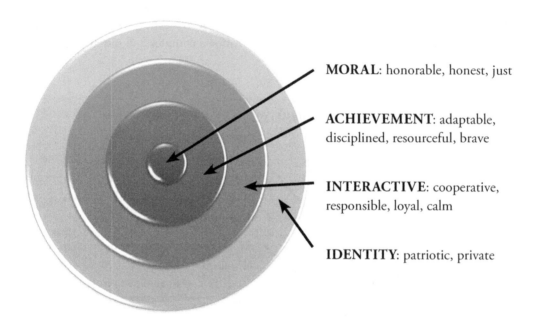

MORAL: honorable, honest, just

ACHIEVEMENT: adaptable, disciplined, resourceful, brave

INTERACTIVE: cooperative, responsible, loyal, calm

IDENTITY: patriotic, private

APPENDIX C

CATEGORY BREAKDOWN

I f your goal is to form a well-rounded character, start by giving him attributes from different categories to help create a balanced personality. Below is a breakdown of the main traits in this thesaurus and which categories each falls under.

Keep in mind that attributes can belong to more than one group. **Enthusiasm**, for example, describes how a character relates to his environment and those around him, but it also factors into how he expresses himself. As such, it can be either an *interactive* or an *identity* attribute. The function of a trait can also vary based on motivation. If a character is **obedient** because he wants to further his career, it's an *achievement-based* trait. But if he consistently complies because he believes it to be the right thing to do, then it becomes a *moral attribute*. For these reasons, the category groupings below are simply a starting point for exploring each character's positive traits and the unique reasons behind them.

ACHIEVEMENT

Adaptable
Adventurous
Alert
Ambitious
Analytical
Bold
Cautious
Centered
Charming
Confident
Cooperative
Courageous
Creative
Curious
Decisive
Disciplined
Efficient
Focused
Idealistic
Imaginative
Independent
Industrious
Intelligent
Mature
Meticulous
Obedient

Objective
Observant
Organized
Passionate
Patient
Pensive
Perceptive
Persistent
Persuasive
Proactive
Professional
Resourceful
Responsible
Sensible
Studious
Talented
Thrifty
Wise

IDENTITY

Adventurous
Affectionate
Ambitious
Bold
Centered
Charming
Confident
Creative

Curious
Disciplined
Easygoing
Enthusiastic
Extroverted
Flamboyant
Flirtatious
Funny
Happy
Honorable
Idealistic
Imaginative
Independent
Innocent
Inspirational
Intelligent
Introverted
Just
Kind
Mature
Merciful
Nature-Focused
Nurturing
Optimistic
Passionate
Patriotic
Pensive

Persuasive
Philosophical
Playful
Proper
Quirky
Sensual
Sentimental
Simple
Sophisticated
Spiritual
Spontaneous
Talented
Traditional
Uninhibited
Whimsical
Wholesome
Witty

INTERACTIVE
Adaptable
Adventurous
Affectionate
Alert
Analytical
Appreciative
Bold
Calm
Cautious
Charming
Confident
Cooperative
Courageous
Courteous
Curious
Diplomatic
Discreet
Easygoing
Empathetic
Enthusiastic
Extroverted
Flamboyant
Flirtatious
Friendly
Funny
Generous

Gentle
Happy
Honest
Honorable
Hospitable
Humble
Imaginative
Independent
Industrious
Innocent
Inspirational
Introverted
Just
Kind
Loyal
Mature
Merciful
Nature-Focused
Nurturing
Obedient
Objective
Observant
Optimistic
Passionate
Patient
Patriotic
Perceptive
Persuasive
Philosophical
Playful
Private
Professional
Proper
Protective
Quirky
Resourceful
Sensible
Sensual
Sentimental
Simple
Socially Aware
Sophisticated
Spiritual
Spontaneous
Spunky

Supportive
Tolerant
Traditional
Trusting
Uninhibited
Unselfish
Whimsical
Wholesome
Witty

MORAL
Appreciative
Centered
Cooperative
Courageous
Courteous
Diplomatic
Empathetic
Friendly
Generous
Honest
Honorable
Hospitable
Humble
Innocent
Just
Kind
Loyal
Merciful
Obedient
Optimistic
Patient
Persistent
Professional
Proper
Protective
Responsible
Socially Aware
Spiritual
Supportive
Thrifty
Tolerant
Trusting
Unselfish
Wholesome

INDEX

This index includes all of the attributes and similar traits listed in this thesaurus. Keep in mind that, due to size limitations and our desire to include as many different attributes as possible, not every trait here has its own entry. But by going to the associated entry for each trait below, you should find ample information on each attribute.

THE NEGATIVE TRAIT THESAURUS

Building Flawed Characters That Readers Will Love

Crafting likable, interesting characters is a balancing act, and finding that perfect mix of strengths and weaknesses can be difficult. Not only does a well-drawn protagonist need positive attributes to help him succeed, he must also have flaws that humanize him and give him something to overcome. The same is true of villains and the rest of the story's supporting cast. So how can writers figure out which flaws best fit their characters? Which negative traits will create personality clashes and conflict while making success difficult?

Inside this volume you will find:

- A vast collection of flaws to explore when building a character's personality. Each entry includes possible causes, attitudes, behaviors, thoughts, and related emotions
- Real examples from literature, film, or television to show how each flaw can create life challenges and relational friction
- Advice on building layered and memorable characters from the ground up
- An in-depth look at backstory, emotional wounds, and how pain twists a character's view of himself and his world, influencing behavior and decision making
- A flaw-centric exploration of character arc, relationships, motivation, and basic needs
- Tips on how to best show a character's flaws to readers while avoiding common pitfalls
- Downloadable tools to aid writers in character creation

The following traits are included in this collection:

Abrasive	Childish	Cruel
Addictive	Cocky	Cynical
Antisocial	Compulsive	Defensive
Apathetic	Confrontational	Devious
Callous	Controlling	Dishonest
Catty	Cowardly	Disloyal

Disorganized
Disrespectful
Evasive
Evil
Extravagant
Fanatical
Flaky
Foolish
Forgetful
Frivolous
Fussy
Gossipy
Greedy
Grumpy
Gullible
Haughty
Hostile
Humorless
Hypocritical
Ignorant
Impatient
Impulsive
Inattentive
Indecisive
Inflexible
Inhibited
Insecure
Irrational
Irresponsible
Jealous

Judgmental
Know-It-All
Lazy
Macho
Manipulative
Martyr
Materialistic
Melodramatic
Mischievous
Morbid
Nagging
Needy
Nervous
Nosy
Obsessive
Oversensitive
Paranoid
Perfectionist
Pessimistic
Possessive
Prejudiced
Pretentious
Promiscuous
Pushy
Rebellious
Reckless
Resentful
Rowdy
Scatterbrained
Self-Destructive

Self-Indulgent
Selfish
Sleazy
Spoiled
Stingy
Stubborn
Subservient
Superstitious
Suspicious
Tactless
Temperamental
Timid
Uncommunicative
Uncooperative
Uncouth
Unethical
Ungrateful
Unintelligent
Vain
Verbose
Vindictive
Violent
Volatile
Weak-Willed
Whiny
Withdrawn
Workaholic
Worrywart

The Negative Trait Thesaurus sheds light on your character's dark side. Written in list format and fully indexed, this brainstorming resource is perfect for creating deep, flawed characters readers will relate to.

For more information, please visit the Writers Helping Writers' bookstore page (https://writershelpingwriters.net/bookstore/).

RECOMMENDED READING

To read further on characters, their development, and other areas of writing craft, we recommend these excellent resources.

Writer's Guide to Personality Types provides profiles of dozens of mental, emotional, and physical personality traits and types to help writers create original characters. (Jeannie Campbell, LMFT)

Writer's Guide To Character Traits will help you gain the knowledge necessary to create distinctive characters whose personalities correspond to their thoughts and actions - no matter how normal or psychotic they might be. (Dr. Linda Edelstein)

Writing Screenplays That Sell, New Twentieth Anniversary Edition teaches all writers to think deeply about their characters' motivations, story structure, and the art of selling. (Michael Hauge)

The Hero's 2 Journeys (CD/DVD) brings the perspective of two storytelling legends who share their practical experience and extensive research regarding story structure, character arc, and how to give your story greater commercial appeal. (Michael Hauge and Christopher Vogler)

Writing Fiction for All You're Worth: Strategies and Techniques for Taking Your Fiction to the Next Level contains a collection of articles and blog posts on writing, easily searchable under the headings of The Writing World, The Writing Life, and The Writing Craft (James Scott Bell)

Outlining Your Novel: Map Your Way to Success will help you choose the right type of outline to unleash your creativity, guide you in brainstorming plot ideas, and aid you in discovering your characters. (K.M. Weiland)

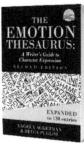

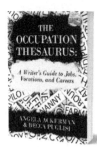

PRAISE FOR...

THE EMOTION THESAURUS

"One of the challenges a fiction writer faces, especially when prolific, is coming up with fresh ways to describe emotions. This handy compendium fills that need. It is both a reference and a brainstorming tool, and one of the resources I'll be turning to most often as I write my own books."

~ **James Scott Bell, International Thriller Writers Award Winner**

THE POSITIVE AND NEGATIVE TRAIT THESAURUSES

"In these brilliantly conceived, superbly organized and astonishingly thorough volumes, Angela Ackerman and Becca Puglisi have created an invaluable resource for writers and storytellers. Whether you are searching for new and unique ways to add and define characters, or brainstorming methods for revealing those characters without resorting to clichés, it is hard to imagine two more powerful tools for adding depth and dimension to your screenplays, novels or plays."

~ **Michael Hauge, Hollywood script consultant and author of *Writing Screenplays That Sell***

THE URBAN AND RURAL SETTING THESAURUSES

"The one thing I always appreciate about Ackerman and Puglisi's Thesauri series is how comprehensive they are. They never stop at just the obvious, and they always over-deliver. Their Setting Thesauri are no different, offering not just the obvious notes of the various settings they've covered, but going into easy-to-miss details like smells and tastes. They even offer to jumpstart the brainstorming with categories on potential sources of conflict."

~ **K.M. Weiland, best-selling author of** *Creating Character Arcs* **and** *Structuring Your Novel*

THE EMOTIONAL WOUND THESAURUS

"This is far more than a brilliant, thorough, insightful, and unique thesaurus. This is the best primer on story—and what REALLY hooks and holds readers—that I have ever read."

~ **Lisa Cron, TEDx Speaker and best-selling author of** *Wired For Story and Story Genius*

THE OCCUPATION THESAURUS

"Each and every thesaurus these authors produce is spectacular. The Occupation Thesaurus is no different. Full of inspiration, teachings, and knowledge that are guaranteed to take your writing to the next level, it's a must. You need this book on your craft shelf."

~ **Sacha Black, bestselling author of** *Anatomy of Prose*

ADD WRITERS HELPING WRITERS® TO YOUR TOOLKIT!

Over a decade of articles are waiting to help you grow your writing skills, navigate publishing and marketing, and assist you on your career path. And if you'd like to stay informed about forthcoming books, discover unique writing resources, and access even more practical writing tips, sign up for our newsletter onsite (https://writershelpingwriters.net/subscribe-to-our-newsletter/).

ONE STOP

F O R

WRITERS

Writers, are you ready for a game-changer?

In a flooded market, exceptional novels rise above the rest, and to get noticed, authors must bring their A-game. One Stop for Writers gives creatives an edge with powerful, one-of-a-kind story and character resources, helping them deliver fresh, compelling fiction that readers crave.

Brought to you by the minds behind *The Occupation Thesaurus,* One Stop is home to the largest show-don't-tell description database available anywhere and contains an innovative toolkit that makes storytelling almost criminally easy. A fan favorite is the hyper-intelligent Character Build-er, which helps you explore a character's deepest layers to uncover their desires, fears, motivations, and needs that drive the story. It will even create an accurate Character Arc Blueprint for you, making it easier to marry the plot to your character's internal journey. And the site's story struc-ture maps, timelines, worldbuilding surveys, generators, and tutorials give you what you need when you need it. So forget about staring at the screen wondering what to write. Those days are over, friend.

If you think it's time someone made writing easier, join us at https://www.onestopforwriters.com and give our **two-week free trial** a spin. If you choose to subscribe, use the code **ONESTOPFORWRITERS** for a one-time discount of 25% off any plan*. We're Writers Helping Writers, remember?

See you at One Stop!

Becca Puglisi & Angela Ackerman

*For full details and conditions, see our Coupon Redemption guidelines at https://onestopforwriters.com/coupon.